Southwest Conference Football 1972

Published by
FOOTBALL HISTORY, INC.
Bellaire, Texas

Edited and Designed by
Ray Herndon

A COMPLETE HISTORY OF THE 1972 SEASON

CONTENTS

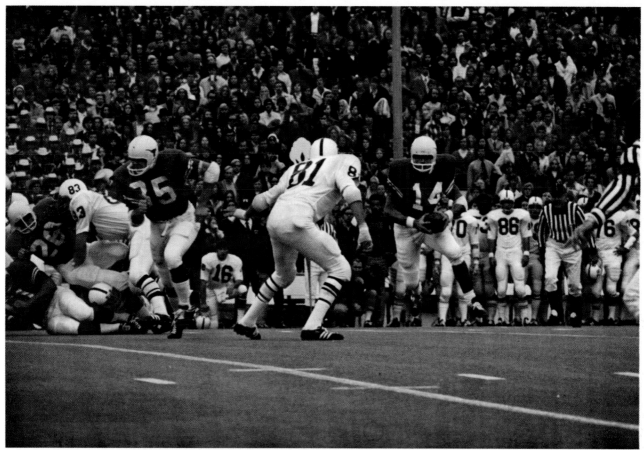

Jim Bertelsen (35) cuts in behind State linebacker John Skorupan (81) as quarterback Eddie Phillips (14) prepares to pitch or keep. Shown kneeling on the sidelines is Lion quarterback John Hufnagel (16).

PENN STATE 30 - TEXAS 6

Nittany Lions make the most of Texas hospitality.

It was a cold, drizzling New Year's Day as a crowd of 72,000 filled the Cotton Bowl to witness the 36th annual football classic. Penn State was returning for its second game here after tying SMU, 13-13, in the 1948 bowl. The Longhorns were old hands as this was their 13th visit to the Cotton Bowl. Maybe all of those 13's was an omen of things to come.

After consecutive mid-season losses to Oklahoma and Arkansas, the Longhorns regrouped and not only won five straight, but beat out the unpredictable Razorbacks for an unprecedented fourth straight Southwest Conference championship. The Nittany Lions had been ranked either fifth or sixth in the nation since mid-season and coming into their last game were victorious in ten straight games. On one of those days where everything goes wrong Tennessee flattened the Lions 31-11. So the Penn Staters were anxious to remove a bad taste from their mouths and to do a little face saving. At the expense of the Longhorns they accomplished both goals.

Their inability to hang on to the football cost Texas dearly in the first half. On their first possession they started at the Texas 14 and drove to the Lion 30, but they were then penalized five yards for offsides. Then, on the next play, quarterback Eddie Phillips lost control of the ball and recovered it at the State 43.

After an exchange of punts the Longhorns were in excellent field position at the Lions 35. Dennis Ladd, Jim Bertelsen and Don Burrisk took turns moving the ball to the 10. Phillips was then snowed under for a two-yard loss. Next a short pass to Rick Davis was incomplete and Steve Valek entered the game for a field goal attempt. The 29-yard boot was on target and with 1:14 left in the first quarter Texas led 3-0.

Early in the second quarter John Skorupan, attempting to tackle Ladd, popped the ball loose and Chuck Mesko recovered for Penn State at the Texas 22. In six plays Lydell Mitchell, Franco Harris and Tom Donchez moved the ball to the five. There Tommy Lee stopped Chuck Herd on a split end reverse and Alberto Vitiello came in and side-winded the ball through the uprights. The 21-yard kick tied the score at 3-3 with 10:38 left before halftime.

The Longhorns received the kickoff and moved from their 29 to the Penn State 25 before facing a fourth down.

3

The Lion's Franco Harris (34) takes out Tommy Lee (45) as Lydell Mitchell (23) scores Penn State's first touchdown. Also pictured is the Longhorn's Mike Rowan (44).

Valek came in and missed a 32-yard field goal attempt as his kick was low and wide to the right.

Late in the second quarter Longhorn linebacker Glenn Gaspard made a one-handed interception of State quarterback John Hufnagel's pass intended for Mitchell. From the Texas 22 Gaspard returned 17 yards to the 39. Phillips now had time running out as he dropped back and passed complete to Pat Kelly at the Lion's 42-yard line. A 19-yard completion and Phillips went to Kelly again on the next play. This also covered 19 yards and put the ball on the Penn State 23 with three seconds between Texas and the gun. Valek entered the game and kicked a 40-yard field goal which established a new distance record for the Cotton Bowl. With time gone the Longhorns took a 6-3 lead into the halftime break.

This was just about the last opportunity for any Longhorn cheers. Last year Texas failed to score in the second half against Notre Dame. The Irish followed suit with two goose eggs for the third and fourth quarters. This year Texas again failed to reach that elusive end zone, but unlike Notre Dame the Nittany Lions were not so bashful.

On the fourth play of the second half Phillips fumbled the ball at the Penn State 47. Jim Laslavic kicked the ball back into Texas territory and Charlie Zapiec recovered for the Lions at the Texas 41. It took State five plays to score, but only three were really needed. Mitchell broke

over right tackle and scampered 19 yards to the 22. Two plays later Hufnagel passed 19 yards to Bob Parsons who was brought down on the Longhorn one. After Tom Donchez was stopped for no gain Mitchell rammed over right guard for the first touchdown of the game. Vitiello kicked the point after and Penn State, with 11:41 left in the third quarter, led 10-6.

Only 2:57 elapsed before the Nittany Lions scored again. This time they did it on two plays. On first down, after taking possession at their 33, Hufnagel kept for a two-yard gain. On the next play split end Scott Skarzynski took off on a fly pattern as Hufnagel rolled right. The ball reached Skarzynski at the Texas 38 and with no one around he waltzed into the end zone. Vitiello added the conversion and the Lions led 17-6.

The Longhorns continued their game of give away late in the third quarter. Bruce Bannon collided with Phillips as he tried to hand off to Jim Bertelsen. The bouncing ball was recovered by Greg Ducatte at the Texas 43. The Lions drove 21 yards to the 22 where, on fourth and two, Vitiello came in and booted a 37-yard field goal. State led 20-6.

On their next series Donnie Wigginton replaced Phillips at quarterback for Texas. The fiery senior, who had so successfully relieved Phillips during the season, could not turn the tide of battle. The die was cast and going into the fourth quarter the Nittany Lions just kept rolling along.

4

The Longhorn's Tommy Woodard (82) stops Tom Donchez (32) as Alan Lowry (40) and Randy Braband (63) rush in to secure the tackle.

Following a Texas punt they took possession at their 22 and drove to the Longhorn one before being thrown back to the nine. On fourth down at the five Vitiello appeared once more and set a new Cotton Bowl record by kicking his third field goal. This one covered 22 yards and with 8:16 left in the game the Lions led 23-6.

Late in the game Penn State cranked up another sustained drive. Starting at their 36 they drove 64 yards in nine plays. Hufnagel got the touchdown on a four-yard scamper around right end. Vitiello capped the scoring with his conversion kick. The Nittany Lions led 30-6 with 3:18 remaining and that is how it ended.

Mitchell, who gained 146 yards on 27 carries, was voted the outstanding player on offense. His teammate Bannon, the Lions defensive left end, took the honors for the outstanding player on defense.

After missed opportunities early in the game the Longhorns just couldn't turn things around. So ferocious was the Penn State defense in the second half, Texas could only muster five first downs and a total gain of 85 yards. In the fourth quarter they had possession of the ball for two minutes and 21 seconds. An unknown factor wasn't discovered until Penn State had scored two quick third quarter touchdowns. Defensive back Mike Bayer was injured in the first half, but was given an OK for second half action. Hufnagel's 19-yard pass to the Texas one was over Bayer. Following that touchdown Bayer should have been covering Skarzynski on the 65-yard bomb. That was when the Longhorns realized too late that Bayer was out on his feet.

The Texas fumbles led to 13 points, two field goals and a touchdown, which is too much to give a team like Penn State. The Nittany Lions had to move only 79 yards for those 13 points.

To add insult to injury this was the first time in 80 games that the Longhorns failed to score a touchdown. In 1964 they beat Rice 6-3, on two field goals, the same as the halftime score here. Senior Tommy Woodard, a co-captain, probably summed it up adequately when he said, "They're stronger than we are and evidently, I'm sorry to say, they wanted to win a little more."

So the weather, cold and miserable, matched the Longhorn followers as they dispersed in the gloom of the 36th annual Cotton Bowl classic.

	Penn State	Texas
First Downs	18	15
Rushes-yards	56-239	52-159
Passing yardage	137	83
Return yardage	0	20
Passes	7-13-1	5-14-0
Punts	5-36	5-33
Fumbles lost	0	3
Yards penalized	0	5

Penn State	0	3	17	10—30
Texas	3	3	0	0— 6

Tex— FG Valek 29
PS—FG Vitiello 21
Tex–FG Valek 40
PS—Mitchell 1 run (Vitiello kick)
PS—Skarzynski 65 pass from Hufnagel (Vitiello kick)
PS—FG Vitiello 37
PS—FG Vitiello 22
PS—Hufnagel 4 run (Vitiello kick)
A—72,000

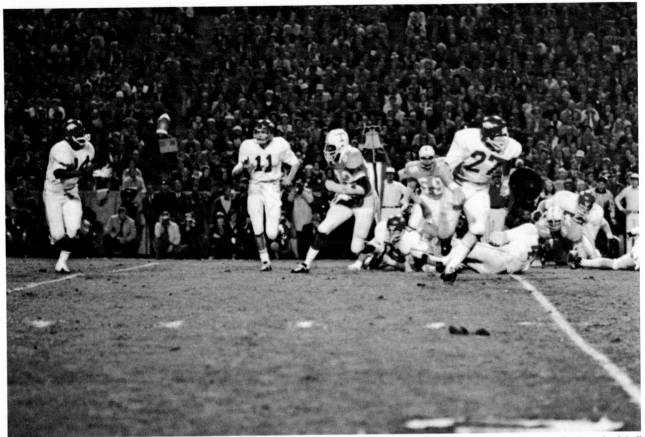

Quarterback Joe Ferguson (11) pitches back to Jon Richardson (24) and Bobby Nichols (27) prepares to lead interference for the Razorback ball carrier.

TENNESSEE 14 - ARKANSAS 13

Controversial calls spell defeat for Razorbacks.

A record 51,410 fans crowded the Liberty Bowl in Memphis on Monday evening December 20 to watch the Volunteers and Razorbacks close out their 1971 football efforts. Sixty-four years had passed since these neighboring state universities met on the gridiron. In 1907 Tennessee hosted and beat Arkansas 14-2.

Tennessee won the toss and elected to receive. After an opening exchange of punts the Vols had possession at their 45. Quarterback Jim Maxwell threw an incompletion then, on second down, handed off to Steve Chancey who ran for nine yards. Bill Rudder gained one and a first down at the Arkansas 45. Rudder ran for two and Maxwell then threw two incomplete passes. Interference was called on the second one against Clark Irwin and the Vols had a first down at the Arkansas 24. Maxwell handed off to Rudder and the Hog defense came up fast to stop the run, but Rudder stopped on his own and threw a halfback pass to wide receiver Emmon Love who was bumped down on the Arkansas three-yard line. On the next play Rudder scored on a power sweep. George Hunt kicked the extra point and with 6:39 left in the first quarter the Volunteers led 7-0.

Early in the second quarter the Hog's Bill McClard tried a 40-yard field goal which was partially blocked and Tennessee took over at their 20. After allowing one first down the Razorbacks held and following a Bobby Majors punt Arkansas took over at their 34. It was then that the Hog offense started clicking. Joe Ferguson passed to Jim Hodge for 18 yards, passed to Jon Richardson for six more and then hit Hodge again for 12 and a first down at the Tennessee 30. A screen pass to Jack Ettinger gained five and Mike Saint cut back against the grain to run for seven yards to the 18. Ferguson gained two on the option keeper, but Hodge was thrown for a six-yard loss on a screen pass at the right sideline. Hodge's emotions got the best of him and he slammed the ball to the ground which cost the Hogs 15 yards, back to the 36, for unsportsmanlike conduct. Hodge more than made up for that mistake as he caught a scrambling Ferguson's pass, on the next play, just before running out of the end zone. McClard tied the game at 7-7 with his successful extra point.

The Volunteers marched from their 20 to the Arkansas 21 where, on fourth down, Hunt missed a 38-yard field goal attempt. With only 52 seconds left the Razorbacks ran out the clock and the two teams went to their dressing rooms tied up 7-7.

Volunteer Bill Rudder (36) scores Tennessee's first touchdown from three yards out. The Razorbacks' Mike Davis (39) helps make the tackle as Rudder falls into the end zone.

Jack Morris returned the second half kickoff to the Arkansas 23. Ferguson continued his aerial assault as he hit Richardson for two and Hodge for 12. Tennessee was then penalized 15 yards for roughing the passer which put the ball on the Vol 45. After an incompletion Ferguson passed to Ettinger for 11 yards, but on the next play the Hogs were penalized back to the Tennessee 48 when they were caught with an ineligible receiver downfield. Ferguson tried to hit Keith French with a bomb and Majors intercepted at the 13 and returned 27 yards to the 40.

Two running plays gained five yards. On third down Louis Campbell intercepted Maxwell at the Arkansas 33. Following an exchange of punts the Razorbacks put the ball in play at their 35. On first down Dicky Morton turned the corner and ran for 29 yards to the Vol 36. Saint then tried to hit Ettinger on a halfback pass. The pass was incomplete, but Tennessee was penalized 15 yards, to their 24, for roughing the passer. Morton ran for four and Saint blasted up the middle for 11 to reach the nine. After Morton picked up two on a sweep he and Ferguson bobbled a handoff and Vol Eddie Brown recovered the fumble at the 11.

Tennessee moved to the Arkansas 47 in seven plays, but there Maxwell lost the center snap and Scott Binnion came out on top of the ball. This gave Arkansas possession on their 46. Morton ran for four then Ferguson hit Richardson on a screen for 20 yards. Saint

picked up 10 on carries of two and eight yards. On a draw play Morton made nine as the third quarter came to an end. Saint ran for two and the Razorbacks had a first and goal at the nine. Morton gained two inside. Ferguson tried to hit Bobby Nichols for the score, but Nichols and Majors collided and the ball fell harmlessly to the ground. Richardson made five up the middle which brought up a fourth and two. After a time out McClard came in and kicked a 20-yard field goal to put Arkansas ahead 10-7.

Moments later the Hogs had the ball on the Volunteer 43 thanks to Campbell's second interception. Richardson made four, then Ferguson found Nichols alone in the left flat and the pass-run gained 24 yards to the 15. Richardson lost five on a run, then made eight on a screen pass. On an attempted sweep Morton was caught for a yard loss and that brought in McClard. He added three more points with a 30-yard field goal and with 6:09 remaining Arkansas led 13-7.

Tennessee was guilty of clipping on the kickoff return and penalized to their 15. Maxwell fired deep on first down and Campbell had his third interception. He went out of bounds at the Hog 49 after the catch.

The Razorback offense kept the pressure on as Richardson ran for three, Saint for four and Richardson again for nine on a screen pass. Two running plays picked up five yards, but Ferguson's third down pass was incomplete. McClard then kicked a 48-yard field goal, but Nichols was called for holding and the three points were

7

Dicky Morton picks up nine yards for the Razorbacks on a draw play. Five plays later Bill McClard kicked a 20-yard field goal to put Arkansas ahead 10-7.

erased and the Hogs moved back 15 yards.

Drew Toole punted into the end zone and Tennessee started play at their 20. Three plays gained eight yards and Majors punted to the Arkansas 30. Saint gained five on two carries. Ferguson threw a screen pass to Richardson who gained two before being swarmed under in front of the Vol bench. After the unpiling a fumble was called and Tennessee's Carl Witherspoon was credited with the recovery at the Arkansas 37. This ruling coupled with the field goal taken away moments earlier demoralized the Razorbacks.

After Chancey gained one yard Maxwell passed to Theiler for 19 yards to the Hog 17. Curt Watson took a pitchout on the next play and went down the right sidelines for the score. Suddenly, with Hunt's extra point, the Vols were ahead 14-13 with only 1:56 left in the game.

Ferguson connected on two passes to Ettinger which gained 20 yards to the Arkansas 40. Firing deep on the next play Ferguson was intercepted and the ball was returned 47 yards to the Arkansas 35. The game ended with Tennessee on the Hog eight thanks to 22 yards in penalties against the Razorbacks.

To say that Arkansas head coach Frank Broyles was upset at the officiating would be a mild way of describing his anger. On the holding call that cancelled the field goal Nichols stated that the defensive end pulled him inside and threw him to the ground. On the fumble recovery Richardson said that he didn't think it was a fumble. He

stated he got up and saw teammate Tom Reed on the ball and he saw Reed hand the ball to the official. This follows closely Reed's version of the incident. Reed said, "I was lying on the ground and I saw the football. Everyone started yelling that it was Tennessee's ball so I grabbed the ball and cradled it to my chest. Three Vols jumped on top of me, but I still held the ball. Finally the official came up and put his hands on the ball. I gave the ball to him and he signalled Tennessee's ball. I asked him if he was kidding and he told me to get my hands off the football." The same Southeastern Conference official called both the holding penalty and fumble recovery.

On the bright side for Arkansas, if there is one, Joe Ferguson was selected the outstanding player in the Liberty Bowl as he broke the record for most completions with 18 and tied the record for most attempts with 28. Louis Campbell was named the outstanding Razorback defender as he set a new Liberty Bowl record with three interceptions. The Arkansas defensive unit held Tennessee to 239 total yards with only 92 of that amount coming in the second half.

	Ark.	Tenn.
First downs	22	15
Rushes-yards	46-167	34-98
Passing yardage	200	142
Return yardage	35	115
Passes	18-28-3	11-22-3
Punts	3-44	5-44
Fumbles lost	2	1
Yards penalized	85	73

Arkansas	0	7	0	6—13
Tennessee	7	0	0	7—14

Tenn—Rudder 2 run (Hunt kick)
Ark—Hodge 36 pass from Ferguson (McClard kick)
Ark—FG McClard 20
Ark—FG McClard 30
Tenn—Watson 17 run (Hunt kick)
A—51,410

The Cougars' Robert Newhouse prepares to put the ball down after scoring the first Houston touchdown on a run of two yards. He also scored the other Cougar touchdown on their next possession. (18) is Colorado defensive back Brian Foster.

COLORADO 29-HOUSTON 17

Cougars lose scoring touch after first quarter.

The seventh-ranked Buffaloes came to the Astrodome to meet the 15th-ranked Cougars in the 13th Annual Bluebonnet Bowl. Although Houston plays their home games there, Colorado was designated the "home" team for the game. Both teams have identical 9-2 records and all four defeats came on the road. A standing room only crowd of 54,720 came to start their New Year's Eve celebration by watching the first ever meeting between the two schools.

Houston kicked off and Colorado started scrimmage on their 30 after a seven-yard return. The Buffaloes thundered the 70 yards in nine plays with Texan Charlie Davis doing most of the thundering. He gained 57 yards with 27 of it coming on the ninth play. J. B. Dean kicked the extra point and with 3:46 gone Colorado led 7-0.

The Cougars retaliated as they received the Buffalo kickoff and moved 79 yards in 15 plays. Robert "Gator" Newhouse carried on eight of those plays and gained a net of 36 yards. His running mate Tommy Mozisek carried three times for 20 yards and quarterback Gary Mullins passed twice complete for 16 yards. Inside the 10

Colorado was offsides two plays in a row. Newhouse went over from the two on third down. Ricky Terrell booted the point after and with 5:22 left in the first quarter the game was tied 7-7.

On the third play after their kickoff Houston found itself with the ball again at the Colorado 34. A third down pass by quarterback Ken Johnson bounced off Davis' fingers and Punchy Hamrick intercepted for the Cougars. Houston scored in seven plays with Newhouse carrying five times, his longest run was 15 yards from the 18 to the three. Earlier, on fourth and two at the 26, Mullins ran the keeper for eight yards to keep the drive alive. Newhouse scored from the three on second down. Terrell's point after was good and Houston led 14-7.

The Buffaloes came right back and moved 61 yards in 10 plays to score. This despite two 15-yard penalties although one was offset by a 15-yard pass interference call on Cougar defender Jeff Bouche. The touchdown came on a third down Johnson to Brunson pass good for five yards. Dean missed the tying point and Houston led 14-13 with the second quarter only 1:40 old.

Butch Brezina (64), Frank Ditta (59), Bill Stohler (81), Burl Fuller (26) and Randy Peacock (31) chase the elusive Charlie Davis. Davis was the leading rusher and voted the outstanding back in the game.

On their next possession the Cougars were stopped at the Colorado 39 and Hal Roberts punted to the Buff five with no return. The "Mad Dog" defense slowed down the Colorado attack this time. Although they moved in close enough for Dean to kick a 32-yard field goal, it took 15 plays and a little over six minutes to do it. The big gainer was a 38-yard run by Johnson on a keeper. With the successful field goal Colorado pulled ahead 16-14.

Wayne Johnson fumbled the Buffalo kickoff and Dave Orvis pounced on the ball for Colorado at the Cougar 33. After a short Johnson to Michele pass gained five yards, Davis carried seven straight times and scored from one yard out on his seventh carry. Dean kicked the conversion point and the Buffaloes led 23-14.

Newhouse returned the kickoff 16 yards to the Houston 39. The Cougars reached the Buff 35 where on fourth down Newhouse lost one yard on a draw. Colorado, with only 13 seconds remaining, ran out the clock as the first half ended.

Houston received to open the final half and raised the hopes of Cougar fans as they moved to the Colorado 11-yard line in only five plays. The big gainer being a Mullins to Del Stanley pass which covered 28 yards. From the 11 Mullins lost three on a keeper, but on second down threw a pass to Riley Odoms who made a great catch and was struggling for the first down when he fumbled the ball.

Lorne Richardson recovered for Colorado at his three.

After eluding the shadow of their goal posts on punt exchanges, the Buffaloes looked like they were on their way to another score as they moved from their 20 to the Cougar 26. Davis then hit the middle for three yards, but fumbled and Burl Fuller recovered for Houston at his 23.

On two straight completions Mullins moved the Cougars 51 yards. Pat Orchin caught the first pass for 27 yards and then Odoms caught the next one for 24 yards and a first down at the Buffalo 26. Two runs by Newhouse and a screen pass to Orchin gave a first down at the 15. Three plays only reached the 12, so Terrell entered the game and kicked a 29-yard field goal. Houston now trailed by six, 23-17.

The Cougars held Colorado to no first downs following the kickoff and after Stearns' punt had the ball on their 35. One play later the third quarter ended. They methodically moved the ball toward Colorado's goal as twice they gambled on fourth down and made it. On fourth and one at the Buff 28 Mullins kept for two yards and on the next series Newhouse picked up three yards on a fourth down play. This brought up a first and 10 at the 13. The third fourth down gamble failed as Stearns knocked down a pass intended for Odoms in the end zone.

Colorado took over at their nine. Three plays later the Buff's faced an almost impossible nine yards needed on

The "Mad Dogs" drop Buffalo quarterback Ken Johnson for a loss on this play. Bill Stohler (81), Thomas Ward (40), Butch Brezina (64) and an unidentified Cougar make the sacking in front of an enthusiastic Houston bench.

fourth down. The center snap to punter Stearns was low and as he stooped to retrieve the ball he looked around to see if there was anyway he could get the punt off. Well, to his surprise all the Cougars had their backs to him running back upfield for the return. Stearns tucked the ball under his arm and ran 12 yards before the startled Cougars regrouped and brought him down. This bit of daring shook Colorado out of the doldrums and they proceeded to cover the remaining 78 yards in 10 plays. During the drive Bill Stohler dumped Johnson for a loss of 12 yards, but on third and 15 Fuller interferred with Cliff Branch on a pass and the 32 yard penalty kept the drive alive. Johnson scored the touchdown on a one-yard keeper. His pass attempt for the conversion was incomplete and the Buffaloes led 29-17 with 3:48 remaining.

Newhouse returned the kickoff 15 yards to the Cougar 28. The drive looked promising until reaching the Buffalo 43. There a Mullins pass, intended for Orchin, was intercepted by Brian Foster at the Colorado 15.

Following two delay penalties and three plays, Stearns punted from the end zone out to the 32. With 1:09 left Mullins passed to Orchin for 24 yards to the 10. Two incomplete passes and a running play gained one yard. On fourth down Mullins overthrew Mozisek.

Only 19 seconds remained when Davis made five yards and ran out the clock. Final score Colorado 29—Houston 17.

It was quite an offensive show as the Buffaloes gained 398 total yards and Houston only six yards less at 392. Both teams lost their scoring touch in the second half. The Cougars rolled up 238 yards and could put only three points on the scoreboard.

Overall the teams broke nine Bluebonnet Bowl records. Davis from West Columbia, returned home and set a new rushing record of 202 yards and was voted the outstanding back of the game. Butch Brezina of Houston was voted the outstanding lineman. Newhouse, the NCAA's second highest yards gainer for one season, ended up a brilliant career with 168 yards and both Cougar touchdowns. Mullins, who quarterbacked the Cougars to 25 victories in his 30 starts, completed 11 of 25 passes for 173 yards. Colorado moved up to third ranked in the final poll and Houston dropped two places to 17th.

	Houston	Colorado
First Downs	19	24
Rushes yards	50-219	62-336
Passing yardage	173	62
Return yardage	0	0
Passes	11-26-1	7-17-1
Punts	2-37	3-32
Fumbles lost	2	0
Yards penalized	47	52

Houston 14   0   3   0—17
Colorado 7   16   0   6—29
CU—Davis 27 run (Dean kick)
UH—Newhouse 2 run (Terrell kick)
UH—Newhouse 3 run (Terrell kick)
CU—Brunson 5 pass from Johnson (kick failed)
CU—FG 32 Dean
CU—Davis 1 run (Dean kick)
UH—FG 29 Terrell
CU—Johnson 1 run (Pass failed)
A—54,720

11

SO YOU'RE A SOUTHWEST CONFERENCE FOOTBALL FAN

Southwest Conference football is exciting today, but it was no different in the many years that have gone by since its inception. One of the most rewarding aspects of this job is researching some of the history and the knowledge gained in doing so. Tie games were counted in SWC percentages for the first time in 1925. In 1934 SWC teams played round-robin for the first time. For five straight years a SWC team led the nation in passing, only once has a SWC player led the nation in total offense.

So you're a Southwest Conference football fan. Below are 25 questions to test you and don't feel bad if your score does not come up to your expectations. The knowledge gained more than offsets the disappointment. Some of the questions have more than one answer. Score one point for each correct answer given in a multiple answer question. Maximum score: 90 - if you achieve a score of 45 you're a SWC football fan. The answers to the questions appear on page 197.

The source for most of the answers is the Official Southwest Athletic Conference Football Roster and Record Book. Published every year and edited by Wilbur Evans and Bill Morgan, the book may be purchased by mailing $2.50 (per copy) to the Southwest Athletic Conference, Box 7185, Dallas, Texas 75209.

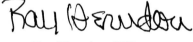

Ray Herndon, Editor

1. Only once, in the same year, have three SWC teams finished in the final Top Ten. Name the three teams and the year. (4 points)
2. Once upon a time the SWC Champion went through the season undefeated and untied four years in a row. Name the two teams involved. (2 points)
3. Name the four schools who were members of the SWC at one time, but are not now. (4 points)
4. What are the nine SWC freshman team nicknames? (9 points)
5. In 1943 and 1944 what SWC school suspended football because of World War II? (1 point)
6. The same four SWC teams played in bowl games for two consecutive years. Who were the teams and what were the years? (6 points)
7. In what Texas city was TCU founded and under what name? (2 points)
8. The record for the most games played by a SWC team in one season is 12, held jointly by Rice, SMU, TCU and Texas A & M. Which school won all 12 games? (1 point)

9. Name the only SWC player to lead the nation in total offense and the year in which he did this. (2 points)
10. Not counting Texas Tech and Houston, name the youngest member of the SWC. (1 point)
11. Twice SWC teams have won National Championships back to back. What were the years and what four teams were involved? (8 points)
12. Only three SWC teams have scored more than 400 points in regular season play. Name the three teams. (3 points)
13. For five straight years a SWC team led the nation in pass offense. What were the years, who were the quarterbacks and what team did they play for? (11 points)
14. One team holds the SWC season record for rushing defense, passing defense and total defense. All three records were set in the same year. Who was the team and what was the year? (2 points)
15. One year two SWC players made All-American, but failed to make the All-SWC team. Who were the players? (2 points)
16. Only once have three teams tied for the SWC championship. Who were the teams and what year did it happen? (4 points)
17. Only three players made All-SWC four times. One year all three made All-American. Who were the players and what year did they all make All-American? (4 points)
18. Name the only team to finish first after being picked to finish last in the SWC Pre-season Poll. (1 point)
19. One team led the SWC in passing for five straight years. Who was the team and what were the years? (6 points)
20. One SWC team played football 40 years before having a losing season. Name the team and the year they had their first losing season. (2 points)
21. What three teams have participated in every SWC season? (3 points)
22. One SWC team went through two seasons unbeaten, untied and unscored on. What team and what years? (3 points)
23. According to the late Kern Tipps, the SWC came of age nationally when two of its members went on the road and on Saturday, October 6, 1934, beat Purdue and Notre Dame. Who were the schools and what were the scores? (4 points)
24. A present SWC team played two present SWC teams three times each during one season. Name the team and the two teams that were played three times. (3 points)
25. Name the teams and the score in the most lopsided game played between two present SWC members. (2 points)

Preview 1972

PREDICTIONS

FINAL 1971 TOP TEN
1. Nebraska
2. Oklahoma
3. Colorado
4. Alabama
5. Penn State
6. Michigan
7. Georgia
8. Arizona State
9. Tennessee
10. Stanford

1972 PRE-SEASON TOP TEN
1. Nebraska
2. Colorado
3. Oklahoma
4. Ohio State
5. Arkansas
6. Penn State
7. Alabama
8. Southern Cal
9. Washington
10. Michigan

FOOTBALL WRITERS PRE-SEASON TOP TEN
1. Nebraska
2. Colorado
3. Oklahoma
4. Penn State
5. Arkansas
6. Michigan
7. Ohio State
8. Arizona State
9. Tennessee
10. Notre Dame

1972 SWC PRESS TOUR
1. Arkansas
2. Texas
3. Texas A & M
4. TCU
5. SMU
6. Texas Tech
7. Rice
8. Baylor

1971 RECORDS

	SEASON W	L	T	SWC W	L	T
HOUSTON	9	2	0	0	0	0
TEXAS	8	2	0	6	1	0
ARKANSAS	8	2	1	5	1	1
TCU	6	4	1	5	2	0
TEXAS A & M	5	6	0	4	3	0
SMU	4	7	0	3	4	0
TEXAS TECH	4	7	0	2	5	0
RICE	3	7	1	2	4	1
BAYLOR	1	9	0	0	7	0

ALL-TIME RECORDS

		W	L	T	PCT.
1.	Texas	518	191	28	.730
2.	Arkansas	386	275	32	.583
3.	Texas A & M	379	275	45	.579
4.	TCU	372	277	50	.573
5.	Houston	143	113	9	.558
6.	Texas Tech	258	205	25	.557
7.	Baylor	334	289	39	.536
8.	SMU	279	247	47	.530
9.	Rice	286	268	27	.516

1972 SCHEDULES

	ARKANSAS	BAYLOR	HOUSTON	RICE	SMU	TEXAS	TEXAS A&M	TCU	TEXAS TECH
Sept. 9	Southern Cal		@ Rice	Houston			@ Wichita State		
Sept. 16		@ Georgia	Arizona State		Wake Forest	@ Nebraska			Utah
Sept. 23	Okla. State	@ Missouri	@ Tulsa	Clemson	@ Florida	Miami	@ LSU	@ Indiana	@ New Mexico
Sept. 30	Tulsa			@Georgia Tech	@ Va. Tech	@ Texas Tech	Army	UTA	Texas
Oct. 7	@ TCU	Miami	@ Va. Tech	LSU	New Mexico State	Utah State		Arkansas	Tulsa
Oct. 14	Baylor	@ Arkansas	San Diego State			Oklahoma	Texas Tech	@ Tulsa	@ Texas A&M
Oct. 21	@ Texas	@ Okla. State	@ Miami	@ SMU	Rice	Arkansas	TCU	@ Texas A&M	Arizona
Oct. 28	North Texas	Texas A&M	Mississippi State	Texas	Texas Tech	@ Rice	@ Baylor	@ Notre Dame	@ SMU
Nov. 4	@ Texas A&M	@ TCU	@ Florida State	Texas Tech	@ Texas	SMU	Arkansas	Baylor	@ Rice
Nov. 11	Rice	Texas	Colorado State	@ Arkansas	Texas A&M	@ Baylor	@ SMU	@ Texas Tech	TCU
Nov. 18	SMU	Texas Tech	New Mexico	@ Texas A&M	@ Arkansas	@ TCU	Rice	Texas	@ Baylor
Nov. 23						Texas A&M	@ Texas		
Nov. 25	@ Texas Tech	@ SMU	Cincinnati	TCU	Baylor			@ Rice	Arkansas
Dec. 2		Rice		@ Baylor	@ TCU			SMU	

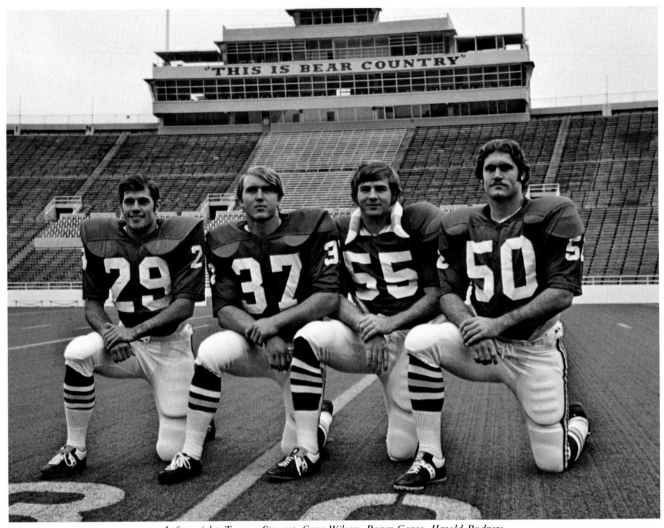

Left to right: Tommy Stewart, Gene Wilson, Roger Goree, Harold Rodgers.

BAYLOR BEARS

Head Football Coach: Grant Teaff

No.	Name	Pos.	Wt.	Ht.	Class Exp.
11	Neal Jeffrey	QB	176	6-1	So
12	Robert Armstrong	QB	192	5-11	So
14	Jerry Jameson	WB	182	6-2	So
17	Randy Cavender	QB	196	6-1	Jr1L
18	Chuck Gossett	QB	190	6-1	JrSq
20	Ricky Duff	DB	174	5-9	Sr2L
21	Brian Kilgore	WB	202	6-3	So
22	Marcus Rogers	TB	194	5-11	So
23	Gary Lacy	TB	194	5-11	JrTr
24	Ira Dean	DB	199	6-0	Sr2L
25	Karl Ray	SE	176	5-9	So
27	Doug Lee	DB	178	5-10	Fr
28	Ray Harper	TB	174	5-10	JrTr
29	Tommy Stewart	DB	168	5-7	Sr2L
30	Billy Wilson	WB	186	5-11	JrSq
31	Pat McNeil	FB	212	6-0	Fr
33	Tom Turnipseede	ROV	187	6-1	So
34	Lester Ealey	WB	185	5-8	JrTr
35	Ralph Funk	TB	204	6-0	Fr
36	Harlan Deem	K	180	6-1	Sr1L
37	Gene Wilson	FB	191	5-10	Sr2L
38	Dwayne Trammell	ROV	193	5-11	Sr2L
39	Larry Bowling	DB	184	5-11	Sr1L
40	Don Drake	DB	151	5-10	JrTr
41	Mike Riley	SE	171	5-11	SrSq
42	Robert Weygandt	DB	175	5-10	So
43	Bubba Hicks	K	160	5-10	So
44	Ed Taylor	LB	213	6-1	Sr2L
45	Wayne Prescher	FB	224	6-0	Sr1L
46	Derrel Luce	LB	208	6-3	So
47	Paul Savage	LB	207	6-1	Sr1L
48	Keith Stone	DB	191	6-2	JrTr
49	Rusty Parrott	K	201	6-1	Fr
50	Harold Rodgers	OG	208	6-1	Sr2L
51	Cary Dorman	C	213	6-0	JrSq
52	Chris Cariker	C	234	6-4	Fr
53	Randy Perdue	DG	192	6-0	Sr1L
55	Roger Goree	DE	201	6-0	Sr2L
56	Harry Pfeffer	LB	227	5-10	JrTr
57	Barry Pledger	DG	210	6-0	So
58	Jeff Mund	C	216	6-1	Fr
59	Gary Barkley	LB	218	5-11	Fr
60	Ronnie Martin	DE	228	6-2	JrTr
61	Dan Stout	OG	219	6-1	So
62	Scott Davis	OG	228	6-1	Fr
63	Tim Mills	OG	210	5-11	So
64	Dennis DeLoach	LB	197	6-0	So
65	Mike Wilder	DT	198	6-1	Jr1L
66	Richard Mason	OT	245	6-5	Jr1L
68	John Oliver	DE	199	6-3	Fr
69	Tommy Bluntzer	C	217	6-4	JrSq
71	David Walters	OG	230	6-4	Sr2L
72	Larry Denton	OT	212	6-2	Sr1L
73	Jon Royal	OT	224	6-3	Fr
75	Phil Perry	OT	236	6-1	JrTr
76	Reade Aulenbacher	OT	236	6-4	Fr
77	Lee Wright	OT	215	6-2	Sr1L
78	Millard Neely	DG	271	6-1	JrTr
79	Joe Johnson	DT	206	5-11	So
80	Dale Lechler	DE	193	6-0	So
81	Lloyd Kitchen	SE	181	5-11	So
82	Steve Watson	DE	198	5-11	So
83	Jeff Haas	SE	180	6-1	So
84	Charles Dancer	SE	156	5-11	JrTr
85	Coy Zunker	OT	220	6-2	So
86	Steve Trainer	TE	221	6-2	Fr
87	Mike Conradt	K	191	6-3	Jr1L
88	Mike Black	DE	210	6-3	Jr1L
89	Rusty Bundy	TE	194	6-2	Sr1L
90	Kenny Townsend	TE	214	6-1	Jr1L

TCU Captains for 1972 - Front row: Lyle Blackwood and Tookie Berry. Second row: Ronnie Peoples and Guy Morriss.

TEXAS CHRISTIAN HORNED FROGS

Head Football Coach: Billy Tohill

No.	Name	Pos.	Wt.	Ht.	Class Exp.
42	Anderson, Greg	P	192	6-0	So
59	Bartlett, Leon	C	209	6-1	JrSq
54	Berry, Tookie	LB	222	6-2	Sr2L
25	Blackwood, Lyle	DB	189	6-1	Sr1L
70	Bond, Sidney	OT	255	6-5	Jr1L
82	Bowen, Lane	TE	211	6-4	Sr2L
32	Braddock, Steve	DB	185	6-3	Jr1L
80	Brown, Danny	TE	209	6-3	So
69	Cowan, Les	OG	267	6-5	JrSq
45	Crouch, J. G.	LB	210	6-3	Fr
71	Davis, Charlie	DT	252	6-3	Jr1L
38	Dixon, David	DB	190	6-1	Sr2L
75	Draper, Lloyd	OT	240	6-2	Sr2L
13	Drennan, Terry	QB	173	5-11	So
88	Duncan, Dave	SE	165	6-2	So
79	Faulk, Tim	OT	236	6-4	JrSq
52	Garnett, Rick	C	207	6-1	Jr1L
84	Grimmett, Frankie	DE	208	6-2	Sr2L
28	Harris, Larry	OHB	190	6-0	Sr2L
81	Heinichen, Jeff	DE	197	6-0	JrSq
48	Hernandez, Gene	DB	175	6-1	So
18	Howard, Don	QB	198	6-2	JrSq
12	Huffman, Royce	DB	189	6-1	Sr1L
35	Kelley, T. L.	FB	207	6-0	Fr
53	Ladner, Dale	LB	197	5-11	Jr1L
14	Littleton, Ronnie	OHB	184	6-1	Fr
23	Luttrell, Mike	OHB	205	6-1	So
27	McGinnis, David	DB	173	5-11	Sr2L
87	McNeel, Phil	SE	196	6-5	JrSq
67	McNiel, Jim	LB	222	6-3	Jr1L
65	McWilliams, John	OG	224	6-1	So
11	Marshall, Kent	QB	189	6-2	Jr1L
68	Morriss, Guy	OG	255	6-4	Sr2L
50	Moser, Gene	LB	227	6-1	So
77	Mraz, Tom	DT	219	6-2	So
10	Muckleroy, Harold	DB	186	6-1	Jr1L
83	Ott, John	TE	208	6-2	JrSq
40	Patterson, Steve	SE	176	5-11	Jr1L
60	Peoples, Ronnie	OG	220	6-3	Sr2L
22	Pouncy, Freddie	SE	170	5-7	Sr1L
85	Putt, Rusty	DE	202	6-2	Sr1L
89	Robinson, Ed	DE	210	6-3	Jr1L
33	Sadler, Billy	OHB	200	6-0	Sr1L
41	Scott, Danny	OHB	179	5-11	So
19	Senn, Perry	QB	186	5-10	JrTr
86	Shipley, Robert	DE	180	6-0	So
34	Silvey, Butch	LB	214	6-0	Sr2L
24	Simmons, Berl	K	204	6-1	Jr1L
73	Steel, Ken	DT	245	6-5	Sr2L
47	Stout, Gary	LB	186	5-9	Sr2L
55	Terveen, Dede	LB	235	6-2	So
37	Utley, Chad	LB	195	6-0	So
72	Van Wart, Tommy	DT	250	6-5	So
51	Walker, Scott	C	220	6-3	Sr2L
62	Wang, Merle	OG	244	6-4	JrSq
74	Wauson, Jerry	OT	221	6-2	Sr2L
30	Webb, Ronnie	FB	200	6-1	So
36	Whitman, Gary	LB	204	6-1	Jr1L
17	Williams, Lee	DB	185	6-0	JrTr
39	Wiseman, Richard	DB	175	6-0	Sr2L
31	Young, Chester	LB	181	5-11	So

Left to right: Puddin' Jones, Burl Fuller, David Bourquin.

HOUSTON COUGARS
Head Football Coach: Bill Yeoman

No. Name	Pos.	Wt.	Ht.	Class Exp.
1 Deryl McGallion	MLB	200	6-1	Jr1L
2 Bubba Broussard	MLB	210	6-4	So
3 D. C. Nobles	QB	180	6-2	JrSq
4 Robert Ford	SE	170	5-7	Sr2L
5 Sandy McCrea	K-SE	170	5-10	Jr1L
6 Frank Scalise	FLK	170	6-0	So
7 Chuck Fairbanks	QB	180	6-2	So
8 Howard Ebow	RS	170	6-0	Jr1L
9 Terry Peel	QB	180	6-0	SrSq
10 David Husmann	RS	190	6-2	So
11 Ronnie Davis	QB	180	5-11	So
13 Marshall Johnson	RB	190	6-1	So
14 Joel DeSpain	QB	200	6-2	Sr1L
15 Ronnie Pickle	LS	195	6-3	So
16 Marty Watts	TE	195	6-3	So
17 Phillip Terrell	LCB	190	5-11	So
19 Del Stanley	FLK	165	6-0	Sr1L
20 David Pecor	LLB	200	6-3	So
22 Clarence Shelmon	FB	190	6-0	So
23 Bryan Willingham	SE	175	6-0	So
24 Robert Giblin	RCB	200	6-2	So
26 Burl Fuller	LS	185	6-0	Sr1L
27 Reggie Cherry	RB	185	6-1	So
28 Tommy Kaiser	LS	190	6-1	So
29 Wayne Johnson	SE	180	6-1	JrSq
30 Puddin Jones	RB	205	5-9	Sr1L
31 Randy Peacock	LCB	190	6-0	Sr2L
32 Steve Elliot	MLB	205	6-1	So
33 Hal Roberts	K-FLK	150	6-0	Jr1L
34 Todd Williamson	RCB	165	5-10	So
35 Larry Houston	RCB	175	6-0	So
36 Mike Wooldridge	RS	170	6-2	So
38 Randy McDaniel	FB	195	6-0	So
40 Roger Mayes	LCB	185	6-0	So
41 Bill Hamrick	RLB	190	6-1	Jr1L
42 Ronnie Joyce	SE	180	6-0	So
43 Ronnie Pegram	LS	185	6-2	So
44 Leonard Parker	FB	205	5-10	Jr1L
46 Milton Ward	FB	215	6-0	So
47 John Paige	FLK	185	6-3	So
49 Richard Arnold	RLB	185	6-0	So
51 Mike Rinehart	C	190	6-1	So
52 Glenn Riske	C	210	6-1	Jr1L
53 Ernie Uzzell	LLB	205	6-2	So
54 Jay Crowell	OLG	210	6-2	So
55 Bert Schupp	C	230	6-2	So
56 Mike Ilaoa	OLT	215	6-1	So
57 Bill Reed	C	225	6-3	So
58 Bill Jones	MLB	200	6-0	So
59 Harold Evans	RLB	215	6-5	So
60 Gerald Hill	DLE	225	6-1	So
61 James Dugas	DRT	210	6-1	So
62 Joe Norton	ORG	205	6-0	So
63 Ken Baugh	OLG	240	6-3	JrSq
64 Larry Keller	DLT	210	6-2	So
65 Steve Brezina	DRT	230	6-0	JrSq
66 Jack King	ORT	240	6-4	So
67 Ronnie Munos	ORG	230	6-2	JrSq
68 David Bourquin	ORG	230	6-2	Sr2L
69 Max Vater	OLG	230	6-1	So
70 Mike Sanguinet	DLT	232	6-1	So
71 Walker Westerlage	OLT	220	5-11	So
72 Charles McKinney	OLG	230	6-0	So
73 Don McIntosh	OLT	225	6-3	So
74 Luke Stungis	ORT	215	6-2	Sr1L
75 Paul Lohn	ORT	225	6-4	So
76 Keith Braun	DLT	250	6-5	So
78 Paul Morrison	LLB	185	6-2	So
79 David Cruthirds	DRT	225	6-3	So
80 Charles Mader	DLE	205	6-1	JrSq
81 Bill Stohler	DRE	205	6-2	Jr1L
82 Johnny Sargent	TE	230	6-4	So
83 Mack Mitchell	DRE	230	6-8	So
84 Eric Muegge	DRE	220	6-3	SrSq
85 Phill Hahn	DLE	240	6-4	JrSq
86 Miller Bassler	TE	205	6-4	So
87 Ricky Terrell	K-DLE	210	6-1	So
88 Steve George	DRT	250	6-5	Jr1L
89 Paul Loukanis	FLK	185	6-1	So

Texas Captains for 1972 - Left to right: Alan Lowry, Randy Braband, Jerry Sisemore.

TEXAS LONGHORNS
Head Football Coach: Darrell Royal

No. Name	Pos.	Wt.	Ht.	Class Exp.
29 Aboussie, Joe	OB	189	5-9	So
70 Adams, Dan	OT	216	6-0	Jr
10 Akins, Marty	QB	190	6-0	Fr
41 Arnold, Jay	DE	189	6-0	Jr1L
21 Bayer, Mike	DB	177	6-0	Sr2L
33 Bennett, Lonnie	OB	182	5-8	Jr
78 Boecker, John	DT	285	6-6	So
63 Braband, Randy	LB	231	6-0	Sr2L
62 Burleson, Rick	C	220	6-4	Fr
25 Burrisk, Don	OB	184	5-10	Jr1L
47 Cannon, Bruce	LB	200	5-10	Jr
37 Childress, R. J.	LB	208	6-2	Sr1L
89 Cromeens, Mike	DE	211	6-3	Jr
61 Crosslin, Don	OG	242	6-0	Jr1L
72 Crowell, Mike	DT	226	6-4	So
23 Cumley, Steve	OE	168	6-0	Jr
80 Currin, Fred	DT	218	6-5	So
65 Dahlberg, Greg	C	214	5-11	Jr1L
81 Davis, Rick	OE	230	6-4	Jr1L
5 Dean, Mike	KS	209	6-0	So
34 Ealey, Donald	OB	205	6-0	Sr1L
74 English, Doug	DT	237	6-5	So
42 Featherston, Coy	OB	180	5-9	So
55 Fenlaw, Rick	LB	193	6-1	Fr
24 Fleming, Steve	OB	187	5-10	Sr1L
18 Ford, Adrian	QB	194	6-0	So
38 Gaspard, Glen	LB	224	6-0	Jr1L
51 Hardage, Mike	C	206	6-2	So
54 Hebert, Bruce	OT	214	6-0	So
86 Hicks, Stan	OE	208	6-1	Sr2L
52 Huber, Tighe	OG	216	6-3	So
49 Isbell, Tommy	DB	180	5-10	So
35 Johnston, Wade	LB	219	6-0	So
12 Keel, Tommy	DB	163	5-10	So
16 Kelly, Pat	OE	172	5-11	Jr1L
36 Krill, David	DB	173	6-0	So
26 Ladd, Dennis	OB	198	6-0	Jr1L
22 Landry, Tom	OB	190	5-11	Jr1L
46 Leaks, Roosevelt	OB	206	5-11	So
85 Lee, Sherman	LB	210	6-1	So
45 Lee, Tommy	LB	214	6-3	Sr2L
60 Lenz, Robert	OG	217	6-3	Jr
15 Lowry, Alan	QB	186	5-10	Sr2L
59 Lyles, Lee	C	215	6-3	Sr
30 Macaluso, Mickey	LB	203	6-2	So
64 Mailey, Bruce	OG	215	6-3	So
19 Melancon, Terry	DB	178	5-9	So
67 Mercado, David	OT	213	6-2	So
48 Minnick, Malcolm	DE	212	6-0	Jr1L
13 Moore, Jim	OE	158	5-9	Jr1L
68 Oxley, Steve	OT	227	6-1	Sr2L
43 Padgett, Pat	DB	170	5-9	So
95 Perry, Fred	LB	196	6-0	So
14 Presley, Mike	QB	194	6-2	So
66 Roach, Travis	OG	251	6-3	Sr2L
44 Rowan, Mike	DB	192	5-10	Sr2L
87 Rutherford, Bill	DE	225	6-2	Jr1L
8 Sarchet, Fred	DB	165	5-10	So
3 Schott, Billy	KS	176	5-8	So
32 Shaw, Howard	LB	205	5-11	Sr1L
79 Sheldon, Rick	OG	225	6-2	So
76 Sisemore, Jerry	OT	260	6-4	Sr2L
71 Smith, Garry	OT	225	6-3	So
20 Steakley, Dan	OB	174	5-9	Sr2L
75 Thurman, Rick	DT	225	6-5	So
57 Tresch, Bob	C	229	6-4	So
77 Walker, Bill	DT	223	5-11	Jr1L
92 Walker, Paul	LB	198	6-0	So
82 Whittier, Julius	OE	205	5-10	Sr2L
67 Wilcox, Will	OT	220	6-3	Fr
11 Workman, Ronnie	DB	200	6-3	Jr
50 Wyman, Bill	C	231	6-1	Jr1L
28 Yeoman, Gary	DB	187	6-0	Jr

Left to right: Wayne Morris, Leonard Carey, Alvin Maxson, Robert Popelka.

SOUTHERN METHODIST MUSTANGS
Head Football Coach: Hayden Fry

No. Name	Pos.	Wt.	Ht.	Class Exp.
10 Casey Ortez	QB	190	6-3	So
11 John Blackburn	QB	185	5-11	So
12 Gene Pouncy	CB	183	6-0	So
14 Raymond Mapps	SE	165	5-9	Sr2L
15 Kenny Harrison	SE	165	6-1	Fr
16 Andy Duvall	S	175	5-11	Jr1L
18 Don Jarma	QB	175	6-1	So
19 Keith Bobo	QB	195	6-3	Jr1L
20 Randy Dossett	S	185	6-1	Sr2L
21 Dennis Howell	FB	200	6-0	Sr1L
22 T. J. Hutchinson	HB	190	5-11	Jr1L
23 Danny Browning	HB	182	6-0	So
25 Wayne Morris	RB	195	6-1	Fr
27 Kelly Overturf	HB	185	6-0	So
28 Alvin Maxson	HB	190	6-0	Jr1L
29 Rayford Clark	FB	210	5-11	Jr1L
30 Clint Hackney	LB-K	205	6-1	So
31 Leonard Carey	LB	220	6-0	Sr1L
32 Sam McLarty	P	170	5-10	Sr2L
33 Jim Farris	LB	195	6-2	So
34 Garry Henderson	LB	210	6-2	JrTr
35 Hawk Shaw	LB	220	6-4	JrTr
37 Corky Hall	LB	190	6-0	So
38 Joe Dickerson	LB	190	6-2	Sr2L
39 Ted Thompson	LB-K	215	6-1	So
40 Joe Pouncy	SE	179	6-0	So
41 Ronnie Robertson	CB	175	5-10	Jr1L
42 Mickey Early	S	180	5-11	So
43 Robert Popelka	S	178	6-0	Sr2L
44 Rusty Fuller	CB	172	5-9	So
45 Robert Smith	CB	168	6-0	So
46 Jim Ryan	LB	190	6-3	Sr2L
47 Mack Rogers	LB	210	6-1	Sr1L
49 Cleve Whitener	LB	195	6-0	Sr2L
50 Bill Wood	OG	215	6-3	So
51 Mike Smith	C	220	6-3	So
52 Jim Upshaw	C	210	6-2	So
54 Steve Stookey	DT	210	6-1	So
55 Mike Haynes	C	200	6-0	Jr1L
56 Herb Johnson	OT	220	6-3	So
57 Bill Thomas	OG	240	6-4	So
58 Kelly Arnold	OT	215	6-4	Jr1L
59 Steve Sims	C	225	6-3	JrSq
60 Charles Carneal	DE	210	6-1	JrSq
61 James Bond	OG	205	5-11	So
62 Doug Terry	DT	182	5-9	JrSq
63 Randy Savage	DT	220	6-2	So
64 Horace Derry	DE	240	6-4	So
65 Guy Thomas	OG	240	6-1	Fr
66 Ed Johnson	DT	240	6-5	JrTr
67 Don Randell	DT	195	5-9	Sr2L
68 Tom Black	OG	225	6-3	Sr2L
69 Marvin Hahn	OT	245	6-5	So
70 Steve Morton	DE	235	6-5	So
71 Phil Jones	OG	210	6-1	So
72 Louis Kelcher	DT	250	6-4	So
73 Henry Sheppard	OG	230	6-6	So
74 Mike Leitko	DT	225	6-4	Jr1L
75 Schaad Titus	OG	230	6-2	So
76 D. Nady	OT	235	6-5	So
78 Tino Zaragoza	DE	190	6-4	So
79 Don Deweber	OT	225	6-2	Sr2L
80 Rufus Shaw	SE	165	5-10	So
81 Randy Goss	FL	180	6-1	Jr1L
82 Rory Best	TE	210	6-2	So
83 Ralph Blount	TE	215	6-4	JrSq
84 David Krischke	FL	185	6-4	So
85 Kris Silverthorn	CB	185	5-11	Jr1L
86 Joe Nobles	TE	200	6-2	So
87 James Lee Robinson	SE	180	5-10	Jr1L
88 Oscar Roan	TE	210	6-6	So
89 Mark Hammond	TE	186	6-1	So
90 Robert Gibson	CB	188	5-11	So
91 Doug Berg	CB	190	6-0	Sr2L
93 Brian Duncan	LB	190	5-11	So
94 Bobby White	S	175	5-11	So
95 Rick Weyand	DE	215	6-4	So

Texas A & M Coach and Captains for 1972 - Front: Coach Emory Bellard, Boice Best (68), Grady Hoermann (31), Todd Christopher (64) and Brad Dusek (44).

TEXAS A&M AGGIES
Head Football Coach: Emory Bellard

No. Name	Pos.	Wt.	Ht.	Class Exp.
10 Lex James	QB	193	6-0	JrTr
11 Tim Trimmier	QB	189	6-4	JrSq
12 Don Dean	QB	190	6-0	So
13 Bill Nutt	P	190	6-0	So
14 Earnest Bean	HB	198	6-0	Fr
15 Bobby Hughes	SE	163	5-8	JrSq
17 Rick Spencer	SE	163	5-6	Jr1L
18 Carl Roaches	SE	155	5-9	Fr
19 Mike Keese	SE	181	6-1	So
20 Mark Green	HB	216	6-3	Jr1L
21 Clifford Thomas	HB	186	5-11	Sr1L
22 Allen Anderson	HB	192	6-0	So
23 Skip Walker	HB	180	6-0	Fr
24 Marvin Tate	S	194	6-1	So
25 Robert Murski	CB	189	6-0	Sr2L
26 Pat Thomas	CB	178	5-10	Fr
28 Ronnie Hubby	HB	196	5-10	Fr
29 Al Thurmond	S	174	5-11	So
30 Jerry Honore	FB	220	6-0	So
31 Grady Hoermann	LB	220	6-0	Sr2L
32 Euger Deets	LB	220	6-1	So
33 Alvin Bowers	FB	210	6-0	Fr
34 Ken Stratton	LB	191	5-10	So
35 Paul Hulin	DE	212	6-0	So
36 Bill Cazalas	LB	210	6-0	So
37 Gary Whitehead	HB	202	5-0	Jr1L
38 Charlie Billingsley	CB	153	5-9	Jr1L
40 David Standish	FB	196	5-11	JrSq
41 Alan Bryant	CB	184	5-9	So
42 Steve Canter	S	186	6-1	So
43 Dwight LaBauve	DT	188	6-1	Jr1L
44 Brad Dusek	FB	212	6-2	Sr2L
46 Larry Ellis	S	172	5-11	Jr1L
47 Mike Newton	S	190	6-1	So
48 Bob Jennings	CB	193	6-0	JrTr
49 Corky Sheffield	CB	180	5-10	Sr1L
50 Buster Callaway	RG	258	6-3	Sr2L
51 Skip Kuehn	C	233	6-0	Sr1L
52 D. J. Hubbert	DE	220	6-0	So
53 Darrell Taliaferro	C	198	6-2	SrSq
54 Mike Mercer	C	187	5-11	JrSq
55 Ted Lamp	DT	215	6-1	So
56 Kevin Owen	DT	231	6-3	So
57 Henry Tracy	C	215	6-2	Fr
58 Mike Park	LT	225	6-4	Sr2L
59 Dennis Carruth	LB	209	5-11	Sr2L
60 Kent Finley	LB	209	6-0	Sr2L
61 Bill Wiebold	DT	228	6-3	Jr1L
63 Ricky Seeler	LT	238	6-3	So
64 Todd Christopher	LG	237	6-2	Sr2L
65 Clifton Thomas	LG	247	6-4	Sr1L
66 Dan Peoples	LG	215	6-2	Jr1L
68 Boice Best	DT	233	6-1	Sr2L
69 Herman Mauch	LT	249	6-3	JrSq
70 Warren Trahan	RT	254	6-1	So
71 Brooks Doughtie	RG	222	6-2	JrSq
73 Robert Gerasimowicz	C	212	6-0	Sr2L
74 Glenn Bujnoch	LT	230	6-4	Fr
75 Bud Trammell	RG	254	6-1	SrSq
76 Ralph Sacra	RT	238	6-5	Sr2L
77 Ed Simonini	LB	200	6-0	Fr
79 Dennis Smelser	LG	250	6-5	Fr
80 Homer May	TE	237	6-3	Sr2L
81 James Dubcak	DE	240	6-6	Sr2L
82 Doug Jordan	TE	217	6-2	So
83 Richard Osborne	SE	210	6-5	Fr
84 Tom Burke	TE	222	6-4	SrSq
85 Mike Bruton	LB	209	6-0	JrSq
86 David McKee	LB	202	6-0	JrSq
87 Max Bird	DE	223	6-0	Sr2L
88 Blake Schwarz	DE	215	6-3	Fr
89 Glenn McNatt	LB	212	6-2	JrSq
90 Randy Haddox	LT	238	6-5	So
91 Gregg Hall	DT	217	6-0	Sr1L
92 Dennis Henderson	DE	235	5-11	So
93 Robert Dennis	LB	195	5-10	So
94 Clay Thorton	LB	196	6-1	SrSq
95 Don Long	DE	237	6-3	So
96 Mike Bertirotti	DT	212	5-11	So
97 Roberto Payan	K	218	6-2	JrSq
98 Rusty Pool	LB	215	6-1	Jr1L
99 Pat McDermott	K	160	5-9	Sr2L

1972 Arkansas Seniors - Front row left to right: Walter Nelson, Louis Campbell, Jon Richardson, Jim Benton, Jim Hodge, Jim Irwin, Les Williams, Mike Reppond. Back row left to right: Scott Binnion, Joe Ferguson, Mike Saint, Mike Griffin, David Reavis, Don Wunderly, Tom Reed, Glen Lowe.

ARKANSAS RAZORBACKS
Head Football Coach: Frank Broyles

No. Name	Pos.	Wt.	Ht.	Class Exp.
86 Applegath, James ..	LB	176	6-1	JrSq
84 Avlos, Nick	TE	223	6-3	JrSq
61 Bankston, Bill	OG	220	6-1	JrSq
52 Bennett, Archie	OT	241	6-0	Sr2L
87 Benton, Jim	LB	212	6-0	Sr2L
36 Binnion, Scott	LB	210	5-11	Sr2L
62 Bolton, Andy	K	206	5-10	So
55 Boozman, John	OG	229	6-3	Jr1L
64 Brand, Rodger	OG	212	6-1	Jr1L
57 Brawner, Jim	DE	209	6-0	Jr1L
19 Bull, Scotty	QB	203	6-4	So
53 Burns, Billy	LB	215	6-1	So
37 Campbell, Louis ...	RC	182	6-1	Sr2L
59 Capshaw, Gary	C	202	6-3	So
88 Craig, Reggie	FL	182	6-0	So
39 Davis, Mike	RC	184	6-0	Jr1L
34 Douglas, Freddie	FS	170	5-10	Fr
54 Drake, Randy	C	230	6-4	So
23 Ettinger, Jack	SE	184	6-2	Jr1L
11 Ferguson, Joe	QB	182	6-1	Sr2L
78 Flesher, Mike	OT	231	6-4	So
50 Freeland, Stuart	C	232	6-3	Jr1L
35 Fryer, Jimmy	FB	210	5-11	Jr1L
42 Fuchs, Rolland	TB	192	5-10	So
79 Glover, Steve	OT	236	6-1	JrSq
66 Griffin, Mike	OT	241	6-2	Sr2L
82 Griffith, Calvin	DE	223	6-3	JrSq
49 Harris, Tommy	SS	182	6-1	Fr
85 Hedgepeth, Steve ..	TE	212	6-3	Jr1L
31 Hirschfield, Hal	FB	210	6-0	So
22 Hodge, Jim	FL	167	5-11	Sr2L
25 Hollingsworth, Mark .	FS	191	6-1	Jr1L
20 Irwin, Clark	SS	187	6-0	Jr1L
15 Irwin, Jim	LC	177	5-11	Sr1L
83 Jordan, Ivan	DE	200	6-2	Fr
70 King, Lee	OT	244	6-3	So
14 Kirkland, Mike	QB	187	6-2	Fr
76 Landrum, Steve	DE	210	6-3	So
71 Lowe, Glen	OG	240	6-3	Sr2L
46 Martin, Ken	LC	170	5-11	So
30 Miles, Wayne	FB	210	6-3	So
80 Morrison, Matt	TE	193	6-2	So
23 Morton, Dickey	TB	170	5-10	Jr1L
21 Moseley, John	LC	188	6-0	So
16 Nelson, Walter	QB	185	6-0	Sr1L
27 Phillips, Larry	RC	185	6-1	So
89 Reavis, David	DT	240	6-3	Sr2L
74 Reed, Tom	OG	235	6-3	Sr2L
26 Reppond, Mike	SE	172	6-0	Sr2L
58 Revard, Ron	OT	235	6-2	Sr2L
60 Rhiddlehoover, Jon .	DT	226	6-1	So
56 Rhodes, Danny	LB	217	6-1	Jr1L
24 Richardson, Jon	TB	188	5-11	Sr2L
51 Rownd, Ed	LB	204	6-1	Jr1L
28 Sadler, Dennis	SE	189	6-3	JrSq
44 Saint, Mike	FB	200	6-0	Sr2L
73 Sims, Chuck	DT	223	6-3	So
40 Smith, Rollen	RC	190	6-1	JrJC
47 Stell, Jack	DE	187	6-2	So
48 Strain, Ray	DE	198	6-1	So
41 Taylor, Jim	SS	189	6-1	Jr1L
29 Toole, Drew	P	207	5-11	Jr1L
17 Warren, Tom	FS	175	5-11	So
68 Wheat, John	LB	210	6-1	Jr1L
32 White, Marsh	FB	209	6-2	So
45 Williams, Les	DE	197	5-10	Sr2L
72 Wunderly, Don	DT	221	6-3	Sr1L
62 Wynn, Ricky	K	220	6-4	Fr
81 Yoder, Douglas	DE	205	6-3	Fr

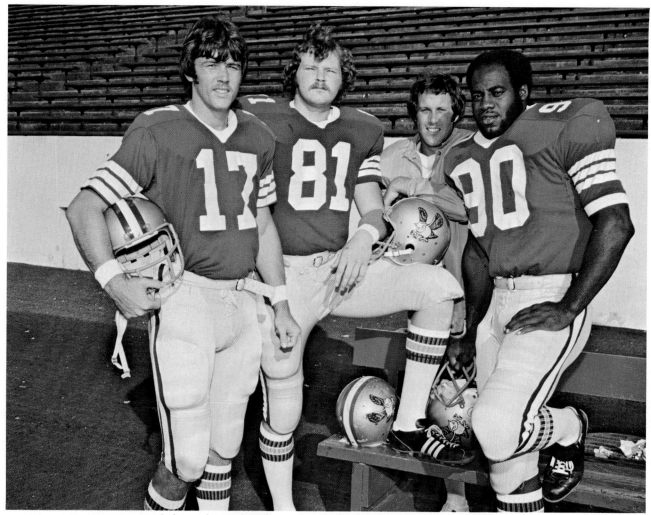

Left to right: Mark Williams, Gary Butler, Bruce Gadd, Rodrigo Barnes.

RICE OWLS
Head Football Coach: Al Conover

No. Name	Pos.	Wt.	Ht.	Class Exp.
10 Bruce Gadd	QB	185	5-11	Sr2L
11 Bill McCabe	QB	183	6-2	So
14 Mike Kramer	QB	189	6-2	SrSq
15 Hank English	K	164	5-10	JrSq
17 Mark Williams	K	186	6-0	Sr2L
19 Johnny Peterson	S	162	5-10	So
20 Ron Arceneaux	R	181	6-2	Jr1L
21 Gary Ferguson	RB	181	5-10	So
22 Steve Ogletree	FB	184	6-1	Jr1L
23 Joe Buck	TE	185	6-1	Sr2L
25 Bill Chilivetis	CB	179	5-9	Jr1L
26 Don Bernshausen ..	CB	174	6-0	Jr1L
28 Buddy Chuoke	CB	172	5-10	So
29 Carl Swierc	R	180	6-1	Jr1L
30 Dennis Pokluda	FB	205	5-11	So
31 David Simpson	FB	197	5-10	Jr1L
33 Harry Higgins	CB	194	6-0	JrSq
34 Larry Brune	MM	190	6-1	So
35 LaRay Breshers	LB	199	6-0	Sr2L
36 Chuck Hudson	DB	185	6-3	Fr
37 Pat Kelly	LB	197	6-0	Jr1L
38 Jake Smitherman ..	LB	208	6-0½	So
39 Brad Tally	MM	180	5-11	Jr1L
40 Preston Anderson ..	MM	172	6-0	Jr1L
41 Cliff Crabtree	FB	187	5-10	Sr2L
42 Tom Clanton	CB	179	5-10	Sr2L
43 Joe Phy	RB	156	5-7	Jr1L
44 John Coleman	RB	186	5-10	Fr
46 Cullie Culpepper	S	160	6-0	So
49 Bruce Henley	S	173	6-2	Jr1L
50 David Snellings	LB	194	6-0	Jr1L
51 Tommy Godard	C	217	6-3	Jr1L
52 Jody Medford	DT	248	6-3½	So
53 Richard Hollas	LB	197	6-1	Jr1L
54 Hap Feuerbacher ...	LB	194	6-0	Jr1L
55 Wade Bode	DT	226	5-11	Jr1L
56 Joe Suggs	C	195	6-0	Jr1L
57 Larry Baugh	LB	195	6-2	Jr1L
58 David Vandiver	OG	220	6-0	Jr1L
60 Bart Goforth	OG	229	6-2	Sr2L
61 Randy Alford	DT	222	6-0	Sr2L
62 Rusty McKeever	OG	215	6-0	So
63 Tobin Haynes	OG	198	6-2	Sr2L
64 Michael Goode	C	202	6-1	Jr1L
65 Steve Pruitt	DE	207	6-2	Jr1L
66 Mike Friend	OG	226	6-4	So
67 Dee McCurry	LB	204	5-10	So
69 Hal Perkins	OG	217	6-0	So
70 Scott Moss	OT	224	6-0	So
73 Larry Medford	DE	234	6-2	Jr1L
74 Sammy Johnson ...	OT	245	6-3	Jr1L
75 Ron Waedemon ...	OT	239	6-5	Sr2L
76 Cornelius Walker ...	DT	249	6-2½	So
77 John Paul Hershey .	OT	224	6-3	Sr2L
78 Robert Walz	OT	223	6-4	So
79 Bryan Daveport	DT	224	6-2	Jr1L
80 Larry Walling	DE	190	6-2	Sr2L
81 Gary Butler	TE	239	6-4	Sr2L
82 John Burtner	DE	211	6-3	So
83 Bubba Berg	R	186	6-0	Jr1L
85 Edwin Collins	R	190	6-1	Jr1L
86 Tracy Terry	TE	198	6-1	Jr1L
88 Jerry Manning	DE	215	6-5	So
89 John Kelly	LB	208	6-1	Jr1L
90 Rodrigo Barnes	LB	210	6-2	Sr2L

Left to right: Donald Rives, Joe Barnes, Doug McCutchen.

TEXAS TECH RED RAIDERS

Head Football Coach: Jim Carlen

No. Name	Pos.	Wt.	Ht.	Class Exp.
11 Don Grimes	KS	169	5-9	Jr1L
12 Joe Barnes	QB	185	5-11	Jr1L
14 Jerry Reynolds	QB	198	6-2	JrSq
16 Jimmy Carmichael	QB	175	6-1	Jr1L
20 Randy Olson	CB	169	5-10	So
21 Steve VanLoozen	FS	185	5-11	Jr1L
22 Gary Bartel	DB	159	5-9	So
23 Danny Willis	SS	176	6-0	Jr1L
24 Tony Green	DB	182	6-1	So
25 Salley Richard	SS	176	5-11	So
26 Randy Levens	SS	150	5-10	So
27 Kenneth Wallace	CB	155	5-11	Jr1L
28 Greg Waters	FS	182	6-1	JrSq
29 Lawrence Williams	DB	175	5-10	So
31 Stuart Tucker	FB	178	5-10	Jr1L
32 Doug McCutchen	TB	205	5-11	Sr2L
33 James Mosley	FB	214	5-8	Jr1L
34 Benjie Reed	TB	185	5-10	Jr1L
35 John Garner	FB	196	6-0	So
36 Cliff Hoskins	FB	196	6-0	So
38 George Smith	TB	176	5-10	JCTr
40 Calvin Jones	F	213	6-4	So
41 Harry Case	TE	217	6-1	Sr2L
42 Ricky Bates	SE	191	6-1	So
43 Curtis Jordan	F	180	6-1	Fr
44 Andre Tillman	SE	224	6-5	Jr1L
45 Pat Felux	TE	208	6-1	So
46 Ronnie Samford	TE	196	6-1	Jr1L
48 Jeff Jobe	F	173	6-2	So
49 Paul Page	F	200	6-2	So
50 George Herro	LB	206	5-10	Jr1L
51 Donald Rives	DG	215	6-2	Sr2L
52 David Knaus	DG	219	6-2	So
53 Randy Lancaster	LB	212	6-1	JrSq
54 Quintin Robinson	LB	212	6-2	Sr2L
56 Tom Ryan	LB	197	6-0	Jr1L
57 Charlie Beery	LB	195	6-2	JCTr
58 Tom Dyer	LB	195	5-11	So
60 Russell Ingram	C	224	6-4	Sr2L
61 Jim Frasure	C	210	6-4	So
62 Harold Lyons	OG	223	5-11	Sr2L
63 Larry Burnett	C	201	6-4	JrSq
64 Gary Monroe	OG	211	6-2	So
65 Dennis Allen	OG	240	6-0	Jr1L
66 Floyd Keeney	OG	217	6-2	So
70 Davis Corley	DT	218	6-3	Sr2L
71 Chuck Zeller	DT	251	6-2	SrSq
72 Tim Schaffner	DT	234	6-2	Sr2L
73 Brian Bernwanger	DT	252	6-0	Jr1L
74 Ecomet Burley	OT	235	5-11	Fr
75 Tom Keliehor	OT	215	6-1	So
76 Doug White	OT	209	6-2	So
77 Fred Chandler	OT	207	6-0	So
78 Gary Shuler	OT	221	6-2	Sr1L
79 Tom Furgerson	OT	225	5-11	JrSq
80 Aubrey McCain	DE	203	6-1	So
81 Tommy Cones	DE	203	6-1	So
83 Randy Griffith	DE	185	6-3	JrSq
84 Gaines Baty	DE	195	6-0	Sr2L
85 Andy Lowe	DE	209	6-2	Jr1L

First Week
September 9

Dickey Morton breaks loose for 18 yards on Arkansas' opening drive of the second half. The Razorback's offensive line clears the path for Morton who overall gained 52 yards on nine carries.

SOUTHERN CAL 31 - ARKANSAS 10

This was an opening game collision between two nationally-ranked powers. The winner could possibly go all the way. A record crowd of 54,461 filled War Memorial Stadium in Little Rock to help usher in another football season. This was the first meeting ever between the Trojans and Razorbacks.

Arkansas won the toss, took the wind, and kicked off. The Trojan's Manfred Moore returned 25 yards before he was jarred loose from the football by Billy Burns. Doug Yoder grabbed the ball in the air and returned two yards to the Southern Cal 28. The Hogs picked up a first down on Dickey Morton's nine-yard run and Jon Richardson's two yard plunge on fourth down. Two running plays and an incomplete pass gained only six. Andy Bolton came in on fourth down and kicked a 27-yard field goal to put Arkansas ahead 3-0.

On the following kickoff Allen Carter fumbled, but Moore covered the ball for USC. The Trojans moved to the Arkansas 39, then were forced to punt. From their 20 the Razorbacks, with the help of a Trojan personal foul, reached their 42 where Drew Toole punted to the Southern Cal 25. On their next possession the Hogs reached the Trojan 33 mainly on the running of Mike

Saint. On third down quarterback Joe Ferguson was rushed hard, fumbled, and recovered for an eight-yard loss. Toole's punt went straight up, but got a good bounce to the USC 21.

As the second quarter opened the Razorbacks were moving again. Ferguson hit Jim Hodge for 15 yards to bring the ball out to the Arkansas 31. Two plays later he connected with Mike Reppond for 10 yards. Saint gained three and Morton broke through a hole as he burst into Trojan territory. The 12-yard gain went for naught as Morton fumbled when hit and Steve Fate recovered for USC at his 40.

This turnover brought some anxious moments to the Razorback defense. The Trojans stormed the Arkansas goal three times before the half ended and came away with only three points. Quarterback Mike Rae first led them to a first and goal at the Hog two. Sam Cunningham gained one, then was held for no gain. Rae kept, after faking to Cunningham, was hit near the goal line and fumbled. USC claimed he scored, Arkansas claimed they had recovered the fumble. The officials put the ball inches away from the goal saying that Rae had not scored and the whistle had blown before the fumble. On fourth down

Mike Saint(44) goes off tackle as Jeff Winans (92) tries to hold on. Tom Reed (74) and Glen Lowe (71) open the hole. Saint led the Razorbacks in rushing with 63 yards on 12 carries

Cunningham was stopped again and Arkansas took over. Next time USC got the ball they reached the nine, but on third and two Rod McNeill lost two and Rae then kicked a 26-yard field goal. Then the Trojans, after reaching the Hog 24, tried a field goal with two seconds remaining. The 41-yard try was wide and the half ended 3-3.

Arkansas received the second half kickoff and with Saint and Morton finding big holes stayed on the ground to reach the USC 18. Ferguson overcame a holding penalty by passing to Matt Morrison for 21 yards to the 16. Southern Cal held and Bolton attempted a 34-yard field goal which was wide.

Before the Razorbacks were in scoring range again the Trojans had scored two touchdowns. They moved 59 yards in five plays with 43 of it gained on a Rae to Edesel Garrison pass. Rae ran five yards for the score and then kicked the extra point. USC led 10-3. Next, linebacker Richard Wood intercepted Ferguson and returned to the Hog 40. The Trojans scored in six plays with McNeill going in from the three. Rae converted and USC led 17-3.

As the fourth quarter opened Bolton missed on an attempt for a 46-yard field goal. After a five-yard penalty put Southern Cal on their 15, Rae lofted a 52-yard pass to Lynn Swann. A face-masking penalty added on gave the Trojans a 67-yard gain to the Arkansas 18. McNeill ran over from there and with Rae's PAT the Trojans led 24-3.

The Razorbacks lowered the deficit to 10 as Ferguson struck with lightning quickness to move 65 yards in four plays. He passed to Hodge for 12, Reppond for 13 and back to Hodge for 39. This put the ball on the USC one and Richardson scored on the next play. Bolton converted and USC led 24-10.

After moving to the Hog 27, Rae missed on a field goal. But Fate intercepted Ferguson and the Trojans were knocking again at the Arkansas 14. Cunningham scored but an illegal motion penalty made him repeat his run from the 17. Rae kicked good and USC led 31-10.

Ferguson led the Razorbacks on a 70-yard drive to the Trojan one, but the final gun stopped the march.

Rae, the senior quarterback who had played in Jimmy Jones shadow for two years, got his chance and came through with a convincing performance for Coach John McKay. On the opposite side Coach Frank Broyles said, "We know we just played a good team and we should be a better team for having played them."

	USC	Arkansas
First downs	24	21
Rushes-yards	52-208	40-168
Passing yardage	269	223
Return yards	75	6
Passes	18-25-0	19-37-2
Punts	4-38-3	5-27-8
Fumbles	3-1	1-1
Yards penalized	8-75	3-43

USC	0	3	14	14—31
Arkansas	3	0	0	7—10

Ark—FG Bolton 27
USC—FG— Rae 26
USC—Rae 5 run (Rae kick)
USC—McNeill 3 run (Rae kick)
Ark—Richardson 1 run (Bolton kick)
USC—McNeill 18 run (Rae kick)
USC—Cunningham 17 run (Rae kick)
A—54,461

Aggie quarterback Lex James (10) follows the blocking of his back, Bubba Dean, on Wichita's Charley Roberts (57). Both James and Bean scored touchdowns in the game.

TEXAS A&M 36 - WICHITA STATE 13

Coach Emory Bellard brought his Aggies to Wichita to open their 1972 season and his head coaching career. Before a Saturday night crowd of 22,659 the Wheatshockers started out as their nickname implies-shockers.

A & M won the coin toss and elected to kick off. The short kick carried only to the 20 where freshman Fred Speck fumbled it briefly before gaining control at his 15. He then darted up the middle past onrushing Cadets and sped 85 yards for a touchdown. John Potts missed the extra point and Wichita led 6-0.

The Aggies kept their cool and marched downfield following the Shocker kickoff, but Brad Dusek fumbled at the Wichita two. Tony Marshall recovered in the end zone for the Shockers. The A & M defense forced a Wichita punt after three plays. Carl Roaches returned the punt 44 yards to the Wichita eight, but A & M was called for clipping which wiped out the return. The second time around the Cadets moved 61 yards in five plays to score. Quarterback Lex James hit tight end Homer May,

who was five yards behind his coverage, for 33 yards and the touchdown. The extra point try was foiled by a bad center snap and the score remained tied at 6-6.

A & M kicked off and Don Gilley caught the ball at his four, went left past two fallen Aggies, and ran down the sideline for 96 yards and a touchdown. Potts hit on the extra point and Wichita led 13-6.

At the end of the first quarter the Cadets trailed 13-6 even though they had held the Shockers to a total of two yards rushing and none passing. But at the end of the first quarter the Aggies were moving downfield and on the third play of the second quarter Bubba Bean scored from two yards out. This capped a 70-yard march which took 16 snaps. The two-point pass attempt for the conversion failed and the Shockers retained their lead at 13-12.

The "shocked" kickoff unit held on the following boot and when Wichita quarterback Tom Owen attempted his first pass it was picked off by Grady Hoermann. The Cadets had possession at the Shocker 31. They scored in

Despite the score the Aggies didn't have everything go their way all the time. Here Shocker linebacker George Whitfield (50) grabs A & M quarterback Lex James (10). With the help of Ken LeBlanc (19) and Ed Collins (32), James was dropped for a loss.

six plays with Mark Green bulling over right tackle from two yards out. The two-point conversion pass was caught out of bounds and this left A & M leading 18-13.

Wichita's offense threatened as they drove to the Cadets 13-yard line. On a fourth and two Hoermann dropped Don Bufford for a two-yard loss. He then came back on the Shockers next possession and intercepted a pass that had been tipped by teammate Dennis Carruth. Hoermann carried his theft 39 yards to the Wichita 14. On first down James pitched out to Gary Whitehead who blasted down the sidelines for the touchdown. Another two-point conversion was missed and with 2:34 left in the first half A & M led 24-13.

The Cadets regained possession at their 45 with 1:30 remaining. James passed to Richard Osborne for 24 yards. On third down 17 James gained around five yards, then pitched back to Green who sped 38 yards down the sideline to score. The conversion attempt again missed. The Aggies led 30-13 and the first half ended 38 seconds later.

Liberal substitutions held down the second half scoring. The only touchdown came on a 10-yard keeper

by James in the third quarter. The Cadets maintained their perfect conversion record by missing their sixth straight. Despite early game setbacks the Aggies remained unruffled and came away with a 36-13 victory.

Roaches made two fine punt returns which were nullified by penalties. Besides the 44-yard return mentioned earlier he made another for 68 yards into the Wichita end zone. It was cancelled out by a roughing the kicker penalty. The Aggie defense held the Wheatshockers to 114 total yards. The Cadets new wishbone offense ground out 363 yards while the pass was used effectively, but sparingly. Some extra points might come in handy next week when the Aggies journey to Lincoln, Nebraska.

	Texas A & M	Wichita
First downs	28	11
Rushes-yards	74-363	24-20
Passing yards	41	0
Passes	5-12-0	13-35-2
Punts	5-38	8-40
Fumbles-lost	6-3	1-1
Penalties-yards	9-125	11-133

Texas A&M	6	24	6	0—36
Wichita	13	0	0	0—13

Wich—Speck 85 kickoff return (kick fails)
A&M—May 32 pass from James (conversion fails)
Wich—Gilley 94 kickoff return (Potts kick)
A&M—Bean 2 run (conversion fails)
A&M—Green 2 run (conversion fails)
A&M—Whitehead 14 run (conversion fails)
A&M—James 10 run (conversion fails)
A—22,659

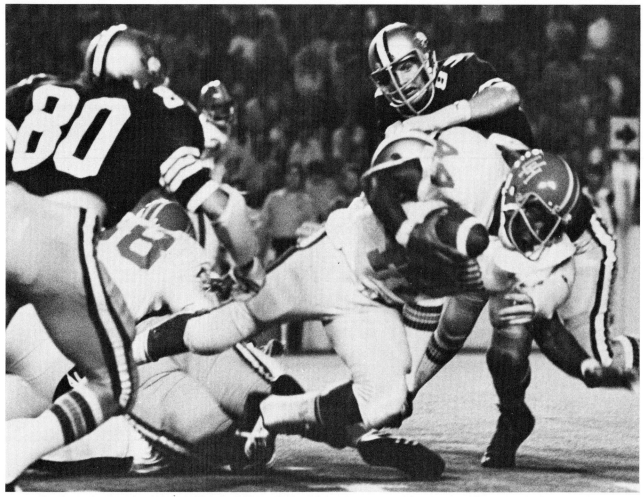

Cougar fullback Leonard Parker, here picking up short yardage between Larry Walling (80) and John Kelley (89), was the leading rusher for the night with 125 yards. He also scored both Houston touchdowns.

RICE 14 - HOUSTON 13

The budding crosstown rivalry between the Cougars and Owls held court for the second time. The encore proved as exciting as last year's two-point victory by Houston. A crowd of 51,000 invaded Rice Stadium and the two teams kept them jumping up and down all during the game. At the end everyone was standing.

There was no scoring in the first quarter although the Cougars threatened after receiving the opening kickoff. With quarterback D. C. Nobles directing the attack they moved from their 28 to the Rice 27. On fourth down and eight Nobles was intercepted at the Owl 10 by Bruce Henley who returned to his 26.

The Owls did not make a first down until their final possession of the opening quarter. When the quarter ended they were on the Cougar 24. Quarterback Bruce Gadd had run for 11 yards and passed to Gary Ferguson for 15 yards to help reach that point. Edwin Collins opened the second period by losing 14 yards on an end around. Mark Williams attempted a field goal from the 45 which was short.

A short Cougar punt gave Rice their next possession at

their 43. In nine plays the Owls had the games' first touchdown. John Coleman, a freshman who had just entered the game, gained steadily on the ground as Rice marched to the Houston 30. From there, on third down, Gadd lofted a high pass into the corner of the Cougar end zone. Edwin Collins, waiting for the ball to come down, out-guessed his double coverage and leaped up to catch the ball. Williams kicked the extra point and with 9:58 left in the first half Rice led 7-0.

The Cougars used up just about all of the time as they ran 19 plays to move 68 yards for the tying touchdown. Leonard Parker and Puddin Jones gained yardage on the ground after a Nobles to Marshall Johnson screen pass of 14 yards had moved the ball into Owl country. At the 11 Nobles returned to the screen pass and hit Robert Ford who was downed at the one. Parker and then Nobles were held for no gain. Following a timeout Parker was called on again and this time he made it. Ricky Terrell kicked the point after and the game was tied 7-7. A minute later the first half ended.

Rice received the kickoff to open the second half. From

David Vandiver (58) and Bart Goforth (60) are the pulling guards on a sweep as quarterback Bruce Gadd (10) hands off to Gary Ferguson (21).

the Owl 37 Gadd hit Ferguson, who made a one-handed catch, for 15 yards. This third and nine play actually gained 30 yards as the Cougars were called for grabbing the face mask. Coleman then ran the ground attack from the 33 with a 14-yard gain putting the ball on the Houston eight. On third down Gadd found Collins behind his man in the end zone and the five-yard pass was good for the go ahead touchdown. Williams added the extra point and Rice led 14-7. The 77 yards covered in 14 plays left 8:32 in the third quarter.

The Owls almost pulled away when LaRay Breshers recovered a Parker fumble at the Cougar 33. Houston got retribution when Collins caught and then dropped a Gadd pass at the 15. Deryl McGallion recovered for Houston.

Toward the end of the third quarter the Cougars were on the move. On the last play of the period Nobles passed to Parker for 10 yards to the Owl 33. Later a 10-yard run by Parker reached the 16. The Rice defense applied the brakes and the Owls took possession at their 12, but moments later Dennis Pokluda fumbled and Bill Jones recovered the ball back at the two. Parker scored on first down. The conversion attempt was bobbled and the kick failed. Rice led 14-13 with 9:56 left.

On their next possession the Cougars reached the Rice 28, but Larry Walling spilled Nobles for a loss of five yards on fourth and one. When they got the ball again there was 2:17 left and they were on their own 23. After an illegal receiver downfield penalty and a time out, their last, Nobles put his arm in high gear. He passed to Johnson for 20 yards, to Puddin Jones for six, back to Johnson for another 20 and two plays later he hit Jones again who fell into the end zone. The officials ruled his knee had touched at the one. Parker was stopped as he tried to dive over and time ran out before the last play got underway although Preston Anderson went through the formalities as he dropped Nobles' attempt to go wide.

It was a great beginning for new Owl coach Al Conover and a bitter ending for the Cougars who did everything but get into the Rice end zone once more. If the first two games between these schools is indicative of things to come they can remove all the seats as everybody will be standing throughout the game.

	Houston	Rice
First downs	21	13
Rushing yards	56-178	46-115
Passing yards	176	115
Return yards	0	21
Passes	16-28-1	8-17-0
Punts	4-38	5-39
Fumbles-lost	2	1
Penalties-yards	4-50	1-9

Houston .... 0 7 0 6—13
Rice .... 0 7 7 0—14
Rice—Collins 30 pass from Gadd (Williams kick)
Hou—Parker 1 run (Terrell kick)
Rice—Collins 5 pass from Gadd (Williams kick)
Hou—Parker 2 run (kick failed)
A—51,000

SYNOPSIS

TOP TEN

1. Southern Cal
2. Colorado
3. Ohio State
4. Oklahoma
5. Alabama
6. Penn State
7. Tennessee
8. UCLA
9. LSU
10. Nebraska

SWC OFFENSIVE PLAYER OF WEEK

John Coleman, Halfback, Rice

SWC DEFENSIVE PLAYER OF WEEK

Grady Hoermann, Linebacker, Texas A & M

UPSET OF WEEK:

UCLA 20 - Nebraska 17

SWC TEAM LEADERS FOR SEASON

OFFENSE
Rushing . . . . Texas A & M 363 yds.
Passing . . . . Arkansas 223 yds.
Total . . . . Texas A & M 432 yds.

DEFENSE
Rushing . . . . Texas A & M   20 yds.
Passing . . . . Texas A & M   94 yds.
Total . . . . Texas A & M 114 yds.

SEASON RECORDS

	W	L	T
Texas A & M	1	0	0
Rice	1	0	0
Houston	0	1	0
Arkansas	0	1	0

Second Week
September 16

39 YEARS AGO
SEPTEMBER 16, 1933
TCU 33 - Austin 0
Rice 7 - Texas A&I 0
North Texas 7 - SMU 0

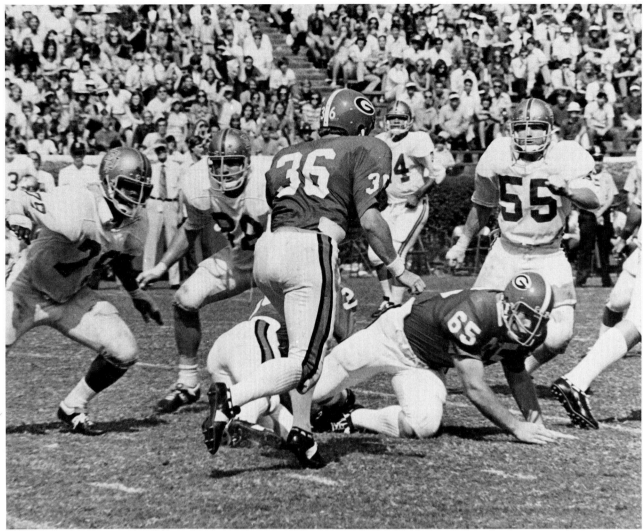

Bulldog Hal Bissell faces the determined Baylor defense as Joe Johnson (79), Mike Black (88) and Roger Goree (55) close in. Goree's got a little help this year. . . no gain.

GEORGIA 24 - BAYLOR 14

A shirtsleeved crowd of 53,201 came to Sanford Stadium in Athens to watch the Bulldogs have a light workout against SWC "Patsy" Baylor. Not too much to get excited about as the Bears had won a grand total of three games the last three years. 'Course this was the first ever meeting between the two schools, so that was something. Georgia, nationally ranked, was a 28 point favorite.

The game started out as a rout as the Bulldogs quickly put 10 points on the scoreboard. Georgia, on their second possession, got a break when a face masking penalty was called on Baylor. This happened when Bulldog quarterback Andy Johnson had just been dumped for a loss on third down. Johnson, with a second chance, passed to Bob Burns for 15 yards to the Bear 20 and two plays later Hal Bissell escaped through the middle for 19 yards and a touchdown. Kim Braswell converted and midway through the first quarter Georgia led 7-0.

The second Georgia break came when, on the following

kickoff, Marcus Rogers fumbled and Don Griffith recovered for the Bulldogs at the Baylor 22. The Bear defense held and Braswell kicked a 22-yard field goal to put Georgia ahead 10-0.

Baylor usually folds about this time, but new quarterback Neal Jeffrey was starting his first game and had no past performances to guide him. He didn't get them across the goal as the new found muscle in the Bear defense shut the door on Georgia, but he took them close enough for Mike Conradt to kick a pair of field goals. One for 38 yards early in the period and another from 37 yards with 8:06 remaining. And that is the way the first half ended, Georgia 10—Baylor 6.

The Bulldog fans sensed something was wrong. Baylor had not scored in an opening game since 1969 and here they trailed by only four points at halftime!

As the second half opened the Bears were threatening to take the lead. Gary Lacy rolled up yardage on the ground as he picked up 11, eight and 15 yards. Georgia's

Bear Gary Lacy follows the blocking of Gene Wilson in this first half action. Lacy ended up as the leading ball carrier for the game

third break came at their 23 when Billy Wilson fumbled and Jim Cagle recovered for the Bulldogs.

Some said that was the turning point, others said it came later in the third quarter when the Bears had a choice of refusing or accepting a Bulldog holding penalty, it would be fourth and 13 or third and 29. They chose third and 29 and on the next play sub quarterback James Ray dropped a bomb in Rex Putnal's hands at the Baylor 15 and Putnal ran it in for six points. The pass-run covered 55 yards. Braswell kicked good and Georgia led 17-6.

The Bulldogs, a running team, abandoned their strength for the pass as they discovered a weakness in the Bear's armour. On their next possession they moved 68 yards in 11 plays. Johnson hit Putnal and Lynn Hunnicut on crucial third down passes to reach the Baylor 20. From there the Bulldogs scored in five plays with Burns going in from the three. Braswell was on target and Georgia led 24-6 with 8:30 left in the game.

The aroused Bears came back and drove 73 yards in 13 plays. Richard Mason opened a hole at right tackle and Lacy scored from the one. Jeffrey passed to Charley

Dancer for two points and the final score read Georgia 24 - Baylor 14.

The Bear defense, led by middle guard Millard Neely, shut down the Bulldogs vaunted running attack. Neely said that when Baylor arrived here they respected Georgia, but now he thinks Georgia also respects Baylor. Statistics, they say, are for losers so let's close with some quotes from Georgia coach Vince Dooley. On a Saturday radio show he said, "All we know about Baylor is that Grant Teaff coached last year at San Angelo State." After the game he looked at the statistics and said, "Who won this game? Baylor is certainly better than they were given credit for. They are a sound team and well-coached. We were outcoached by Baylor today even though we won." There, isn't that better than statistics?

	Bay	Geo
First downs	20	12
Rushes-yards	39-131	45-132
Passing-yards	183	135
Return yards	9	26
Passes	18-32-1	5-12-0
Punts	4-39-0	7-36-0
Fumbles-lost	6-4	2-1
Penalties-yards	4-30	4-46

Baylor 0   6   0   8—14
Georgia 10   0   7   7—24
Geo—Bissell 19 run (Braswell kick).
Geo—FG 22 Braswell.
Bay—FG 38 Conradt.
Bay—FG 37 Conradt.
Geo—Putnal 55 pass from Ray (Braswell kick).
Geo—Burns 3 run (Braswell kick).
Bay—Lacy 1 run (Dancer pass from Jeffrey).

33

Linebacker Jim Farris (33) recovers a Deacon fumble, which had bounced back into their end zone, for an SMU touchdown. Other Mustangs converging on the ball are Charles Carneal (60) Ted Thompson (39), Randy Dossett (20) and Robert Gibson (90).

SMU 56 - WAKE FOREST 10

The Mustangs were playing their first game in the new Texas Stadium and early rain showers held the crowd down to 20,175. Not since Maris and Mantle has there been such a devastating M & M duo as Alvin Maxson and Wayne Morris. At the end Maxson totaled 169 yards in 22 carries and Morris gobbled up 154 in 18 cracks. Maxson also managed to squeeze in four touchdowns along the way. This was the first meeting ever between the Deacons and Mustangs and the Deacons are probably still wondering which way did he go.

SMU scored 10 points in the opening quarter. The first came on a 30-yard field goal by Clint Hackney which was set up when Kris Silverthorn intercepted a pass thrown by Deacon quarterback Chuck Ramsey. This put SMU in front 3-0.

Wake Forest came back and entered field goal range, but Doug Berg blocked Ramsey's attempt from the 37.

Donnie Brown had intercepted Mustang quarterback Casey Ortez to set up the blocked kick.

Ortez then hit swift Rufus Shaw on a fly pattern and the play covered 68 yards into the Deacon end zone. A holding penalty nullified it all and put SMU back on its 17. There they moved 83 yards to score. Other than an Ortez to Shaw pass for 16 yards, Maxson picked up all the yardage on his ground assault. He faked, darted and dashed his way the last 13 yards for the touchdown. Hackney kicked good and SMU led 10-0.

Early in the second quarter the Mustangs got a "cheapie" when Andy Duvall recovered Ed Campbell's fumble on the Wake Forest 15. On first down Maxson swivel-hipped in and SMU led 16-0. The conversion attempt was blocked.

In between Mustang touchdowns the Deacons squeezed in a 40-yard field goal by Ramsey. But another

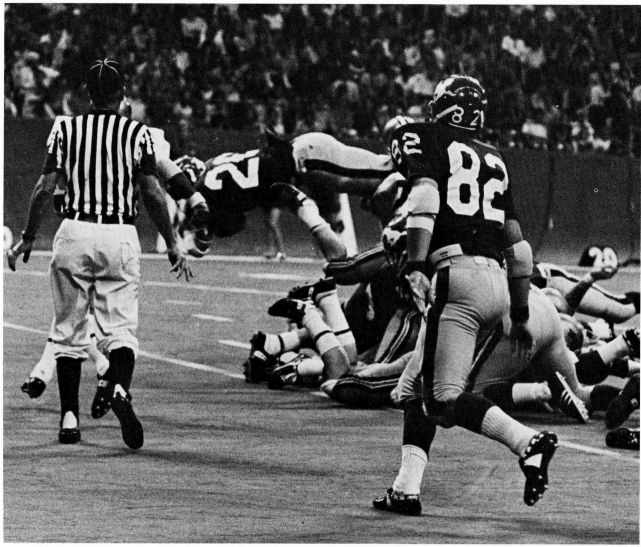

Alvin Maxson (28) flies across the Wake Forest goal for this third touchdown. Tight end Rory Best (82) observes Maxson's leap. For the day Maxson scored four touchdowns in all.

interception of a Ramsey pass, this one by Cleve Whitener, at the Deacon 21 set up SMU for another score before halftime. A pass interference penalty on Wake Forest put the ball on the six. Maxson got his third touchdown two plays later. Hackney converted and at intermission the Ponies led 23-3.

The third quarter action slowed considerably. But toward the end Morris entered the game and woke everyone up with a 50-yard touchdown run. Hackney kicked good and SMU led 30-3.

On the final play of the third quarter Silverthorn returned a Deacon punt 59 yards to the Wake Forest nine. Sub quarterback John Blackburn kept for five and on second down scored from the four. Hackney missed the conversion and early in the fourth quarter SMU led 36-3.

The Mustangs were to score three more touchdowns and all were set up by Wake Forest mistakes. Charles Carneal recovered a Deacon fumble at their 39 and the Ponies scored in four plays with Maxson getting his fourth TD from the 11. Next, new quarterback James

Ryan fumbled a pitchout at his 10 and the ball bounced back into the Deacon end zone where Jim Farris covered it for an SMU touchdown. Finally, Ryan fumbled again and the Mustangs had possession at the Wake Forest 32. Morris accounted for 26 yards and third quarterback Keith Bobo scored from the four. Hackney made two out of three in the extra point department and SMU led 56-3.

Before it all ended the Deacons finally got to the Mustang end zone. Starting quarterback Ramsey passed eight yards to Carl Lowe for the touchdown and Ramsey kicked the extra point. Final score: SMU 56 - WF 10.

	Wake Forest	SMU
First downs	13	25
Rushes-yards	54-97	52-356
Passing yards	115	159
Return yards	7	159
Passes	8-18-2	5-15-1
Punts	6-44	4-35
Fumbles-lost	9-5	1-0
Penalties-yards	5-48	6-57

Wake Forest.....0 3 0 7—10
SMU ....10 13 7 26—56

SMU—FG Hackney 30
SMU—Maxson 13 run (Hackney kick)
SMU—Maxson 15 run (kick blocked)
WF—FG Ramsey 40
SMU—Maxson 1 run (Hackney kick)
SMU—Morris 50 run (Hackney kick)
SMU —Blackburn 4 run (kick failed)
SMU—Maxson 11 run (Hackney kick)
SMU—Farris, fumble recovery in end zone (kick failed)
SMU—Bobo 4 run (Hackney kick)
WF—Lowe 8 pass from Ramsey (Ramsey kick)
A—20,175

Quarterback Joe Barnes (12) pitches back to George Smith (38) who had quite an auspicious beginning as he rushed for 153 yards on 11 carries.

TEXAS TECH 45 - UTAH 2

For the season opener a crowd of 38,180 came to Jones Stadium in Lubbock to see the Red Raiders play the Utes for the first time ever. They were apprehensive about what to expect this year from Tech. Last year hopes were high and methodically progressed down with each game. The offense had a put-you-to-sleep rhythm which put more pressure on the Tech defense than on the opponents defense. One game is not a season, but things may be a little different this year.

Quarterback Joe Barnes followed the opening kickoff with a 71-yard drive to the Utah four. There the Raiders got their only turnover of the game out of the way. A bad center quarterback exchange caused the fumble. Tech had to go to the well three times before getting a drink. They came right back and missed a field goal before going all the way on their next threat. It was an 87-yard drive in

17 plays. The clock had entered the second quarter when Barnes went in from the two. Doug McCutchen had set up Barnes run when he ran 28 yards up the middle to the two. Don Grimes converted and Tech led 7-0.

Midway through the period Grimes was successful on a 34-yard field goal attempt which boosted Tech's margin to 10 points. The drive covered 73 yards.

As time was running out another long drive was kept alive with an interference call on a third and 20 situation. Next Barnes, under tremendous pressure, just got his pass away to Ronnie Samford in the end zone. With 18 seconds remaining the Raiders had scored again. This drive covered 69 yards. Grimes kicked good and at halftime Tech led 17-0.

Utah tried to get things going their way as the second half opened. A roughing the kicker penalty against Tech

Tight end Ronnie Samford grabs a 20-yard pass from Joe Barnes for a Red Raider touchdown just 18 seconds before halftime.

got the Utes out of the starting blocks. Quarterback Don Van Galder had a hot hand as Utah picked up three straight first downs. A penalty had started the drive and a penalty ended it. Guilty of holding, the Utes settled for a 59-yard field goal attempt which fell short.

Their defense then held through three downs and the Raiders were forced to punt. The center snap went over punter John Garner's head and he retreated and fell on the ball in Tech's end zone. A safety for Utah brought the score to 17-2.

Later in the third period newcomer George Smith shattered whatever hopes the Utes had of getting closer. He took a quick pitch-out and tightroped down the right sideline to score from 56 yards out. Grimes kicked the conversion and the Red Raiders led 24-2.

As play moved into the final quarter the dam finally burst. Linebacker Quintin Robinson intercepted a pass thrown by Steve Marshall and ran the ball back 78 yards for a touchdown. Grimes was on target again and Tech

led 31-2. Then punter Garner, playing fullback, scored up the middle from 15 yards and sub Cliff Hoskins closed the scoring as he dashed 79 yards to score with over eight minutes still left in the game. All of this brought the score up to 45-2 Tech, which is how it ended.

The Tech defense, living up to its reputation, limited the Utes to 55 yards on the ground. The offense had three runners over 100 yards. Smith had 153, Hoskins 117 and McCutchen 102. James Mosely just missed the 100 mark as he totaled up 93. Barnes completed 10 of 18 pass attempts for 134 yards and one touchdown.

	Utah	Tech
First downs	15	28
Rushes-yards	35	53
Passing yards	225	134
Return yards	31	101
Passes	12-29-4	10-20-0
Punts	5-41	2-39
Fumbles-lost	4-1	5-1
Penalties-yards	5-63	9-121

Utah	0	0	2	0—	2
Texas Tech	0	17	7	21—	45

Tech—Grimes 2 run (Grimes kick)
Tech—FG Grimes 21
Tech—Sanford 20 pass from Barnes (Grimes kick)
Utah—Safety Garner tackled in end zone
Tech—Smith 56 run (Grimes kick)
Tech—Robinson 79 pass interception (Grimes kick)
Tech—Garner 15 run (Grimes kick)
Tech—Hoskins 79 run (Grimes kick)
A—38,180

This play started the Cougars amazing fourth quarter comeback. Marty Watts catches a pass from D. C. Nobles and scores to complete the 17-yard touchdown play. Ken Robinson (20) couldn't stop Watts.

ARIZONA STATE 33 - HOUSTON 28

Last year these two explosive teams were supposed to have a scoring spree when they met. Well, it turned out to be a defensive duel. This year before an Astrodome crowd of 24,628 and a national television audience the Sun Devils and the Cougars more than made up for last year.

Things started out badly for Houston, in fact things couldn't have been worse. With Arizona State in possession at their own 45 quarterback Dan White passed deep to Joe Petty. Randy Peacock and Burl Fuller had Petty covered like a blanket and the ball was batted up in the air. Behind all three players was Sun Devil Steve Holden. He snatched the ball out of the air and trotted in for a touchdown. Juan Cruz converted and State lead 7-0.

Less than two minutes later Holden was in the Cougar end zone again. From the Sun Devil 48 White passed to Holden over the middle who caught the pass in heavy traffic. He almost lost his balance as one hand went to the turf, but regained it, cut to the outside and outran everyone down the sideline. Phil Hahn blocked the conversion and State led 13-0.

Next Bruce Kilby broke through and blocked Hal Roberts' punt and returned it six yards to the Cougar 22. Woody Green scored from the nine and Cruz converted to make it 20-0 and the first quarter had five minutes to go.

If there was ever a time for Houston to pull an "el foldo" this was it. But the Cougars did just the opposite and before those five minutes passed they had put 14 points on the scoreboard and going into the second quarter only trailed by six points.

First Robert Ford recovered a punt fumble by Holden at the Arizona State 24. Seven plays later quarterback D. C. Nobles scored from one yard out. Two plays after the Houston kickoff linebacker Harold Evans intercepted a White pass in the flats and returned 20 yards for a touchdown. Ricky Terrell converted after each score.

The Sun Devils retaliated in the second quarter. Bo Warren intercepted a Nobles pass at his 35 and returned to the 41. State covered the 59 yards in 14 plays. Fullback Brent McClanahan scored on a run of two yards. Cruz kicked good to put Arizona State ahead by 27-14.

This was the heartbreaker. Marshall Johnson (13) is heading for the winning touchdown. Just behind, Puddin' Jones (30) throws a block on Larry Shorty (72). This was ruled a clip and it was all called back. Robert Ford (4) and Ken Baugh (63) are trailing Johnson.

Cruz came back in 56 seconds before halftime and kicked a 44-yard field goal. The Sun Devils had widened the gap to 30-14 as the first half ended.

The third quarter came and went with neither team scoring. This left the Cougars 15 minutes to overcome 16 points. The first break came when Hahn recovered a fumble by McClanahan at the Cougar 47. Houston scored in six plays with the payoff coming on a 17-yard Nobles to Marty Watts pass down the middle. Terrell converted and Houston trailed 30-21.

With 10:53 to go Cruz kicked a 38-yard field goal which widened the gap to 12 points at 33-21. Only six minutes remained when Cruz came in for another field goal effort which, if successful, would just about salt away a Sun Devil victory. Evans blocked the kick and Gerald Hill grabbed the ball and returned 28 yards to the State 46.

On first down Nobles made it all the way in one play. He passed to Marshall Johnson for 46 yards and a touchdown. Terrell's kick was good and with 5:52 to play the Cougars were back in the thick of it 33-28.

With less than four minutes remaining the Cougars had possession again and Nobles looped a screen pass to Johnson in the left flat. Johnson, leaving Sun Devils strewn all over the field, made a brilliant run from left to right corner on a slant all the way with what looked like the winning touchdown. It was not to be as a clipping call on Houston put the ball back to the State 24. Nobles kept right and made 15 to the nine. On an incomplete pass State was guilty of roughing Nobles which put the ball on the four. On first and goal, with 3:21 left, Nobles kept right again. He fumbled when hit and Ken Johnson recovered not only the ball for Arizona State, but the whole ballgame.

When Houston got the ball back only 37 seconds were left and they had run out of miracles.

	Arizona State	Houston
First Downs	19	10
Rushes-yards	67-353	38-154
Passing yards	149	239
Return yards	25	104
Passes	6-20-2	15-36-1
Punts	4-44	8-35
Fumbles-lost	3-2	2-2
Penalties-yards	5-42	7-63

Arizona State	20	10	0	3—33
Houston	14	0	0	14—28

ASU—Holden pass from White (Cruz kick)
ASU—Holden 52 pass from White (kick failed)
ASU—Green 9 run (Cruz kick)
Hou—Jones one run (Terrell kick)
ASU—Evans 20 interception return (Terrell kick)
ASU—McClannahan 2 run (Cruz kick)
ASU—FG Cruz 44
Hou—Watts 17 pass from Nobles (Terrell kick)
ASU—FG Cruz 38
Hou—Johnson 46 pass from Nobles (Terrell kick)
A—24,628

A & M's Brad Dusek (44) grabs a fourth down pass from Lex James and gains 16 yards. Dusek had to leave the game because of a knee sprain suffered on the tackle by Dave Mason (25). Also shown are the Aggies' Todd Christopher (64) and Nebraska's Rich Glover (79).

NEBRASKA 37 - TEXAS A&M 7

The Cornhuskers returned to Lincoln for their home opener before a record crowd of 76,042. It wasn't a triumphant return as the UCLA Bruins blind-sided them a week ago and escaped with a victory. Now the partisan crowd wanted revenge, the 'Huskers wanted revenge and the Aggies were the enemy although they had nothing to do with the hard feelings.

Nebraska opened up on their second possession as quarterback Dave Humm directed them 86 yards in eight plays. The big play was a pass to wide receiver Johnny Rodgers which covered 42 yards. Humm scored from the one on a sneak and Rich Sanger coverted to give Nebraska a 7-0 lead.

The Aggies received the kickoff and moved to the 'Husker 45 where Roberto Payan tried a 62-yard field goal. Rodgers returned the short effort 33 yards and Nebraska kept its forward momentum to reach the Aggie 11. There a fourth down pass fell incomplete and the

Cadets took over. On second down Mark Green fumbled a pitchout from quarterback Lex James and Steve Manstedt recovered for Nebraska at the A & M 10. On the third try Humm again sneaked across from the one. Sanger converted and Nebraska led 14-0 with only moments left in the first quarter.

The Cadets made a great effort to get on the scoreboard after the kickoff. Green returned to his 33. On a daring gamble at the 37, James passed to Brad Dusek on fourth down. It was good for 16 yards, but Dusek had to leave the game with a knee sprain. James kept the drive going as later, on third and seven, he hit Richard Osborne for nine yards and a first and goal at the Nebraska nine. Forsaking an almost sure field goal, James' fourth down pass from the five was batted down by 6'7" John Dutton.

Nebraska was penalized for illegal motion to their two, then marched methodically 98 yards for a touchdown. Maury Damkroger scored from the one and

Nebraska's John Hyland (58) grabs for Skip Walker (23) as he tries to skirt end. John Bell (66) follows the play.

with Sanger's kick the 'Huskers led 21-0. The big gainer in the drive was a controversial pass from Humm to Frosty Anderson for 37 yards. Anderson dove for the ball with both feet off the ground and came down on his back out of bounds, but it was ruled complete.

The Aggies had one more shot at it before halftime. They moved from their 25 to the Nebraska 27. On fourth down James passed to Homer May in the end zone, but the ball was tipped away by Randy Borg.

In the third period the A & M defense again held the Cornhuskers deep in Aggie territory when Larry Ellis intercepted Humm at the seven. In almost a replay of first quarter action, Jerry Whitehead fumbled on second down and Dave Mason recovered for Nebraska at the Cadet 10. On third down Humm passed to Jerry List for nine yards and six points. Sanger kicked the seventh point and Nebraska led 28-0.

In the fourth quarter the Cornhuskers tacked on a 54-yard Sanger field goal and the subs were sent in to wear down the already worn out Aggie defense. Quarterback Steve Runty passed 12 yards to flanker Ritch Bahe for the

final 'Husker score. The extra point was missed so Nebraska led 37-0.

With 7:20 remaining in the game the Aggies got their first first down of the second half. Don Dean replaced James at quarterback and after 80 yards the Cadets finally reached paydirt. The big gainers in the drive were a 19-yard pass to Osborne and a 29-yard completion to May which produced the score. McDermott converted and with 3:29 to play the 'Huskers led 37-7.

The game ended with Nebraska on the A & M five. With a little luck the game could have wound up 23-17 Nebraska, but a little luck is like hindsight...it's never there when you need it.

	Texas A & M	Nebraska
First downs	13	26
Rushes-yards	37-75	62-252
Passing yards	154	216
Return yards	1	111
Passes	15-27-0	13-21-1
Punts	5-37	2-29
Fumbles lost	5-3	1-0
Penalties-yards	2-10	2-18-7

Texas A&M......0   0   0   7— 7
Nebraska.......14   7   7   9—37
Neb—Humm 1 run (Sanger kick)
Neb—Humm 1 run (Sanger kick)
Neb—Damkroger 1 run (Sanger kick)
Neb—List 9 pass from Humm (Sanger kick)
Neb—FG Sanger 54
Neb—Bahe 12 pass from Runty (kick failed)
A&M—May 29 pass from Dean (McDermott kick)
A—76,004

SYNOPSIS

2

TOP TEN

1. Southern Cal
2. Oklahoma
3. Colorado
4. Ohio State
5. Tennessee
6. UCLA
7. Alabama
8. LSU
9. Nebraska
10. Arizona State

SWC OFFENSIVE PLAYER OF WEEK

Alvin Maxson, Halfback, SMU

SWC DEFENSIVE PLAYER OF WEEK

Harold Evans, Linebacker, Houston

UPSET OF WEEK:

Bowling Green 17 - Purdue 14

SWC TEAM LEADERS FOR SEASON
OFFENSE

Rushing . . . . Texas Tech 481 yds.
Passing . . . . Arkansas 223 yds.
Total . . . . Texas Tech 615 yds.

DEFENSE

Rushing . . . . Texas Tech 55 yds.
Passing . . . . SMU 115 yds.
Total . . . . SMU 212 yds.

SEASON RECORDS

	W	L	T
Rice	1	0	0
SMU	1	0	0
Texas Tech	1	0	0
Texas A & M	1	1	0
Baylor	0	1	0
Arkansas	0	1	0
Houston	0	2	0

Third Week
September 23

Fullback Ronnie Webb scores the Horned Frog's first touchdown from the one. Blocking for Webb are Scott Walker (51) and Ronnie Peoples (60).

TCU 31 - INDIANA 28

The Horned Frogs opened their 1972 football season in Bloomington, Indiana before a crowd of 34,004. The Purple Gang tried to run and hide from the Hoosiers but were never able to breathe easy as persistent Indiana kept right on their coattails.

Indiana made the first threat as they took the opening kickoff and moved to the Frog 13. A holding penalty blunted their drive and Chris Gartner came in for a field goal attempt. The center snap went through the ball holder's hands and Ed Robinson recovered at the TCU 43.

The Frogs scored on their first possession of the season as they drove 57 yards in 12 plays. Quarterback Kent Marshall ran keepers and Mike Luttrell and Billy Sadler ran the flanks as TCU faced a third down only once in the drive. Ronnie Webb scored from the one and Berl Simmons converted to put the Horned Frogs ahead 7-0 with the first quarter almost gone.

The Hoosiers got a break when on the Frogs' next possession a Marshall fumble turned the ball over at the TCU 15. On second down quarterback Ted McNulty ran the option to his left and pitched back at the last second to empty space. The rest of the backfield had gone right. Rusty Putt covered the ball for TCU at his 30.

As play moved into the second quarter Lyle Blackwood returned an Indiana punt 27 yards, but a clip put the ball back on the TCU 28. On first down Marshall pitched back to Luttrell who swung around right end, eluded one tackler at the 50 and won the foot race to the end zone. The 72-yard run coupled with Simmons' extra point gave the Frogs a 14-0 advantage.

Unlucky Blackwood ran back the next Indiana punt 70 yards into the end zone, but another clipping penalty rubbed it all out. This hurt because the Hoosiers squeezed in a touchdown just before the half. A fumble by Sadler gave them possession at the TCU 18. Two McNulty to Glenn Scolnik passes carried to the one and Ken Starling scored with 20 seconds left. A two-point pass conversion missed and at intermission TCU led 14-6.

44

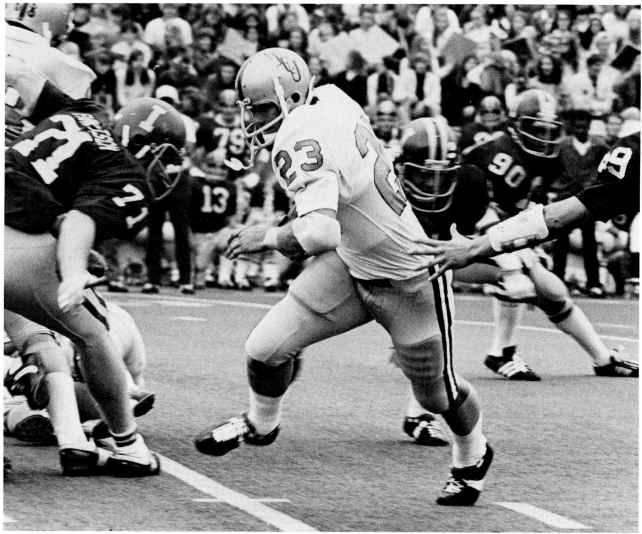

Horned Frog Mike Luttrell (23) scored two touchdowns, one on a run of 72 yards. He gained 140 yards rushing on 19 carries during the game.

The Horned Frogs wasted no time as the second half opened. They moved from their 37 to the Indiana four with Marshall's 30-yard run being the big gainer. The Hoosiers held and Simmons kicked a 22-yard field goal. TCU led 17-6.

Indiana came right back and on the strength of a 61-yard pass from McNulty to Scolnik moved 80 yards to score. The points came when on fourth down McNulty hit Scolnik again for one yard. Gartner kicked good and TCU led 17-13.

As play moved into the fourth quarter the Frogs were on the move again. Marshall again supplied the fireworks on a 35-yard run. Luttrell scored from the one on fourth down to cap a 75-yard drive. Simmons converted and the Frogs led 24-13.

Then the combination of McNulty to Scolnik was still clicking as a 40-yard completion reached the TCU eight. Starling made the eight on one play and Gartner kicked good. TCU led 24-20.

The Horned Frogs put pressure back on Indiana as they scored again from 73 yards out. Most of the yardage and the touchdown came on one play. Marshall found Sadler wide open downfield and the completion and run covered 62 yards. Simmons kicked the extra point and TCU regained their 11-point lead 31-20.

The Hoosiers just wouldn't stay down. Starling and Ken St. Pierre did the running and McNulty did the passing as they moved downfield to the Frog eight. Almost like a broken record it was McNulty to Scolnik for the eight yards and a touchdown. A two-point conversion run by Starling put Indiana a field goal behind at 31-28 with 4:47 left.

Indiana got the ball back with 3:09 remaining, but the Frog defense rose to the challenge and forced four incompletions. TCU then ran out the clock to preserve their hard-earned victory.

	TCU	Ind.
First downs	15	20
Rushes-yards	57-291	49-58
Passing yards	99	291
Return yards	107	139
Passes	4-6-0	24-37-0
Punts	5-42	6-37
Fumbles lost	3-2	5-2
Penalties-yards	5-45	6-52

Indiana 0   6   7   15—28
Texas Christian . 7   7   3   14—31

TCU—Webb 1 run (Simmons kick)
TCU—Luttrell 72 run (Simmons kick)
Ind—Starling 1 run (pass failed)
TCU—FG Simmons 22
Ind—Scolnik 1 pass from McNulty (Gartner kick)
TCU—Luttrell 1 run (Simmons kick)
Ind—Starling 8 run (Gartner kick)
TCU—Sadler 62 pass from Marshall (Simmons kick)
Ind—Scolnik 8 pass from McNulty (Starling run)
A—34,004

Bruce Gadd hands off to John Coleman (44) as pulling guards Mike Friend (66) and David Vandiver (58) lead interference.

RICE 29 - CLEMSON 10

Since 1949 the Owls and Tigers had met five times with Clemson holding the edge in victories 3-2. Rice made it three apiece as quarterback Bruce Gadd really flew. He broke two school records with 31 completions and 368 total passing yards. Edwin Collins caught 10 of Gadd's passes which also set a new Rice record. All of this before a home crowd (in 70,000 seat Rice Stadium) of 19,500. A lot of echoes were awakened Saturday night.

Clemson got off on the wrong foot on the opening kickoff. David Thomas fumbled when hit by Pat Kelley. David Snellings recovered for Rice at the Tiger 28. On third down Gadd passed to Cliff Crabtree for 14 yards and a first down at the eight. John Coleman carried twice to reach the three. Then a delay of game penalty set the ball back to the eight and one down later the Owls settled for a Mark Williams field goal of 25 yards. Rice led 3-0.

The Owls next drove from their 43 to the Clemson 11, but ran out of downs and Williams missed a 27-yard field goal attempt. He got another chance at the end of the first

quarter. Gadd's four completions covered 39 yards and Gary Ferguson's two carries picked up 26 yards on the way to the Tiger 13. A reverse pass to Collins lost eight yards and Ferguson then lost three on a run. Williams hit this time on a 35 yarder and Rice led 6-0.

Early in the second quarter Gadd had the Owls on the move again. Passes to Gary Butler and Bubba Berg accounted for 52 yards and they reached the Tiger 15. Once again a delay of game penalty stopped the Owls and their "twelfth" man, Williams, kicked a 28-yard field goal to account for all the points as Rice led 9-0.

Clemson recovered a punt fumble by Bruce Henley. Stan Hopkins fell on the ball at the Rice 24 and it was the first time the Tigers had been in Owl territory for the night. Nothing came of it as the Rice defense forced a field goal attempt by Ed Seigler from 47 yards out. The kick was short.

Rice took possession at their 20 and moved the 80 remaining yards in eight plays to give Williams a rest.

Rodrigo Barnes (90) stops Tiger Smiley Sanders (23) as LaRay Breshers (35), Cornelius Walker (76) and Larry Walling (80) close in to help.

Gadd's passes accounted for 69 yards with the score coming on a 29 yard toss to Collins just inside the flag. Williams converted and 30 seconds later the Owls took a 16-0 lead to intermission.

An unusual set of circumstances brought about Rice's next score. A Williams punt went out of bounds at the Tiger three. Rice was offsides and Williams punted again, dead on the two. Rice was holding and Williams third punt was caught by Jeff Siepe. When hit he fumbled and Ron Arceneaux, reaching for the ball, batted it into the end zone. David Vandiver fell on the ball and the Owls had a touchdown. A two-point pass failed and Rice led 22-0.

Clemson threatened as they moved 35 yards in eight plays, twenty-seven coming on a pass from quarterback Ken Pengitore to Gordy Bengel. To give you an idea of the job the Owl defense was doing, it took seven plays to make the other eight yards. This all brought up a field goal try by Siegler and he connected on a 43-yard kick. With the third quarter half over Rice led 22-3.

A rare thing happened on the next Owl scoring drive. Gadd was dumped for a loss attempting to pass. This was

the first time this year and it came after 57 attempts. To make up for this bit of adversity he completed five passes on the way to the Tiger end zone, the last one to Collins for 28 yards and a touchdown. Williams converted and with 28 seconds before the fouth quarter Rice led 29-3.

Clemson, early in the final period, moved 60 yards in four plays to score a touchdown. A run by Pengitore was good for 18 yards. Moments later Jay Washington turned the left corner and scrambled 41 yards down the sideline for the score. Siegler converted and Rice led 29-10.

One last Tiger threat was snuffed out by the Owl defense at the Rice seven. A fourth and one effort missed and Rice took over with 13 seconds remaining.

	Clemson	Rice
First downs	12	24
Rushes-yards	47-152	32-107
Passing yards	114	368
Return yards	11	4
Passes	6-14-0	31-47-0
Punts	7-35-4	4-35-2
Fumbleslost	2-6	1-1
Penalties-yards	2-16	5-45

Clemson	0	0	3	7—10
Rice	6	10	13	0—29

Rice—FG Williams 25
Rice—FG Williams 35
Rice—FG Williams 28
Rice—Collins 29 pass from Gadd (Williams kick)
Rice—Vandiver recovered fumble in end zone (pass failed)
Clem—FG Sieger 43
Rice—Collins 28 pass from Gadd (Williams kick)
Clem—Washington 41 run (Seigler kick)
A—19,500

47

State quarterback Brent Blackman (10), the game's leading rusher, is forced to the outside by Hog tackle Don Wunderly (72).

ARKANSAS 24 - OKLAHOMA STATE 23

The Razorbacks and Cowboys had met 36 times, beginning in 1912, and only once had they tied. That was a 21-21 affair at Stillwater in 1946. Well, they won't come any closer to a standoff than they did Saturday night in rainy Little Rock before 54,431. Both teams had opportunities to break the game wide open, but most went begging. It all came down to a conversion, not for two points, just an automatic extra point with 6:23 remaining.

OSU kicked off and Arkansas started at their 24. Mainly on the running of Dickey Morton the Razorbacks reached the Cowboy 38 before Tommy Cheyne punted to Alvin Brown. Brown fumbled the ball and Jim Hodge recovered for the Hogs at the State 13. Morton gained seven, Jon Richardson lost six and quarterback Joe Ferguson passed incomplete. Mike Kirkland's 28-yard field goal attempt was wide.

When Arkansas got the ball again Ferguson fumbled at the State 33 and Barry Price recovered for the Cowboys at

his 35. On third down four quarterback Brent Blackman kept and ran 49 yards to the Razorback 10. On fourth and two Blackman was stopped at the one.

After a short punt went to the Arkansas 33 the Cowboys came back and got the field goal that they passed up moments earlier. Eddie Garrett kicked good from 40 yards and OSU led 3-0.

Following the kickoff Ferguson was intercepted by Darryll Stewart at the Hog 33 and Stewart returned to the seven. On second down Blackman fumbled and Louis Campbell got the ball for Arkansas at his 10.

Cheyne eventually punted out to the Razorback 49. As play moved into the second quarter the Cowboys, on fourth and one at the 40, lined up in punt formation. The snap went to the short man, James Mann, who handed off to Al Nelms going left. Nelms kept on going for 40 yards and a touchdown. Garrett converted and OSU led 10-0.

The Razorbacks then cranked up and moved 72 yards in 16 plays to get back in the game. Two big Ferguson

Scott Bull (19) leads interference for Dickey Morton (33) as Cowboy tackle Barry Price (65) gives chase.

passes helped keep things going. One of 19 yards to Mike Reppond, following a 10-yard loss on a fumble, and one of 15 yards to Hodge. Richardson scored on fourth and one from the one. Kirkland kicked good and OSU led 10-7. That was the score at the half 7:18 later.

The Hogs had three possessions in the third quarter and scored every time. A 36-yard Ferguson to Hodge pass set up the first one and Ferguson scored from the one on a keeper. Kirkland's kick was good and Arkansas led 14-10. A punt return of 38 yards by John Moseley set up a 40-yard field goal by Kirkland for the next score. The Razorbacks led 17-10.

Before the next Arkansas score the Cowboys got in the act. They moved 80 yards in four plays. James Nunn ran for 24 yards, Fountain Smith gained one and then Blackman kept for 26 yards. A personal foul on Arkansas put the ball on the 14. Blackman then passed to Garrett for the touchdown. Garrett also kicked the point and the score was tied 17-17.

With 2:40 left in the third quarter Richardson returned the kickoff to the Arkansas 35. Ferguson passed 15 yards to Matt Morrison at the 50. Richardson ran for 10, then

carried again for 19 to the OSU 21. Morton covered the distance on three straight carries and with Kirkland's kick the Razorbacks led 24-17.

As play moved into the fourth quarter a 14-yard punt by Cheyne gave the Cowboys a chance at a field goal, but Garrett missed the 32-yard attempt. Midway thru the last period State got another chance when Ferguson was intercepted by Ray Ennis at the Hog 43. Ennis returned to the 36. On first down Blackman lofted a high one which Gant ran under at the 10 and barreled into the end zone. Garrett's conversion attempt hit one of the uprights and was no good. Arkansas led 24-23.

Mike David doused the Cowboys last hopes when he intercepted Blackman with 1:26 left. With the ball at the OSU 46 Ferguson ran out the clock with three keepers.

	Okla. St.	Ark.
First downs	16	25
Rushes	59-343	59-215
Passing-yards	50	190
Return yards	33	50
Passes	2-9-1	14-30-2
Punts	7-39	6-29
Fumbles	5-2	3-1
Penalties	3-25	2-30

Oklahoma State	3	7	7	6—23
Arkansas	0	7	17	0—24

OSU—FG Garrett 40
OSU—Nelms 40 run (Garrett kick)
Ark—Richardson 1 run (Kirkland kick)
Ark—Ferguson 1 run (Kirkland kick)
Ark—FG Kirkland 40
OSU—Garrett 14 pass from Blackman (Garrett kick)
Ark—Morton 13 run (Kirkland kick)
OSU—Gant 36 pass from Blackman (kick failed)
A—54,431

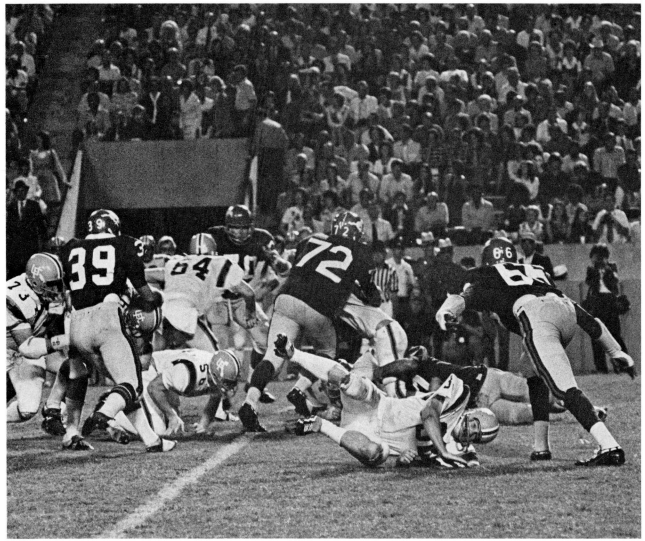

The Mustang defense swarms on the ball carrier. Don Randall (67) makes the tackle and Louis Kelcher (72) stops the forward progress. Other Mustangs are Ted Thompson (39), Steve Morton (70) and Ed Johnson (66).

SMU 21 - FLORIDA 14

On a cool Saturday night in Tampa, Florida the Mustangs, before 42,849, won their second straight outing of the season. The Florida Gators eventually became the victim, but not until some very anxious moments had passed in the fourth quarter.

SMU let one opportunity escape right at the start. On the second play of the game Andy Summers fumbled and Robert Popelka recovered for SMU at the Florida 31. After a run and two incomplete passes Clint Hackney tried a 48-yard field goal which fell short of the crossbar.

The Gators held on to the ball next time, but couldn't move and were forced to punt. Kris Silverthorn fielded the ball at his 32-yard line, a couple of blocks opened a hole and he was long gone. The 68-yard return coupled with Hackney's conversion gave SMU a 7-0 lead with only 3:44 gone.

The next Mustang possession came at their seven. Quarterback Casey Ortez passed to Randy Goss for 22

yards, but a motion penalty wiped it out and put the ball on the three. From there SMU marched to the Gator 21 as twice Ortez hit Goss on third down passes of 21 and 17 yards. Wayne Morris had a run of 21 yards in the drive. On third down at the 21 Tyson Sever intercepted an Ortez pass at his 13 and returned to the Florida 49.

In the second quarter Ortez was intercepted again and Florida had possession at their 42. Quarterback Chan Gailey tossed a screen pass to Kenny Lucas which gained 30 yards. After a third down Gailey run reached the 17 the Gators were just shy of a first down. Vince Kendrick got the call and Popelka met him at the line of scrimmage to stop the play for no gain.

The first half ended with the Mustangs nursing their seven point advantage.

Morris and Alvin Maxson struck quickly as the second half opened. At the Mustang 25 Morris found the middle hole and made 24 to the 49. T J. Hutchinson gained three

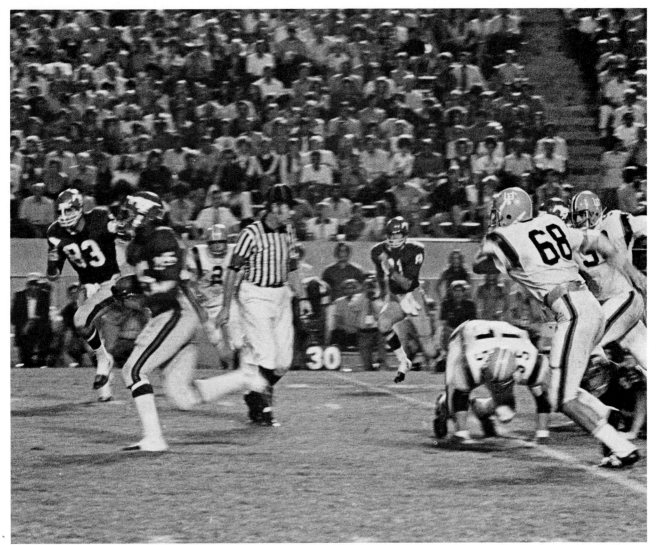

Wayne Morris (25) is almost a blur as he explodes through the line to pick up 24 yards on SMU's second touchdown drive. Ralph Blount (83) and Randy Goss (81) are trying to catch up to the flying Morris.

to reach the Gator 48. Maxson took an Ortez pitchout, got a good block, and eluded the remaining Florida defenders to go all the way. Hackney kicked good and SMU led 14-0.

Late in the third quarter an Ortez screen pass was intercepted by Alvin Butler but the Mustang defense shut down the Gators.

As the fourth quarter opened SMU had possession at their 15. Ortez returned to the pass and hit Goss for 14 and Rufus Shaw for 31 yards. Moments later a 22-yard pass to Oscar Roan reached the Gator 16. On third and six at the 12 Ortez rolled to his right under heavy pursuit and threw on the run to Morris who was downed on the two. Maxson scored on the next play. Hackney converted and with 12:28 left SMU led 21-0.

Florida's receivers finally started holding on to new quarterback David Bowden's passes. He moved the Gators 65 yards to a touchdown with the score coming on a six-yard toss to Nat Moore. Elwood Aust converted and SMU led 21-7.

A Morris fumble gave Bowden another chance and

Popelka saved a score when he intercepted a pass at SMU's 13 and ran it back 57 yards to the Florida 30. Maxson lost a fumble at the 31 on the next play. Here came Bowden again and he was stopped this time by Andy Duvall who intercepted at the SMU 15 with 3:54 remaining.

The next time Florida got the ball the Bowden onslaught continued and he reached the Mustang end zone on a 43-yard pass and run play to Willie Jackson. Fortunately only three seconds were left. Aust kicked good and SMU had won 21-14.

Almost overshadowed was the Mustang defense against the run. On 34 rushes the Gators came up with a minus 15 yards. That kind of line play would be hard to improve on.

	Sou. Methodist	Florida
First downs	16	17
Rushes-yards	43-216	34-0
Passing yards	134	295
Return yards	133	54
Passes	9-22-2	23-40-2
Punts	4-40	9-38
Fumbles lost	4-2	1-1
Penalties-yards	5-65	0-0

Southern Methodist	7	0	7	7—21
Florida	0	0	0	14—14

SMU—Silverthorn 68 punt return (Hackney kick)
SMU—Maxson 48 run (Hackney kick)
SMU—Maxson 2 run (Hackney kick)
Fla—Moore 5 pass from Bowden (Aust kick)
Fla—Jackson 43 pass from Bowden (Aust kick)
A—42,849

Texas' Randy Braband (63) plugs up the middle as Fred Currin (80) swoops in on Miami quarterback Ed Carney (11).

TEXAS 23 - MIAMI 10

The Florida Hurricane came to Memorial Stadium to inaugurate the new lighting system and to meet the Longhorns for the first time ever. A crowd of 62,000 sat through a light rain that lasted through the first half. Both teams had trouble holding on to the ball. Each fumbled five times and lost two of them. But the Texas defense intercepted three Miami passes and that may have been the difference.

Texas got off to a running start on their first possession. They moved 42 yards to the Hurricane 20 mainly on two keepers of 15 yards each by new quarterback Alan Lowry. There the drive was shut down and Billy Schott kicked a 37-yard field goal. Texas led 3-0.

A 16-yard Miami punt set up the next Longhorn score. They took over at the Hurricane 49. On first down Lowry handed off to Lonnie Bennett who found a huge hole off right tackle. After clearing the line of scrimmage he cut back to the center of the field and outran the Hurricane

defenders to the end zone. Schott converted and with 7:16 left in the first stanza the Longhorns led 10-0.

Texas let the next one get away. A Miami fair catch was bungled and Bill Wyman recovered on the Miami 30. On third down Roosevelt Leaks fumbled at the end of a 13-yard run. Al Palewicz recovered for Miami at his 18.

The inspired Floridians then drove 82 yards in 13 plays. Their leading rusher from last year, Chuck Foreman, was moved to flanker and gathered in passes of 18 and 12 yards from quarterback Ed Carney. Woody Thompson got the touchdown from the one. Mike Burke converted and Texas led 10-7 with 13:28 left in the first half.

Another fumble, this one by Lowry on the center snap, got the Miami machine moving again. Mike Barnes recovered on the Miami 37. On the play before Rick Davis had put the ball on the Miami 33 with a 50-yard pass and run play. The Hurricane moved 56 yards to the Texas seven before they had to settle for a 20-yard field

Longhorn back Lonnie Bennett looks for an opening on this run. Bennett scored the first Texas touchdown of 1972 on a run of 49 yards.

goal by Burke. With 3:56 before halftime the game was tied 10-10.

Lowry took to the air as he raced the clock. He hit Julius Whittier, moved to tight end this year, for 31 yards then later hit Davis for 14 yards to the Miami eight. The Hurricane defense held and with 24 seconds left Schott kicked his second field goal, this one for 24 yards, to give Texas a 13-10 lead at halftime.

The Longhorn defense got together in the second half and shut out Miami. The offense couldn't get their running game moving and Lowry turned to the air. He passed to Pat Kelly for 13 and to Jim Moore for 17 to reach the Miami 33 on the Longhorns' first possession of the second half. A holding penalty forced a 56-yard field goal attempt by Mike Dean, which was short.

On their next possession Lowry found Moore behind his coverage and the completed pass covered 41 yards to the Miami 36. On the next play Lowry fumbled the snap, picked it up, then burst through the line and ran 35 yards to the one. On second down Leaks scored. Schott kicked good and Texas led 20-10.

Another opportunity slipped from Texas' grasp when Ronnie Workman recovered a Carney fumble at the Miami 25. The Longhorns got to the Hurricane seven before being stopped and Ken White blocked Schott's field goal attempt from the 16.

Play moved into the fourth quarter and the defense set up the Longhorns last counter. Glenn Gaspard intercepted Carney at the Miami 42 and returned 20 yards. Only four yards were gained in three downs. Schott entered and closed out the scoring with a 33-yard field goal. Texas led 23-10.

Later Workman intercepted a Miami pass at their 49 and Texas had reached the 23 when the game ended.

	Miami	Texas
First downs	14	16
Rushes-yards	45-159	55-232
Passing yards	113	182
Return yards	22	30
Passes	8-22-3	8-13-0
Punts	5-33-6	2-34-5
Fumbles-lost	2-5	2-5
Penalties-yards	6-60	4-35

Miami	0	10	0	0—10
Texas	10	3	7	3—23

TEX—FG Schott 37
Tex—Bennett 49 run (Schott kick)
Mia—Thompson 1 run (Burke kick)
Mia—FG Burke 20
Tex—FG Schott 24
Tex—Leaks 1 run (Schott kick)
Tex—FG Schott 22
A—62,000

Doug McCutchen (32), shown here after receiving quarterback Joe Barnes'(12) handoff, broke the game open early in the second half. He scored three consecutive touchdowns. Jeff Jobe (48) confronts his foe eyeball to eyeball.

TEXAS TECH 41 - NEW MEXICO 16

Last year the Lobos beat the Red Raiders for the second time in 17 tries. At home in Albuquerque they hoped to make it two in a row before 24,860, mostly New Mexico, fans. Two fumbles lost, two pass interceptions and a costly holding penalty led to their defeat along with a spirited band of Red Raiders.

Tech drove 75 yards to score the first time they had the ball. Quarterback Joe Barnes scored from the four on third down one. Don Grimes kicked the extra point and the Raiders led 7-0.

Another promising drive began at the Tech 15 after a good punt return by Lawrence Williams was erased by a clip. Barnes used the running of George Smith and James Mosley to power down to the New Mexico eight. On first down Doug McCutchen lost a yard. Andre Tillman dropped a pass in the end zone on second down. On third down John Garner had a huge hole open but mishandled

the pass from Barnes. Grimes entered and Tech settled for three points to up its lead to 10-0.

The Red Raiders kicked off and on the Lobos' second play from scrimmage quarterback Bruce Boone fumbled. Davis Corley recovered for Tech at the New Mexico 23. Barnes passed to Smith for a first down at the 12. Two incompletions later Barnes was caught for a two-yard loss and in came Grimes. His kick was good from 31 yards out and Tech led 13-0.

The Lobos had died by the run so they decided to live by the pass. Boone hit Paul Labarrere, on the fly, for 57 yards and a touchdown early in the second quarter. McDonald kicked the point after and Tech led 13-7.

The Rex Raiders matched their first quarter scoring when Smith scored on a 14-yard run. Grimes kicked good and Tech led 20-7.

New Mexico came roaring back as Boone hit his tight

54

George Smith (38), who scored the Red Raider's second touchdown, sweeps to the outside here as he find the middle plugged.

end Ken Smith for 46 yards. This put the ball on the Tech 13. Three plays later Rich Diller scored from the two. McDonald converted and Tech led 20-14.

Grimes tried a 42-yard field goal as the first half ended. It was short.

Early in the third quarter a holding penalty turned the game around for Tech. Boone hit Smith with a 33-yard scoring pass which apparently had tied the Raiders with the extra point to come. The holding call wiped it all out and the Lobos were never in the game after that.

McCutchen then scored three consecutive touchdowns. The first came from the New Mexico three ending a 76-yard drive that took 11 plays. Grimes kicked good and Tech led 27-14.

Greg Waters set up the next one with his interception of a Boone pass. After a clipping penalty Tech had possession at their 47. Smith picked up a first down at the Lobo 32 on a 10-yard run and three plays later McCutchen wild-bulled his way 21 yards for the score. Grimes was on target and Tech led 34-14.

New Mexico then made another contribution when John Garner's punt was fumbled and Tech reclaimed the ball at the Lobo 27. Jimmy Carmichael, who had just replaced Barnes at quarterback, passed to Calvin Jones for 13 yards to the 14. McCutchen ran for four, then got his third straight on a 10 yard blast as the fourth quarter was just underway. Grimes kicked good and Tech led 41-14.

The Lobos closed out the scoring with a safety. A bad center snap went over punter Garner's head and out of the end zone. Final score, Tech 41—16. Next week the season gets down to the nitty-gritty for Tech.

	Tech	N Mexico
First downs	30	17
Rushes-yards	68-351	53-217
Passing yards	124	159
Return yards	79	16
Passes	10-18-0	7-18-2
Punts	5-38	7-38
Fumbles lost	2-0	2-2
Penalties-yards	9-97	8-83

Texas Tech	10	10	14	7—41
New Mexico	0	14	0	2—16

Tech—Barnes 4 run (Grimes kick)
Tech—FG Grimes 26
Tech—FG Grimes 31
UNM—Labarrere 57 pass from Boone (McDonald kick)
Tech—Smith 14 run (Grimes kick)
UNM—Diller 2 run (McDonald kick)
Tech—McCutchen 21 run (Grimes kick)
Tech—McCutchen 3 run (Grimes kick)
Tech—McCutchen 10 run (Grimes kick)
UNM—Safety Garner tackled in end zone
A—24,860

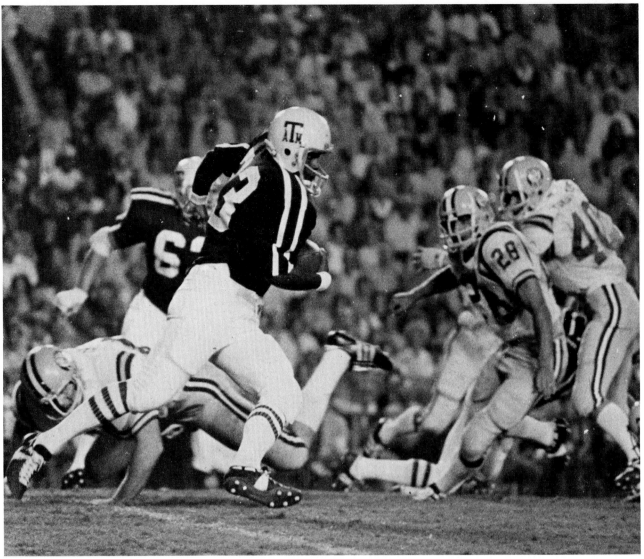

The Aggies' Alvin Bowers (33) gains good yardage on this run. Jimmy Knecht (28) veers to cut off Bowers as Mark Yokubaitis is blocked out of the play.

LSU 42 - TEXAS A&M 17

Playing the Bengal Tigers in Baton Rouge before 68,538 maniacal fans is an experience that very few ever forget. That is because very few survive to forget.

For the Aggies, coming off a bad trip to Omaha, it was a traumatic evening. The first half built up hopes for a close game, but LSU responded with a "scorched earth" offense in the second half. The burnt grass was between the line of scrimmage and the Cadet goal line. A & M had a total offense of seven yards in the final 30 minutes.

LSU scored on their second possession of the game by moving 61 yards in nine plays. Quarterback Bert Jones did most of the damage through the air as he hit Brad Boyd for 12 yards, Gerald Keigley for 14 and one more to Boyd for 24 yards and the touchdown. Rusty Jackson kicked the conversion, his first of six, and LSU led 7-0.

A catastrophe was averted after Earnest Bean fumbled on the first play after the Tiger kickoff. LSU's Brinks Miciotto recovered at the Aggies 28. But Brad Davis fumbled it back to Larry Ellis at the line of scrimmage. The Cadets then moved 45 yards in nine plays with Mark Green gaining a total of 31 on the ground. A & M had to settle for a 44-yard field goal by Pat McDermott. LSU led 7-3 as play had just entered the second quarter.

Paul Lyons replaced Jones at quarterback and the ground game took over on the Bengal's second touchdown drive. Seventy five yards in 14 plays was started by Steve Rogers who ran for 13 yards. Jim Benglis kept it going with 12 more and Lyons ended it when he ran across from the four. With the PAT the Tigers led 14-3.

The Aggies moved 62 yards, following the kickoff, to the LSU 21 where quarterback Lex James lost the ball on a fumble. Dennis Carruth gave the Cadets new life when he intercepted Jones at the LSU 44. A 13-yard loss by James was nullified when the Tigers were found guilty of

Tiger Paul Lyons (16) alternated at quarterback with Bert Jones and led LSU to two touchdowns. Aggies pictured are Bill Wiebold (61), Max Bird (87) and Don Long (95).

holding. This put the ball on the LSU 13. Two plays later Skip Walker scored around right end from the 12. McDermott's kick put the Aggies down by four, 14-10.

With 3:20 left in the half the Cadets almost scored again. Carl Roaches, wide open, was overthrown. Then James passed to Walker for 18 to the LSU 18. Richard Osborne let a James pass get away in the end zone and McDermott's 54-yard field goal effort was short on the last play in the first half.

LSU went 80 yards with the second half kickoff to up the margin to 21-10. The score came on a Jones pass to Keigley for 13 yards.

Four minutes later Norm Hodgins grabbed a James pass in the right flat and raced untouched for 40 yards and a touchdown. LSU led 28-10.

Forty yards was again the distance when the Bengals scored the fifth touchdown. On the sixth play Lyons handed off to Ken Fakier who passed to Keigley for the final 26 yards. The Tigers now led 35-10.

Roaches received the LSU kickoff at his three and returned 97 yards for an Aggie touchdown. McDermott converted and LSU led 35-17.

Jones threw to Jimmy LeDoux for LSU's last touchdown. The pass covered 10 yards and brought the score to 42-17. The Tiger coach sent Jones back in later and time outs were called to try to get one more score. Actually a 13-yard TD pass to LeDoux was washed out by a penalty with nine seconds left. The LSU coach said he wasn't trying to run up the score. He wanted Jones to break the Tiger passing record.

	Texas A & M	LSU
First downs	17	20
Rushes-yards	27-83	54-158
Passing yards	119	178
Return yards	12	37
Passes	16-9-2	23-14-1
Punts	5-36	6-50
Fumbles lost	5-4	2-1
Penalties-yards	2-20	5-83

Texas A&M......0 10   0   7—17
LSU 7   7 14 14—42
LSU—Boyd pass from Jones (Jackson kick)
A&M—FG McDermott 44
LSU—Lyons 4 run (Jackson kick)
A&M—Walker 12 run (McDermott kick)
LSU—Keigley 13 pass from Jones (Jackson kick)
LSU—Hedgins 45 pass interception (Jackson kick)
LSU—Keigley 26 pass from Fakier (Jackson kick)
A&M—Roaches 97 kickoff return (McDermott kick)
LSU—LeDoux 10 pass from Jones (Jackson kick)
A—68,538

Baylor's Gene Wilson (37) finds a huge hole in the Missouri line as he scrambles for good yardage. Other Bears pictured are Jon Royal (73), David Walters (71) and Richard Mason (66).

BAYLOR 27 - MISSOURI 0

"All good things come to those who wait." The Baylor faithful have been waiting a long time for a game like this. Before a shocked crowd of 42,000 in Columbia, Missouri the eight-point underdog Bears shut out the Tigers. It could have been worse...Baylor played everyone that made the trip. The Bruins defense was tremendous. They intercepted four passes and recovered four Missouri fumbles. Not once did the Tigers penetrate the Baylor 10-yard line.

The first quarter was a defensive struggle as neither team could get on the scoreboard. Mike Conradt tried a 52-yard field goal for Baylor, which missed. Well into the second quarter it was still all defense. Up till this point Mike Black and Tommy Turnipseede had recovered Tiger fumbles in Baylor territory to stop two Missouri drives. Then midway through the second period Tommy Stewart intercepted Tiger quarterback John Cherry at the

Bear 31 and returned to the Missouri 45. Seven plays, which included a 19-yard run by Gene Wilson and a 16-yard pass from quarterback Neal Jeffrey to Brian Kilgore, reached the Tiger three. There, facing fourth and goal Conradt entered and kicked a 21-yard field goal with 5:43 left in the first half. Baylor led 3-0.

Following the Bears kickoff Missouri was forced into another turnover. Millard Neely rushed Cherry hard and stripped the ball from the Tiger quarterback. Black was there to make his second fumble recovery at the Missouri 29. On third down and seven Jeffrey tossed a screen pass to Ray Harper who swivel-hipped 23 yards to the Tiger 3, but fumbled when hit. Bruin Lee Wright, following from the rear, pounced on the ball at the two. Jeffrey ran it over on the next play. Conradt converted and Baylor led 10-0 with 3:24 remaining.

Missouri came roaring back with their best drive, 65

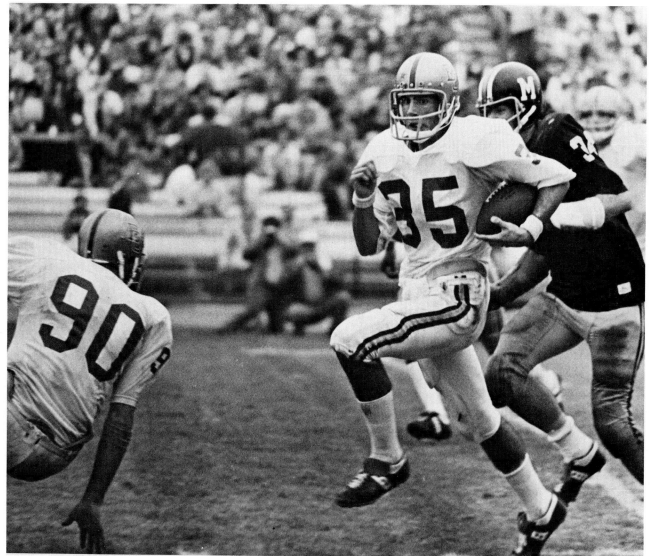

Bear quarterback Neal Jeffrey (35) who had to replace his regular No. 11 jersey, picks up good yardage on this run. Number 90 is tight end Ken Townsend. Chasing Jeffrey is Tiger Tom Kellett (34).

yards, to reach the Bear 13. With 12 seconds left and no time outs, Cherry faked right and bootlegged left. Roger Goree zapped him down on the Missouri 23 for a 10-yard loss. End of threat and end of first half.

In the third period the Bears went .500 as they lost one and won one. The lost one occurred when Jeffrey ran a keeper for 24 yards to the Missouri three. He fumbled when tackled and Tiger J. L. Doak recovered in his end zone. Baylor overcame that setback to march 64 yards in seven plays. The big gainer was an over-the-shoulder catch of a Jeffrey pass by Charles Dancer which covered 38 yards. Gary Lacy and Wilson ran the ball to the three. On third down Jeffrey crossed up the stacked Tigers as he tossed a scoring pass to Ken Towsend who was wide open in the end zone. Conradt kicked the extra point and with 9:01 left in the third quarter the Bears led 17-0. Also in this period the Baylor defense again rose to the occasion. The Tigers drove from their 29 to the Bruin 21. Four plays later the Bears took over with the ball still on their 21.

In the fourth quarter Baylor added 10 points to their total. Darrel Luce picked off a deflected Missouri pass and returned 33 yards to the Tiger six. Four plays later new quarterback Randy Cavender scored from the one. Conradt's kick put Baylor in front 24-0.

Conradt opened and closed the scoring. After Steve Watson intercepted Cherry on the Missouri 28 the Tigers held and Conradt kicked a 45-yard field goal. The distance was a personal record for him. This put Baylor ahead 27-0.

Dennis DeLoach intercepted for Baylor moments later to blunt any Tiger scoring hopes.

The game ball was presented to Coach Grant Teaff. His first victory as the new Bear head coach. Arriving in Waco the team was greeted by jubilant Bear partisans who were delirious...even in the rain.

	Baylor	Missouri
First downs	14	15
Rushes-yards	61-229	53-134
Passing yards	72	111
Return yards	67	20
Passes	7-11-0	5-19-4
Punts	5-30.2	4-28.3
Fumbles lost	7-3	4-4
Penalties-yards	3-35	4-30

Baylor	0	10	7	10—27
Missouri	0	0	0	0—0

Bay—FG Conradt 21
Bay—Townsend 3 pass from Jeffrey (Conradt kick)
Bay—Jeffrey 2 run (Conradt kick)
Bay—Cavender 1 run (Conradt kick)
Bay—FG Conradt 45
A—42,000

Somewhere under Deryl McGallion and Gerald Hill is an unidentified Cougar and the Tulsa ball carrier. Howard Ebow (8) and Larry Keller (64) watch their "Mad Dog" teammates.

HOUSTON 21 - TULSA 0

The Cougars came to Tulsa for their third game of the season and looking for their first victory. After two heart breaking losses Houston really needed this one to get back on the right track. Coach Bill Yeoman shook up his defensive unit and it paid off by setting up all three touchdowns. The offense still wasn't able to throw off its inconsistency as mistakes kept surfacing. Six fumbles were thrown up for grabs by the Cougars and they recovered half of them. Would you believe that Houston had the ball only nine minutes out of the first 30 and left the field at halftime leading 14-0? Skelly Stadium held 23,000 at kickoff time.

The first quarter was a study in frustration for the Cougar offense. They moved the ball well, but failed to get on the scoreboard. The Tulsa 33, 37 and eight were reached. Two field goal tries by Ricky Terrell were

unsuccessful. The first, even with the wind, proved to be too long at 54 yards. The second from just 25 yards was wide right.

The defense came through about midway of the second quarter. Gerald Hill broke through the middle and blocked Art Bennett's punt. Bubba Brousard fell on the bouncing ball at the Hurricane one. Reggie Cherry was stopped for no gain, but on the next play quarterback D. C. Nobles kept around the left side and scored. Terrell converted and with 7:44 left in the half Houston led 7-0.

Only 2:33 elapsed before the Cougars were back in the Tulsa end zone. The Hurricane faced a fourth and five at their 38 when Bennett dropped back to punt. The center snap cleared his head by three feet. Bennett ran back, picked up the ball, and tried to get his kick off. Cougar linebacker Harold Evans got a hand on the ball and it

New running back Reggie Cherry (27) gave the Cougar ground game and outside threat with his speed. Here he is tripped up by Gary Mathis (70).

bounced high in the air. Larry Keller grabbed it at the 15 and returned to the Tulsa eight. On third and goal at the three Nobles fired a quick pass to Puddin' Jones for the touchdown. Terrell converted and with 5:11 before halftime the Cougars led 14-0.

Tulsa made their deepest penetration as they reached the Houston 23, but time ran out there to end the first half.

Houston split ball control with Tulsa during the second half, but once again the defense set up their only score. One touchdown and a fist fight was all that came to pass in the final 30 minutes.

The Cougar touchdown came midway through the third quarter. Safety Burl Fuller cut in front of Tulsa's Steve Shores and intercepted his intended reception at the Hurricane 48. The offense didn't let this opportunity escape as they covered the distance in six plays. Nobles got the score on a keeper from one yard out. Terrell kicked his third conversion and Houston led 21-0.

With about 10 minutes remaining in the game Cougar cornerback Robert Giblin was covering Tulsa flanker Drew Pearson step for step on a third down pass play. The ball hit Giblin in the back and fell incomplete. Giblin and Pearson exchanged a few verbal blows and from the sideline came T. C. Blair with helmet in hand. Blair swung the helmet and hit Giblin in the face. Both benches emptied onto the field before officials regained control.

The game ended with the Cougars preserving their shutout 21-0. Houston now leads the rivalry 12 wins to 10 for Tulsa.

The revamping of the defense was a success as Tulsa's highly touted ground game made 43 yards on 47 attempts. For this game the Cougars best offense was their defense.

	Houston	Tulsa
First downs	15	13
Rushes yards	259	43
Passing yards	65	168
Return yards	58	21
Passes	5-13-0	16-30-1
Punts	4-41.3	10-29.4
Fumbles-lost	6-3	2-1
Penalties-yards	55	9-61

Houston	0	14	7	0	21
Tulsa	0	0	0	0	0

Hou—Nobles 1 run (Terrell kick)
Hou—Jones 8 pass from Nobles (Terrell kick)
Hou—Nobles 1 run (Terrell kick)
A—23,000

SYNOPSIS

TOP TEN

1. Southern Cal
2. Oklahoma
3. Colorado
4. Tennessee
5. Ohio State
6. Alabama
7. Nebraska
8. Michigan
9. LSU
10. Notre Dame

SWC OFFENSIVE PLAYER OF WEEK

Bruce Gadd, Quarterback, Rice

SWC DEFENSIVE PLAYER OF WEEK

Roger Goree, End, Baylor

FRESHMAN RESULTS:

Rice 24 - Houston 14

UPSET OF WEEK:

Baylor 27 - Missouri 0

SWC TEAM LEADERS FOR SEASON

OFFENSE	AVG.
Rushing	Texas Tech 408 yds.
Passing	Arkansas 206 yds.
Total	Texas Tech 545 yds.

DEFENSE	AVG.
Rushing	SMU 41 yds.
Passing	Texas 113 yds.
Total	SMU 246 yds.

SEASON RECORDS

	W	L	T
Rice	2	0	0
SMU	2	0	0
Texas Tech	2	0	0
TCU	1	0	0
Texas	1	0	0
Baylor	1	1	0
Arkansas	1	1	0
Texas A & M	1	2	0
Houston	1	2	0

Fourth Week
September 30

39 YEARS AGO
SEPTEMBER 30, 1933
Arkansas 42 - Oklahoma Baptist 7
Baylor 20 - St. Edwards 6
LSU 13 - Rice 0
Texas 22 - College of Mines 6
SMU 14 - Texas Tech 0
Texas A&M 13 - Tulane 6
TCU 13 - North Texas 0

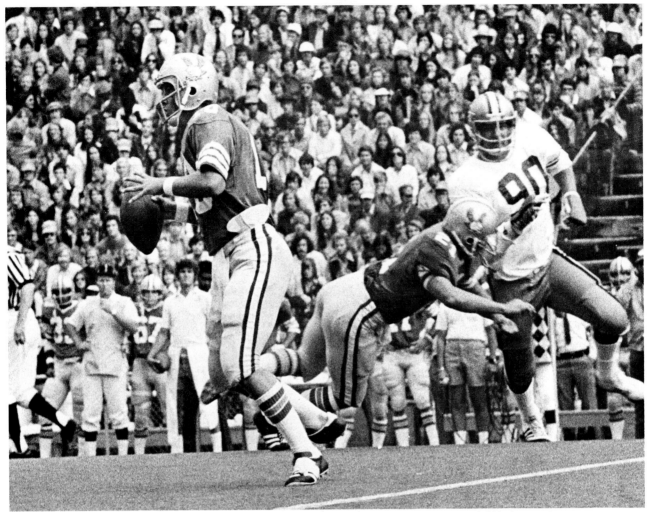

Gary Ferguson (21) throws a block as Owl quarterback Bruce Gadd (10) looks downfield before passing.

RICE 36 - GEORGIA TECH 36

The Owls traveled to Atlanta to take on the Ramblin' Wreck and were 13 point underdogs. Each school had new head coaches. Al Conover for Rice and Bill Fulcher for Tech. In 1960 the Yellow Jackets came to Houston and beat Rice 16-13 and the following year they beat Rice in Atlanta 24-0. The script wasn't followed this year as Georgia Tech had to race the clock to escape with a tie after defeat almost had a foot in the door. A crowd of 41,179 was still on hand to watch the Tech "miracle".

The favorite tag looked prophetic when Tech jumped off to a quick 14-0 lead. The first score came after Gary Carden recovered a fumble by Rice's Dennis Pokluda at the Owl 36. Five plays later quarterback Eddie McAshan hit Jim Robinson with a 22-yard scoring pass. Bobby Thigpen converted and the Yellow Jackets led 7-0.

Before the first quarter was half over Tech had another touchdown. This score was set up when Rice quarterback Bruce Gadd suffered his first interception of the season at his 30. On third down McAshan passed complete to Jim Owings for 25 yards and six points. Thigpen kicked good and Tech led 14-0.

As time was running out in the first period Rice's Bruce Henley recovered a fumbled Tech pitchout at the 50. Gadd then put his arm to work and took the Owls into pay dirt on four plays and a Wreck holding penalty. He passed complete to Gary Butler, to Gary Ferguson and to Joe Buck. The latter for five yards and the TD. Mark Williams converted and Rice trailed 7-14.

The scoring then started coming like automatic rifle shots. Rice got a safety when a center-snap went over punter Bob Jobson's head from the Tech 37. Jobson recovered in his end zone and Rice trailed 9-14. Gadd was intercepted again, this time by Bruce Elliott at the Owl 49. On second down McAshan threw long to Robinson who caught the ball at the sidelines and went in for the score. The play covered 55 yards. Thigpen converted and Georgia Tech led 21-9. Several minutes later Rice was in the Wreck end zone again. Bill Chilivetis intercepted McAshan and returned 25 yards to the Tech 28. Williams kicked the conversion and Rice trailed 16-21.

The Owls took up where they left off as the third quarter opened. Ferguson got loose for 18 yards and

John Kelly (89) picks off one of Tech quarterback Eddie McAshan's five intercepted passes. Coming up fast for convoy is Don Bernshausen (26).

Gadd passed complete to Steve Ogletree, Butler and Ron Arceneaux to reach the Tech 16. The Wreck held and Williams kicked a 33-yard field goal. Rice trailed 19-21. Next Henley received a Wreck punt at his 48 and returned it 52 yards for another Rice touchdown. Williams converted and Rice led 26-21.

As the fourth quarter opened the Owls stunned the Yellow Jackets once more. Preston Anderson intercepted McAshan at the Rice one-yard line and returned his theft 99 yards for a touchdown. Williams kicked good and Rice led 33-21.

Tech then made their move and went 80 yards in nine plays for a much needed touchdown. McAshan's passes did the damage in reaching the Owl one. After Rice stopped two running plays McAshan passed to Tom Lang for the score. Thigpen kicked good and Rice led 33-28.

With 6:43 to play Williams kicked a 47-yard field goal to give the Owls more breathing room. They now led by eight points, 36-28.

Henley stopped one Tech drive as he intercepted McAshan at the Rice five. But moments later the Yellow Jackets got the ball back again at their 39. Two McAshan passes put Tech on the Rice 33. Chilivetis appeared to intercept McAshan on the next play, but the officials said

no. Mark Fields caught a pass for 21 yards to the Owl 12. On the next play pass interference was called on Tom Clanton and that gave Tech first and goal at the one. On second down McAshan passed to Owings for the score. To gain the tie McAshan went to Owings again for the two-point conversion.

The game ended seconds later, but the players didn't want to quit and a fight started which emptied both benches. McAshan was intercepted five times, but he also passed for five touchdowns which, along the way, broke a career record at Georgia Tech. The old record was held by Frank Broyles.

	Rice	Ga. Tech
First downs	15	29
Rushes-yards	41-75	54-137
Passing yards	153	371
Return yards	204	45
Passes	13-28-4	23-38-5
Punts	8-38	4-40
Fumbles-lost	3-1	4-3
Penalties-yards	4-36	6-42

A—41,179

Rice	0	16	10	10—36
Georgia Tech	14	7	0	15—36

Tech—Robinson 22 pass from McAshan (Thigpen kick)

Tech—Owings 25 pass from McAshan (Thigpen kick)

Rice—Buck 5 pass from Gadd (Williams kick)

Rice—Safety Jobson downed ball in end zone following high center snap

Tech—Robinson 55 pass from McAshan (Thigpen kick)

Rice—Swierc 28 pass from Gadd (Williams kick)

Rice—FG Williams 33

Rice—Henley 52 punt return (Williams kick)

Rice—Anderson 99 interception return (Williams kick)

Tech—Long 1 pass from McAshan (Thigpen kick)

Rice—FG Williams 47

Tech—Owings 2 pass from McAshan (Owings pass from McAshan)

65

Texas Tech quarterback Joe Barnes (12) finds a big hole behind the block of Harold Lyons (62) as Longhorn Jay Arnold takes up the chase.

TEXAS 25 - TEXAS TECH 20

There is nothing like success to bring out the fans. Jones Stadium has a listed capacity of 47,000. Saturday night it was overflowing with a crowd of 52,187. Both the Red Raiders and Longhorns were unbeaten as they prepared to open the 1972 Southwest Conference season. Despite not being able to cross the Texas goal Tech still led at the half. They added to their misery in the second half when they started giving the ball away. The Longhorns never look gift horses in the mouth.

Texas started by having difficulty holding on to the ball. On their third play of the game Roosevelt Leaks fumbled, but recovered the ball. On a punt return Pat Padgett lost the ball, but teammate Sherman Lee recovered. Midway through the first quarter quarterback Alan Lowry finally succeeded in losing the ball for Texas. He fumbled on a keeper and Tim Schaffner recovered for the Red Raiders at his 43.

George Smith ran for 10 yards and Texas was penalized for a personal foul to move the ball to the Longhorn 32. Quarterback Joe Barnes passed complete to Ronnie Samford for 22 yards. James Mosely picked up four but Texas

held at their four and Don Grimes came in and kicked a 21-yard field goal. Tech led 3-0.

As the first quarter came to a close the Longhorns were on the march. They moved 89 yards in six plays. Don Burrisk ran for 11, Lowry passed to Lonnie Bennett for 24 yards, the second quarter started, Lowry kept for eight and Tech drew a facemasking penalty. Leaks exploded for 20 up the middle and then carried over from the one on the next play. Billy Schott's extra point gave Texas a 7-3 lead.

The Red Raiders bounced right back as Barnes launched another scoring drive by hitting Calvin Jones for 45 yards with Jones making a great catch. Barnes then passed to Mosley for 16 to the Texas 16. The Longhorns defense shut down the Raider Express and Grimes kicked a 31-yard field goal. Tech now trailed 6-7.

The Longhorns got back in their fumble groove. They drove from their own 23 to the Tech 27 where Bennett fumbled and Kenneth Wallace recovered for Tech. The Red Raiders couldn't get across the goal so they decided to let Grimes kick Texas to defeat. Barnes passed to Smith

Longhorn quarterback Alan Lowry hands off to Roosevelt Leaks as Red Raiders Davis Corley (70), Tim Shaffner (72) and Aubrey McCain (80) converge on the ballcarrier.

for 31, ran for 12 and then six to reach the Texas 17. Three plays lost three yards and Grimes kicked a 37-yard field goal. Tech led 9-7.

Mike Dean missed a 55-yard field goal for Texas just before the first half ended.

Tech took up where it left off as once more they moved into field goal range. Barnes passed to Jones for 14 then found Andre Tillman open and hit him with a 35 yarder. Texas held at its 19 and Grimes kicked a 32-yard field goal which gave Tech a 12-7 lead and tied a SWC record for most field goals in a game.

Following a 10-yard punt Tech had possession at its 45, but the turnover gremlin switched sides as Adrian Ford intercepted Barnes' deep pass and returned 18 to the Texas 42. Lowry got a first down at the Tech 48. Leaks hit the quick opener for 16 yards. Burrisk ran for nine and Lowry kept for 13 to the eight. Lowry scored on the next play then passed to Leaks for a two-point conversion. Texas led 15-12.

Tech gambled on a fourth and four at the Texas 29 and Malcolm Minnick caught Barnes for a loss and the Longhorns took over. The 'Horns were forced to punt and on Tech's third down Barnes' fumble was recovered by Minnick at the Raider 38. Texas scored in nine plays

with Lowry going across from the seven. Schott converted and Texas led 22-12.

On first down following the kickoff Barnes fumbled at the Tech 22 and Jay Arnold recovered for Texas. The Longhorns settled for Schott's 36-yard field goal and upped their lead to 25-12.

Barnes was intercepted by Sherman Lee on the Raiders' next possession. With time running out the men from Lubbock finally crossed the Longhorn goal. After a penalty had put the ball on the Texas 28 Barnes passed to John Garner for 12, then hit Jeff Jobe for 16 yards and a touchdown with seven seconds left. A two-point pass to Tillman made the final score Texas 25 - Tech 20.

The Red Raiders could only get field goals from Texas mistakes while the Longhorns got touchdowns on two Tech bobbles. That was the difference in a hard fought conference opener.

	Texas	Texas Tech
First downs	16	21
Rushes-yards	59-277	46-141
Passing yards	90	282
Return yards	23	-12
Passes	7-14-0	16-25-2
Punts	5-36	3-40
Fumbles-lost	6-2	5-2
Penalties-yards	7-107	6-65

A—52,187

Texas	0	7	8	10—25
Texas Tech	3	6	3	8—20

TT—FG Grimes 21
Tex—Leaks 1 run (Schott kick)
TT—FG Grimes 31
TT—FG Grimes 37
TT—FG Grimes 32
Tex—Lowry 8 run (Leaks pass from Lowry)
Tex—Lowry 7 run (Schott kick)
Tex—FG 36 Schott
TT—Jobe 16 pass from Barnes (Tillman pass from Barnes)

James Lee Robertson makes a leaping catch of a Casey Ortez pass as Gobbler Chuck Perdue (21) arrives too late and Randy Goss (81) looks on.

VIRGINIA TECH 13 - SMU 10

It was a bad day at Blacksburg for the unbeaten Mustangs. The Gobblers, who had lost two on the road, returned home to play before 26,000. They didn't disappoint their followers as they handed SMU its first loss of the season. Credit must be given to the Mustangs in going for a win when a tie was almost a certainty.

The game started out as a give away contest with six turnovers in the first quarter. Tech had four and SMU two. The Mustangs could muster only seven points on the four Gobbler turnovers. Kris Silverthorn and Andy Duvall each recovered a Tech fumble. Ted Thompson and Robert Popelka each intercepted a pass. Thompson's interception led to the Mustang s only touchdown. Gobbler quarterback Don Strock tried to hit Kit Utz near the sideline and Thompson raced in front of the intended receiver. From the Tech 22 he returned to the four. Alvin Maxson scored on first down as he broke through over left tackle. Clint Hackney kicked the extra point and with 4:30 gone in the first period SMU led 7-0.

Meanwhile Tech had their chances too as they recovered in Mustang territory twice on fumbled punts. SMU's defense stopped the opportunities, one of which ended on Popelka's interception and run back of 27 yards to the Gobbler 38.

Nothing came of that as Ralph Blount, after catching a pass from quarterback Casey Ortez, lost the ball when hit at the Gobbler 28. Strock then got Tech moving and on the first play of the second quarter he threw deep for Donnie Reel. Defender Silverthorn fell as Reel caught the ball on the four and scored. The quarterback's brother, Dave Strock, kicked the extra point to tie the score at 7-7.

Ortez then got the Mustangs moving for the first time, but was intercepted on a pass meant for Oscar Roan. Kent Berry made the interception for Virginia Tech at his 47. The Gobblers marched to SMU's nine before Dave Strock kicked a 34-yard field goal. Tech led 10-7.

John Blackburn replaced Ortez at quarterback. On first down at the Mustang 20 Maxson took the handoff

Another leaping catch of an Ortez pass. This one by Rory Best (82) at the Tech nine-yard line giving SMU a first and goal with less than a minute to play. All three Gobbler linebacks arrived too late.

and weaved his way 68 yards to the Tech 11. A clipping penalty on the run brought the ball back to the Gobbler 42. Wayne Morris swept end for 22 yards and the Mustangs eventually reached the nine. On third down Blackburn was trapped for a five-yard loss. This brought in Hackney who kicked a 31-yard field goal to tie the score at 10-10. The first half ended 29 seconds later.

The winning points came in the third quarter and it was only fitting that they were the result of a fumble and blocked kick. The fumble turnover came when Mike Smith pounced on the ball for SMU at the Tech 32. The Gobbler defense continued their mastery over the Mustangs and Hackney came in to try a 51-yard field goal. Tech's Donnie Sprouse burst through to block the kick. He then picked up the ball and reached the SMU 17 before the ball-holder, Sam McLarty, caught him. The Mustangs held at the nine and Dave Strock booted a 26-yard field goal to put the Gobblers on top 13-10.

The scoring was over, but the turnovers continued. Ortez was intercepted and a fumbled handoff between Blackburn and Rayford Clark accounted for two more charitable contributions by the Mustangs. Thompson intercepted Strock, Popelka and Ed Johnson each recovered a Tech fumble, but nothing came of either. Johnson's recovery led to the last gasp for SMU. With 2:52 remaining it gave the Mustangs possession at the Tech 32. On fourth and eight Blackburn passed complete to Rory Best, who leaped high to make the catch at the Gobbler 12 and then backed up three more to the nine. Maxson made four, three and then one on three carries. With the clock fast approaching zero Blackburn kept and was stopped short of the goal. The Mustangs passed up the tying field goal and went for the win and they lost.

Tech also won in turnovers 7-5.

	SMU	VPI
First downs	12	13
Rushes-yards	54-130	37-94
Passing yards	112	206
Passes	11-23-2	16-29-3
Return yards	59	46
Punts	9-37	6-42
Fumbles-lost	3	4
Penalties-yards	4-40	3-47

Southern
Methodist 7   3   0   0—10
Virginia Tech 0   10   3   0—13
SMU—Maxson 4 run (Hackney kick)
VPI—Reel 42 pass from Don Strock (Dave Strock kick)
VPI—FG Dave Strock 34
SMU—PG Hackney 31
VPI—FG Dave Strock 26
A—26,000

69

Razorback Dickey Morton (33) tries to elude Tulsa's George Haynes (43) after receiving hand off from quarterback Joe Ferguson (11). Morton was the leading rusher in the game.

ARKANSAS 21 - TULSA 20

Not counting highschools, Tulsa was the fourth school to ever meet Arkansas in a football game. It was known as Henry Kendall when the two played twice in 1899. Arkansas won the first game and the second was a scoreless tie. Since then they have met 47 times with the Razorbacks winning 31. This is an old, old rivalry which down through the years has built quite a tradition. In Razorback Stadium 40,003 came to sit in on the 50th meeting covering a span of 73 years.

On their second possession of the game, the Golden Hurricane quick-kicked to the Hog 36. From there the Razorbacks moved 64 yards in eight plays. Dickey Morton got things rolling when he consecutively gained 18 yards each time on two running plays. From the Tulsa 28 Scott Bull ran for eight. Morton gained five then ten, Bull two, Joe Ferguson one and Bull went over from the two. Mike Kirkland converted and Arkansas led 7-0.

On the first play of the second quarter Tulsa's Sam Henry missed on a 39-yard field goal attempt. Next time they got the ball the Hurricane went all the way. An unnecessary roughness penalty on the Hogs gave the drive a send off and a daring gamble kept it going. On fourth down and 11 punter Arthur Bennett passed complete, from punt formation, to Drew Pearson for 22 yards to the Arkansas 22. Quarterback Steve Bowling kept on third down and made 17 yards to the two. On second down Ed White ran one yard for the touchdown. Henry kicked good and with 5:58 gone in the second period the game was tied 7-7.

Just before the half John Moseley stopped a Tulsa drive, which had reached the Razorback 22, when he intercepted Bowling at the Hog 12. The first half ended shortly.

Raymond Rhodes fumbled on Tulsa's first scrimmage play after the second half kickoff. Danny Rhodes recovered for Arkansas at the Hurricane 32. Morton picked up most of the yardage as Arkansas moved down to the six. On third down Ferguson used Morton as a

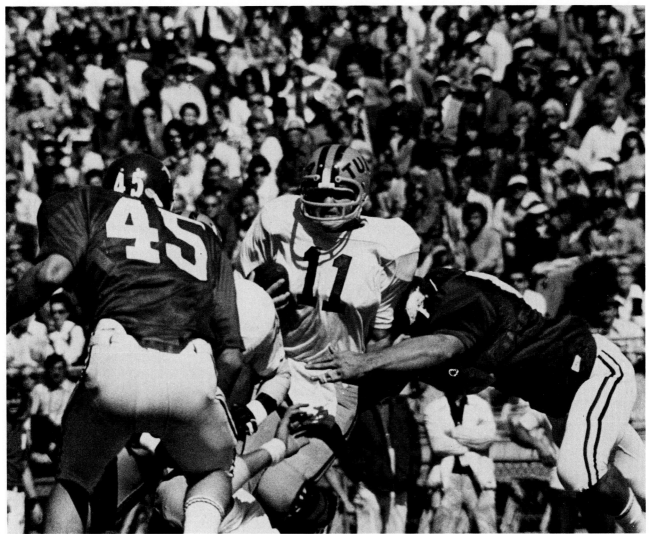

Hurricane quarterback Steve Bowling (11) is grabbed by Hog linebacker John Wheat (68) as Les Williams (45) prepares to give Wheat help.

decoy and passed to Mike Reppond for the score. Kirkland converted and Arkansas led 14-7.

There was no relaxing for the Razorbacks. Tulsa returned the kickoff to their 17, then proceeded to score in five plays. Rhodes ran for 25 to the 42. White made two and Bowling kept for 20 to the Arkansas 36. Buddy Tate gained two and on the next play he ran 34 for the TD. Henry kicked good and once again it was a tie game 14-14.

The Hurricane wasted no time in taking the lead when the Hogs couldn't move following the kickoff. Drew Toole's punt was blocked by Arthur Moore and Tulsa had possession at the Arkansas 31. Not being able to move, Henry came in and kicked a 49-yard field goal to put Tulsa ahead 17-14.

On their next possession Tulsa again drove down to field goal range, moving from their 47 to the Hog 13 in eight plays. On fourth down needing 11, Henry kicked a 31-yard field goal and with 1:27 left in the third quarter Tulsa led 20-14.

On first down at the 20 following the kickoff Morton carried for 18 yards. Ferguson passed to Jim Hodge for eight and after an incompletion Richardson gained two

for a first down. On the first play of the fourth quarter Ferguson hit Reppond for 11 yards at the Tulsa 34. Two plays later he passed to Reppond again, this time for 12 yards. Richardson reached the 12 on a nine-yard run. On first down at the 10 Ferguson passed nine yards to Hodge. Richardson scored on the next play. Kirkland kicked the game winning point and Arkansas led 21-20 with 13:02 left.

To preserve the victory Louis Campbell recovered a Tate fumble at the Hog 39 and later Danny Rhodes intercepted Bowling at the Tulsa 48 and returned to the 42. From there Arkansas ran out the clock.

Tulsa had more first downs, more yards rushing, more yards passing, and more return yardage but Arkansas had more points...one more. Statistics really are for losers.

	Tulsa	Ark.
First downs	20	16
Rushes-yards	59-267	48-182
Passing yards	132	75
Return yards	69	16
Passes	8-21-2	10-23-1
Punts	5-33	9-37
Fumbles-lost	2-2	2-0
Penalties-yards	6-58	5-58

Tul	0	7	13	0—20
Ark	7	0	7	7—21

Ark—Bull 2 run (Kirkland kick)
Tul—White 1 run (Henry kick)
Ark—Reppond 6 pass from Ferguson (Kirkland kick)
Tul—Tate 34 run (Henry kick)
Tul—FG Henry 49
Tul—FG Henry 31
Ark—Richardson 1 run (Kirkland kick)
A—40,003

A & M quarterback Lex James (10) sprints out behind a block by tackle Mike Park (58) to gain nine yards to the Army four. The Aggies scored on the next play.

ARMY 24 - TEXAS A&M 14

The Black Knights of the Hudson were humiliated last week on National TV. This week they weren't on the tube,but the Aggies had 46,680 on hand at Kyle Field. This was a record for a home opener. Well, Army wasn't humiliated this time and the Aggies were a little red-faced at the end.

On their first possession Army, under the direction of quarterback J. Kingsley Fink, marched 75 yards for a touchdown. Bruce Simpson and Robert Hines supplied the running and Fink the passing. He completed an 18-yard pass to Joe Miller, one of 14 yards to James Ward, then back to Miller for 13 which put the ball on the Aggie 10. Simpson scored from the two to cap the 13-play drive. James Barclay coverted and Army led 7-0.

Late in the first period A & M covered 55 yards in eight plays to tie the game. Quarterback Lex James kept the drive alive when he passed 14 yards to Richard Osborne

on a third down and 11 play. He then came back to Osborne for 20 yards to reach the Army 12. James then rolled right and pitched back at the last instant to Bubba Bean who streaked into the end zone. Pat McDermott kicked the extra point and with 1:12 gone in the second quarter it was 7-7.

Following the A & M kickoff Simpson fumbled on first down and Robert Murski recovered for the Aggies at the Army 39. The Aggies scored in five plays overcoming a motion penalty in the process. Bean gained five yards, Alvin Bowers powered his way for 17 and Skip Walker ran for nine to the eight. Next, Walker's eight-yard score was wiped out by the motion penalty. James got nine on a keeper and Bean scored from the four on the next play. McDermott converted and A & M led 14-7.

The Black Knights came right back to go 73 yards and were aided greatly by a holding penalty which cost A & M

Split end Richard Osborne (83) turns upfield after catching a Lex James pass. Stephen Bogosian (86) pursues Osborne. On the ground is Aggie center Skip Kuehn (51).

33 yards. Max Bird broke through to drop Fink for a seven-yard loss on Army's 20. But Corky Sheffield was caught holding downfield and with the yards stepped off from the point of the foul it gave Army the ball on the Aggie 47. Instead of second down and 17 the West Pointers gained 33 yards. Hines' running got the ball to the 25. Fink passed eight yards to Ward, then ran a keeper to the three and Peter Ramsberger scored from the one. Barclay converted to tie the game at 14-14.

The Aggies' McDermott tried a 57-yard field goal, before the half, which was short.

Mistakes continued to plague the Aggies in the second half. They failed to score and two miscue's set up both Army scores. In the third quarter a clipping penalty wiped out a good punt return and A & M was set back to its 17. On first down James cut upfield to his right for two yards, then lofted a pitchback to Bean. Army's Courtney Whitman picked off the ball in mid-air at the 19. Ramsberger ran through tacklers to the 12 and a personal foul got half the distance to the six. Hines gained four and Ramsberger

scored from the two. Barclay converted and Army led 21-14.

Early in the fourth quarter the Aggies were on the move as they reached the West Point 35. James fumbled near the sidelines when hit and Grover Dailey recovered for Army at his 34. This led to a 52 yard field goal attempt by Barclay which was wide to the right. Moments later he got another chance when Matt Wotell intercepted James at the A & M 31. On fourth down Barclay hit from 44-yards out. This put Army ahead 24-14 and with 8:03 left that is the way it ended.

Through four games the Aggies have almost averaged five turnovers a game. They have a season total of 19.

	Army	Tex A&M
First downs	12	17
Rushes-yards	51-157	54-196
Passing yards	81	66
Return yards	39	23
Passes	8-11-0	4-16-3
Punts	7-38	6-38
Fumbles-lost	1-1	5-2
Penalties-yards	3-26	7-95

Army ....7 7 7 3—24
Texas A&M.....0 14 0 0—14
Army—Simpson 2 run (Barclay kick)
A&M—Bean 12 run (McDermott kick)
A&M—Bean 4 run (McDermott kick)
Army—Ramsberger 1 run (Barclay kick)
Army—Ramsberger 2 run (Barclay kick)
Army—FG Barclay 44
A—46,680

Frog fullback Ronnie Webb (30) gets three yards on this carry. R. A. Coppedge (40) closes in from the rear.

TCU 38 - UTA 14

This was the third meeting between these two Tarrant County schools. The 22,300 in Amon Carter Stadium saw the Mavericks give the Horned Frogs fits in the first half and gain the lead at one time. In the second half it was a different story.

UTA, who needed all the help they could get, started off badly when Sid Sims lost the ball on the Mavericks second play of the game. Dede Terveen recovered for TCU at the UTA 45. The Frogs scored in 14 plays as the Mavericks gave ground grudgingly. Mike Luttrell got the touchdown from the three. Berl Simmons converted and TCU led 7-0.

The Frogs cranked up another drive on their next possession. They moved 55 yards in 10 plays, but this time UTA forced a field goal. Simmons responded with a 36-yard effort, which was successful, and TCU led 10-0 with four minutes left in the first quarter.

The Mavericks started at their 16 following the kickoff. They drove to TCU 46 and from there quarterback Bobby Hill passed to the crossing Scott Highsmith who had come out of the backfield. Highsmith caught the ball and sped down the east sideline for a touchdown. R. A. Coppedge kicked good and TCU now led 10-7.

The Purple Gang widened the gap as the second quarter started. Tommy Van Wart tipped a Hill pass and Ed Robinson grabbed it for TCU as he fell at the Maverick 25. A 13-yard combination run by quarterback Kent Marshall and Ronnie Littleton was voided when Marshall's lateral was ruled illegal. On fourth down Simmons kicked a 33-yard field goal. TCU led 13-7.

UTA received the kickoff and couldn't move. On fourth down and four at the 22 Joe Whitney dropped back in punt formation. Whitney didn't punt, he ran, and for 38 yards to the TCU 40. Two plays later Hill threw in

Gary Whitman (36) puts the stopper on Maverick Scott Highsmith (28) with help coming from Kent Steel (73).

the flat to end Felley Donaldson who evaded David McGinnis and ran 39 yards for a touchdown. With Coppedge's extra point the Mavericks led TCU for the first time ever, 14-13.

With time running out in the first half Marshall gathered his forces and drove to the UTA 22. The Mavericks held though and Simmons came in to kick his third field goal, from 40-yards this time. At the half TCU clung to a two-point 16-14 lead.

The Frogs came out like lions in the third period, but after a 70-yard scoring march they then turned to lambs. Luttrell, Billy Sadler and Ronnie Webb ran for most of the yardage on the scoring drive with Luttrell going over on a two-yard run. Simmons added the point after and TCU led 23-14.

Later, at the Maverick 38, a fourth down snap went over Frog punter Greg Anderson's head and he was downed at the TCU 31. After UTA reached the Frog 14 Terveen saved a possible score when he intercepted Hill and ran back to the 50.

Lyle Blackwood returned a Maverick punt 54 yards to UTA's 33. On second down an errant pitchout was recovered by UTA linebacker John Brown. Blackwood then intercepted Hill at the TCU 17. After a punt by Anderson, UTA had possession at their 15. Vic Morriss replaced Hill at quarterback and promptly fumbled to Terveen at the 11. In five plays the Frogs scored, Webb going the final yard. Simmons converted and TCU led 30-14 as the fourth quarter was one-third gone.

TCU added one more touchdown nine seconds before the final gun. Terry Drennan had replaced Marshall and he took the Frogs 81 yards in 15 plays. The score came on a 10-yard keeper by Drennan. Perry Senn ran across for a two point conversion.

	UTA	TCU
First downs	14	22
Rushes-yards	29-99	76-227
Passing yards	233	100
Return yards	201	161
Passes	14-30-3	9-16-0
Punts	5-40.2	4-40.4
Fumbles-lost	2-2	3-1
Penalties-yards	7-60	4-50

A—22,300

Texas-Arlington	.7	7	0	0—14
Texas Christian	.10	6	7	15—38

TCU—Luttrell 3 run (Simmons kick)
TCU—FG Simmons 36
UTA—Highsmith 46 pass from Hill (Coppedge kick)
TCU—FG Simmons 33
UTA—Donaldson 30 pass from Hill (Coppedge kick)
TCU—FG Simmons 40
TCU—Luttrell 2 run (Simmons kick)
TCU—Webb 1 run (Simmons kick)
TCU—Drennan 10 run (Senn run)

SYNOPSIS

TOP TEN

1. Southern Cal
2. Oklahoma
3. Ohio State
4. Alabama
5. Michigan
6. Nebraska
7. Notre Dame
8. LSU
9. Texas
10. Tennessee

UPSET OF WEEK:

Oklahoma State 31 - Colorado 7

SWC OFFENSIVE PLAYER OF WEEK

Alan Lowry, Quarterback, Texas

SWC DEFENSIVE PLAYER OF WEEK

Bruce Henley, Safety, Rice

FRESHMAN RESULTS:

Arkansas 23 - SMU 12
Texas A&M 30 - Rice 7
Texas Tech 27 - TCU 0

SWC TEAM LEADERS FOR THE SEASON

OFFENSE	AVG.	DEFENSE	AVG.
Rushing..................... Texas Tech 324 yds.		Rushing......................... SMU 59 yds.	
Passing .... Rice 212 yds.		Passing .... Baylor 123 yds.	
Total...................... Texas Tech 504 yds.		Total............................ Baylor 256 yds.	

SEASON RECORDS

	W	L	T
TCU	2	0	0
Texas	2	0	0
Rice	2	0	1
SMU	2	1	0
Texas Tech	2	1	0
Arkansas	2	1	0
Baylor	1	1	0
Houston	1	2	0
Texas A & M	1	3	0

CONFERENCE

	W	L	T
Texas	1	0	0
Texas Tech	0	1	0

Fifth Week
October 7

39 YEARS AGO
OCTOBER 7, 1933
Texas Tech 33 - Dixie 0
Arkansas 13 - TCU 0
Texas A&M 34 - Sam Houston 14
Nebraska 26 - Texas 0
SMU 27 - Texas Mines 6
Rice 13 - Loyola 0
Centenary 19 - Baylor 0

Tech quarterback Joe Barnes, who led his team in rushing, sets up to pass on this play behind the blocks of Doug McCutchen (32) on Richard Dixson (85) and Dennis Allen (65) on Al Humphrey (99).

TEXAS TECH 35 - TULSA 18

The Red Raiders and Golden Hurricane had quite a rivalry going back in the 40's and 50's. Starting in 1943 they met for 17 straight years with Tulsa holding the edge in victories, 10 to seven. This was their first meeting since 1959. A crowd of 34,175 was on hand to see if Tech could bounce back after a disheartening loss to Texas last week. Unlike that game the Red Raiders this time gave Don Grimes the night off in the field goal department as they scored four times from short range.

Tech couldn't move on their first possession and John Garner punted to Tulsa's Drane Scrivener who fumbled the ball. Larry Burnett recovered for Tech at the Hurricane six. Three plays made four yards, but on fourth down Doug McCutchen crashed into the end zone from the two. Grimes kicked the extra point and the Raiders led 7-0.

Late in the first quarter Tulsa moved from their nine to the Tech 15. Raymond Rhodes had a run of 23 yards. Quarterback Steve Bowling passed to Drew Pearson for 22 yards and in between Tech drew a 15-yard penalty. Those were the big plays in the drive. Upon reaching the 15 the Hurricane also reached fourth down and Sam Henry kicked a 33-yard field goal on the first play of the second quarter. Tech led 7-3.

Quarterback Joe Barnes and James Mosley shouldered the load as Tech moved in for its second touchdown midway through the quarter. Mosley got the score from the five on a crunching run and with Grimes' conversion Tech led 14-3. The eight play drive covered 65 yards.

The Red Raiders really overcame adversity on their next drive. It too covered 65 yards but included two 15-

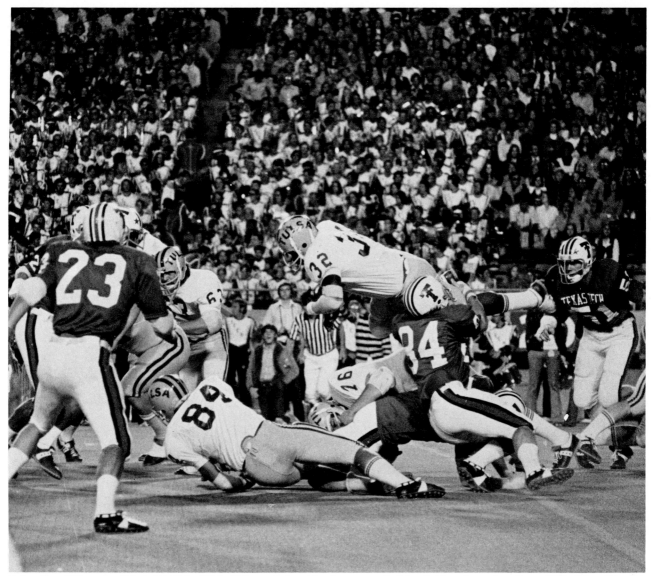

Gaines Baty (84) catches Tulsa's Ed White (32) in flight and brings him down to earth. Other Raiders pictured are Danny Willis (23) and Donald Rives (51).

yard penalties. One for offensive interference which also cost a down and the second on a holding violation. Barnes overcame the latter when he ran for 30 yards to the Tulsa 13. On the next play Barnes passed to George Smith for the touchdown. Only 16 seconds remained before halftime. Grimes converted and Tech led 21-3.

Tech failed to score in the third quarter as Tulsa did likewise. Kenneth Wallace returned a Hurricane punt 24 yards to start the Raiders toward their fourth touchdown. McCutchen ended the drive by running three yards for the score. Grimes kicked the extra point and the Red Raiders led 28-3.

Todd Starks came in at quarterback for Tulsa and passed the Hurricane to a first down at the Tech 12. He then passed to Steve Shores at the back of the end zone for a touchdown. Henry converted and Tech led 28-10.

Jimmy Carmichael relieved Barnes at quarterback and took Tech 55 yards in six plays for the final Red Raider touchdown. At the three he faked a handoff and fooled

Tulsa badly as he turned right end on a keeper and scored untouched. Grimes kicked good and Tech led 35-10.

Starks then led Tulsa to another touchdown in the closing moments of the game. The drive covered 78 yards in eight plays. From the Tech 10 he passed to Pearson for the score. On a fake kick for the conversion Tulsa was stopped, but Tech was penalized for interference. The Hurricane passed for the two points on their next attempt, which again failed, but Tech was guilty of interference again. On their third attempt Rhodes ran for the two points. Final Score: Texas Tech 35 - Tulsa 18.

	Tulsa	Tech
First downs	17	19
Rushes-yards	42-120	63-325
Passing yards	209	70
Return yards	5	67
Passes	14-26-0	5-9-0
Punts	7-42-1	8-35-1
Fumbles lost	4-3	3-3
Penalties yards	7-64	12-92

Tulsa .... 0 3 0 15—18
Texas Tech ....7 14 0 14—35
  Tech—McCutchen 1 run (Grimes kick)
  Tulsa—FG Henry 33
  Tech—Mosley 5 run (Grimes kick)
  Tech—Smith 14 pass from Barnes (Grimes kick)
  Tech—McCutchen 3 run (Grimes kick)
  Tulsa—Shores 12 pass from Starks (Henry kick)
  Tech—Carmichael 3 run (Grimes kick)
  Tulsa—Pearson 10 pass from Starks (Rhodes run)
  A—34,175

Rice fullback Steve Ogletree (22) follows a wall of blockers on this carry as David Vandiver (58) blocks in the background.

LSU 12 - RICE 6

The Owls and Tigers first met in 1915 and have played 40 times since. Overall LSU holds the edge with 25 victories to 12 for Rice. There have been four ties. Sixty thousand fans came to Rice Stadium to watch this year's game which could have gone either way. Turnovers played a big part in the outcome as LSU lost three fumbles and had one pass intercepted. The Owls matched LSU in lost fumbles and five of their passes were intercepted by the Bayou Bengals.

The Tigers first move died at their 41 and Rusty Jackson punted only 24 yards to the Rice 35. LSU's Jimmy LeDoux downed the ball and the Tiger offensive unit was trotting off the field when an official ruled that the ball had touched an Owl and it was still LSU's ball. Rice's defensive troops held again and Juan Roca kicked a field goal from 46 yards to give the Tigers a 3-0 lead.

Rice couldn't move and Mark Williams punted 59 yards to the LSU nine. Quarterback Bert Jones then directed the Tigers to the Owl one-yard line. Jones did the

passing and Chris Dantin the running to move LSU out of the shadow of their goal post. On second and goal Preston Anderson belted Brad Davis hard and Larry Walling recovered for Rice at their three. A 90-yard drive, the longest one of the night, all for naught.

The Owls offense then started clicking as quarterback Bruce Gadd passed to Gary Butler for 21 yards. Moments later another completed pass to Butler covered 16 yards and reached the Rice 46. Two LSU offside penalties moved the ball across midfield. The drive ended when Edwin Collins fumbled a Gadd pass and Tommy Butaud recovered for LSU at his 24.

Rice got the ball back when Roca missed on a 60-yard field goal attempt. Gadd went to the air and his passes to Steve Ogletree, Gary Ferguson and Ron Arceneaux took the Owls to the LSU 40. A run by Ferguson picked up a first down and Gadd then passed to Arceneaux at the Tiger 17. Gadd next found Collins free in the end zone and passed to him for an apparent touchdown. An

The Owls' Preston Anderson (40) knocks Brad Davis (48) loose from the football at the Rice one-yard line. Larry Walling recovered for Rice at the three.

offsides penalty wiped it out. The Owls could give up eight turnovers. Turnovers were common, touchdowns were rare. They lost the touchdown and possibly the game on an offside infraction. Williams tried a 48-yard field goal which fell short.

LSU got into field goal territory, but Roca missed a 47 yarder. This didn't discourage Roca as he got another chance and kicked his longest field goal ever, 53 yards. With eight seconds left in the first half LSU led 6-0.

Neither team could score in the third period. Williams and Roca both missed on field goal attempts. Late in the quarter Gadd was intercepted, but Dantin fumbled on first down and Wade Bode recovered for Rice at the LSU 23. Warren Capone then intercepted Gadd at his 19 as the fourth quarter opened. At the end of three quarters the field goal battle was 2-0 in favor of LSU. Rice had missed two, the Tigers three.

Later Williams got off his second 59-yard punt of the game to put the ball on the Tiger three. Dantin fumbled on first down and Steve Pruitt got the ball for Rice. At least Pruitt thought he recovered, but an official ruled that LSU still had possession.

Rice had another opportunity when an LSU punt gave them possession at the Tiger 39. On third down at the 28 Ferguson fumbled and Norm Hodgins recovered for LSU at his 28. The Tigers scored in six plays. Paul Lyons quarterbacked the drive. Jim Benglis ran the final 23 yards after finding a hole in the middle of the Rice line. LaRay Breshers blocked the conversion and with 6:43 left LSU led 12-0.

John Coleman dove over from the one with 1:47 remaining to cap a nine-play 73-yard drive. The big play came on an end-around pass from Collins to Butler at the Tiger three. A conversion pass missed and LSU led 12-6.

The following Owl onside kick was unsuccessful and LSU ran out the clock.

	LSU	Rice
First downs	21	17
Rushes-yards	65-298	34-67
Passing yardage	114	285
Return yardage	58	24
Passes	7-16-1	20-45-5
Punts	6-39-8	5-48-2
Fumbles	5-3	5-3
Penalties yards	3-15	4-30

LSU .... 3 3 0 6—12
Rice .... 0 0 0 6— 6
LSU—FG Roca 46
LSU—FG Roca 53
LSU—Benglis 23 run (kick failed)
Rice—Coleman 1 run (pass failed)
A—60,000

Longhorn quarterback Alan Lowry gets a bear hug on this play. Lowry gained 145 yards on the ground to lead all rushers.

TEXAS 27 - UTAH STATE 12

The Aggies came to Texas' Memorial Stadium with a former Longhorn directing their attack. Quarterback Tony Adams was on the same freshman team with Longhorn linebacker Randy Braband and Tommy Lee. The crowd of 58,122 failed to see the ex-Texan lead his Utah team to victory, but it wasn't because he didn't try.

The Aggies opened the scoring on their second possession which started at the State 43. They drove to the Texas 25 with the big play being a pass from Adams to Tom Forzani good for 17 yards. At the 25 Adams dropped back and tossed a screen pass to Jerry Hughes who followed his blocking all the way to the Longhorn end zone. Mickey Doyle missed the extra point and with the first quarter half over the Aggies led 6-0.

In the meantime the Longhorns couldn't dent the State defense. On their first three possessions they reached their 28, 26 and 36-yard lines. The fourth time they had the ball, courtesy of an interception by Ronnie Workman at the

State 35, Mike Dean missed a 47-yard field goal effort. Another interception, this one by Glen Gaspard, set Texas up on the Utah State 28. This led to Billy Schott's missed 41-yard field goal try.

As the second quarter opened Doyle tried a 50-yard field goal for State which was short. Texas started at its 20 and finally wracked up their first first down of the game as they moved to their 45-yard line. On the next play quarterback Alan Lowry kept left and gained 30 yards before lateralling back to the trailing Tom Landry. Landry bobbled the pitch but regained possession eight yards later and ran the remaining distance for a touchdown. The play covered 55 yards and with Schott's conversion the Longhorns led 7-6.

The Aggies regained the lead when Doyle kicked a 33-yard field goal. With 1:26 before halftime State led 9-7. But the Longhorns went to the dressing room in the lead as they raced the clock to move 54 yards to the Aggie

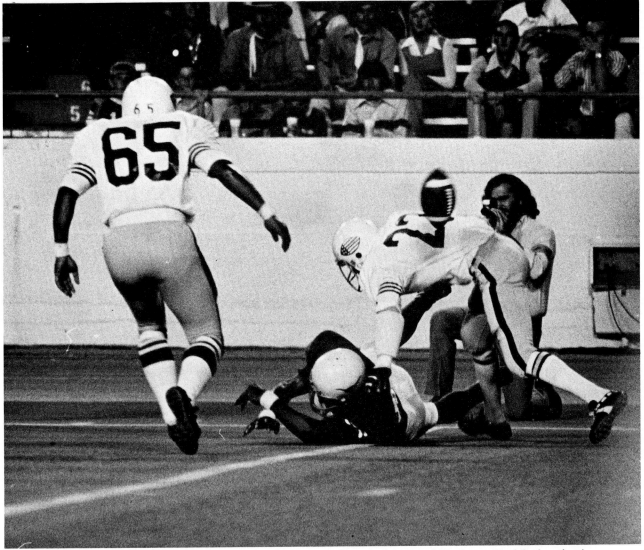

This pass for Lonnie Bennett fell incomplete as Utah State's Willie Halaufia (65) and Jim Boccio (23) defend on the play.

21. The big gainer was a 38-yard pass from Lowry to split end Jim Moore. Only 19 seconds remained when Schott kicked a 38-yard field goal that just cleared the bar. At the half Texas led 10-9.

Utah State moved to the Texas 29 with the second half kickoff, but was stopped when Malcolm Minnick recovered a Hughes fumble. The defenses took over for most of the third quarter and Glenn Gaspard set up the next Longhorn score when he intercepted Adams at the State 28. On third down and the first play of the fourth quarter Dean kicked a 45-yard field goal. Texas led 13-9.

The Aggies came back to threaten when Adams passed to Hughes with the pass and run play gaining 36 yards. But Adams fumbled the snap at the Texas 24 and Minnick again recovered for the Longhorns. Lowry then moved Texas 72 yards on 11 plays. Three successive plays were the big gainers. Lowry passed to Moore for 23 yards, then ran a keeper for 16 yards and on the next down passed to Lonnie Bennett for 19 yards. After his catch Bennett was knocked out of bounds at the Aggie three. Utah State's line stiffened like starch and it took the Longhorns four

downs to score. Landry plunged over from the one and fumbled, but the score was made and Schott's conversion put Texas ahead 20-9.

Utah State drove from their 20 to the Longhorn 25 which included a successful fourth and one gamble by Adams at his own 29. Three incomplete passes brought in Doyle who kicked a 42-yard field goal. With 3:50 left Texas led by eight points, 20-12.

The Longhorns then controlled the ball for the rest of the game which culminated in a nine-yard touchdown run by Lowry on the last play of the game with no time remaining. Schott converted and Texas had won 27-12, for their third straight victory.

	Utah State	Texas
First downs	20	15
Rushes-yards	34-84	54-283
Passing yards	252	83
Return yards	23	18
Passes	26-42-2	4-13-1
Punts	4-39	4-38
Fumbles lost	2-2	3-1
Penalties-yards	3-29	1-5

Utah State	6	3	0	3—12
Texas	0	10	0	17—27

US—Hughes 25 pass from Adams (kick failed)
Tex—Landry 55 run (Schott kick)
US—FG Doyle 33
Tex—FG Schott 38
Tex—FG Dean 45
Tex—Landry 1 run (Schott kick)
US—FG Doyle 42
Tex—Lowry 6 run (Schott kick)
A—58,122

Wayne Morris (25) sets up the final Mustang touchdown with this 24 yard run to the State 35-yard line. The Aggies' Cal Dietz (78), Eric Hoyte (47) and Al Gee (48) converge on Morris. Converging with them is SMU's Ralph Blount (83). Blocking downfield is Rufus Shaw (80).

SMU 55 - NEW MEXICO STATE 6

Last year the Aggies gave SMU fits before losing by three points. For the first half the 27,221 fans saw the heavily favored Mustangs do anything but dazzle their visitors from New Mexico State. Then in the second half the sleeping giant awoke and stomped its opposition into the artificial turf of Texas Stadium.

In the first quarter the Mustangs got a break when the Aggie punter, Doug Baker, dropped the ball and in turn was dropped by Ted Thompson. SMU had possession at the State 36. A pass from quarterback Casey Ortez to Rory Best got 17 of the yards needed to reach the seven. There, on fourth down, Alvin Maxson got the first down and three plays later Ortez passed to Wayne Morris for four yards and a touchdown. Clint Hackney converted and SMU led 7-0.

The next time the Mustangs snubbed a field goal things didn't turn out so good. They had driven to the Aggie five-yard line early in the second quarter. On fourth down Ortez's pass in the end zone was way off target.

SMU again got inside the Aggie 10 and again came away empty handed. Kris Silverthorn started things off by returning a State punt 32 yards to the Aggie 28. After reaching the nine someone put the machinery in reverse gear. First a holding penalty cost them 15 yards and then on the following plays Ortez was sacked for 14 yards in losses.

The Aggies then started moving. Quarterback Joe Pisarcik hit on three of four passes to gain the SMU 11-yard line. One of those completions was to Hank Cook for 44 yards. His fourth completion in the 80-yard drive was to Scooter Warren for six yards and a touchdown. Doug Berg got through to block Dennis Ware's conversion and SMU led 7-6.

The Mustangs took the one-point lead to the dressing room at halftime, but for a bobbled punt attempt they could have been trailing 6-0.

Thompson started the second half avalanche when he intercepted Pisarcik, early in the third quarter, at the

SMU's Leonard Carey (31) and Louis Kelcher (72) combine to drop Aggie tailback Zack Robinson for a loss on this play. G. T. Lewis (63) blocks out Steve Morton (70). The Mustang's Ed Johnson (66) is shown just above Lewis.

Aggie seven. Maxson scored from the one and with Hackney's kick SMU led 14-6.

Silverthorn, second in the nation in punt returns, returned a State punt 77 yards for another Mustang touchdown. Hackney converted and SMU led 21-6.

Unfortunately for New Mexico State, Keith Bobo took over at quarterback on the Mustangs' next possession. He got a touchdown, five in all, on every possession he was in the game.

First it was a 58-yard drive in six plays. Bobo picked up 30 of those yards on two keepers. Maxson scored from the four. Next time SMU had the ball Bobo pitched out to Morris and behind a good block by Bill Thomas he sped 85 yards down the sidelines for a touchdown. Then the Mustangs came back and moved 88 yards in nine plays. Two pass interference calls, costing State 58 yards, aided the drive greatly. The second one put the ball on their one. Maxson scored from there. Hackney missed on one of his five conversion attempts in the third quarter and as play moved into the final quarter SMU led 41-6.

On Bobo's fourth possession he passed to Ken Harrison for 13 yards, then came back to Harrison on a bomb. The play covered 54 yards for a touchdown. On his final possession of the game the Mustangs scored again. Morris started it by running 24 yards. Bobo passed to Harrison for 11 yards to the Aggie 24. On third down he passed 15 yards to Rufus Shaw for the touchdown. Hackney kicked both extra points and SMU led 55-6.

The Mustangs had scored on their first seven possessions in the final half. Their third quarterback, John Blackburn, went in on the eighth and the Mustangs were forced to punt. Seven out of eight ain't bad. Final score: SMU 55 - New Mexico State 6.

	NMS	SMU
First downs	13	23
Rushes-yards	25-1	53-276
Passing yards	284	198
Return yards	25	141
Passes	18-47-2	14-24-0
Punts	10-45-9	6-39-5
Fumbles lost	4-0	2-1
Penalties yards	9-119	6-70

New Mex. State........0 6 0 0— 6
SMU ....7 0 34 14—55
SMU—Morris 4 pass from Ortez (Hackney kick)
NMSU—Warren 6 pass from Pisarcik (kick blocked)
SMU—Maxson 1 run (Hackney kick)
SMU—Silverthorn 77 punt return (Hackney kick)
SMU—Maxson 4 run (kick failed)
SMU—Morris 82 run (Hackney kick)
SMU—Maxson 1 run (Hackney kick)
SMU—Harrison 54 pass from Bobo (Hackney kick)
SMU—Shaw 15 pass from Bobo (Hackney kick)
A—27,221

This touchdown pass from D. C. Nobles to Miller Bassler (86), who is all by his lonesome in the end zone, brought the Cougars to within six points of Virginia Tech. The play covered six yards.

HOUSTON 27 - VIRGINIA TECH 27

This Cougar team of 1972 just doesn't know when to quit, but they are probably wondering what it takes to win. After a normal win against Tulsa last week, they returned to form this week and overcame tremendous odds to tie Tech. Their glorious quest for victory ended when the extra point kick was missed. To appreciate more the accomplishments of the "Comeback Cougars" you have to take into consideration that Don Strock, the opposing quarterback, completed 34 passes out of 53 attempts for 527 yards. All told both teams gained 1,080 yards with 733 of that total coming on passes.

Tech got to rolling in the first quarter and marched 80 yards in nine plays. A pass interference call at the Cougar eight kept the drive alive. Quarterback Strock scored from the three and brother Dave Strock converted. With 2:43 gone VPI led 7-0.

Two possessions later the Gobblers were stopped at the Cougar 36 and Dave Strock entered for a field goal

attempt. It was blocked and Howard Ebow returned to the Houston 20, but officials called a roughing the kicker penalty which gave Tech the ball at the 14. Houston Coach Bill Yeoman, trying to find out what was going on, was penalized and that put the ball on the seven. James Barber scored from the two on second down. Dave Strock missed the conversion and VPI led 13-0.

In the second quarter backup quarterback Terry Peel led the Cougars 95 yards in 13 plays for their only score of the first half. A bad snap kept the drive alive. Hal Roberts was back to punt on fourth and three. The bad snap forced him to run and he made the Tech 43. After Houston reached the 30, Peel ran when his receivers were covered and made 26 yards to the four. Puddin' Jones scored from there and with Ricky Terrell's kick Houston trailed 7-13.

Strock completed five of six passes and Barber dove over from the one-foot line as the Gobblers scored with 35

Brian Willingham (23) catches a 20-yard pass from D. C. Nobles for the tying touchdown with just over one minute left in the game. The Gobblers Randy McCann (33) arrives too late.

seconds left in the first half. Brother Dave didn't get to kick as his brother Don ran for the two-point conversion. VPI led 21-7 at halftime after missing a last second field goal from the Cougar 17.

In the third quarter Dave Strock kicked two field goals to put the Gobblers up 27-7 and then the comeback began.

A Tech turnover gave Houston the ball at the VPI 20. Jones scored from the seven with 3:09 left in the third quarter. Terrell converted and VPI led 27-14. Regular quarterback D. C. Nobles returned and moved the Cougars 84 yards in 13 plays mainly relying on screen passes to flanker Robert Ford. Ford followed the blocking of Luke Stungis for good gains. A pass to Miller Bassler from the six was good for six with the fourth quarter half gone. Terrell converted and VPI led 27-21.

The Cougars cranked up another drive and it ended when Nobles was forced out of bounds at the Gobbler six on fourth down. Time was getting short as the Houston defense held and Andy Hromyak's 50-yard punt went to Bryan Willingham. Fielding the ball at his 30 Willingham took off and returned 37 yards to the Tech 33-yard line.

From the 20, with 1:15 left, Nobles passed to the left corner of the end zone and Willingham hauled it in for a touchdown. The snake bit again as Terrell missed the conversion and the Cougars had to settle for a tie instead of victory. Final score: Houston 27 - Virginia Tech 27.

It was a tremendous game from the 26,000 fans viewpoint as a total of 195 offensive plays took place. Puddin' Jones led all rushers as he gained 162 yards on 24 carries. Nobles after hitting on one of seven in the first half, came back to connect on 16 of 29 in the second half. For the Cougar defense Deryl McGallion came up with 18 tackles. The penalty called on Coach Yeoman was his first since being at Houston.

	Houston	VPI
First downs	23	30
Rushes-yards	47-269	41-78
Passing yards	206	527
Return yards	44	10
Passes	20-41-1	34-53-2
Punts	7-42	4-44
Fumbles lost	6-2	10-4
Penalties	5-69	5-35

Houston 0   7   7 13—27
Va. Tech 13   8   6   0—27

VPI—Don Strock 3 run (Dave Strock kick)
VPI—Barber 2 run (kick failed)
Hou—Jones 4 run (Terrell kick)
VPI—Barbar 1 run (Don Strock run)
VPI—FG Dave Strock 22
VPI—FG Dave Strock 26
Hou—Jones 6 run (Terrell kick)
Hou—Bassler 6 pass from Nobles (Terrell kick)
Hou—Willingham 20 pass from Nobles (kick failed)
A—26,000

Baylor quarterback Neal Jeffrey (11) pitches out at the last second as Lee Wright (77) rises to make a block.

BAYLOR 10 - MIAMI 3

The Bears came home after breaking even in two road games. For that accomplishment the faithful really turned out and the crowd of 35,000 was the largest ever for a home opener.

The offense put the Bears out front in the first half and a ferocious defense held off repeated Miami threats in the second half to preserve the victory. Special praise must go to the Baylor secondary comprised of Ira Dean, Ricky Duff, Tommy Turnipseede, Tommy Stewart and Keith Stone. Stone replaced Duff after he broke his ankle in the second quarter. They shut down the Hurricane passing game when it was the only thing that could get Miami back in the game.

Coach Grant Teaff showed that Baylor wasn't going to play conservative football this season when they took the opening kickoff and moved to the Miami 32 and then went for it on fourth down and three. Pat McNeil was stopped a yard short, but that didn't discourage the Bears as they tried the same thing again later.

The Hurricanes' offense took over possession and moved down field to the Bear 30 where they faced a fourth down needing six. Mike Burke came in and attempted a 46-yard field goal which was wide to the right.

Starting from their 20 the Bears moved steadily downfield on the running of Brian Kilgore, Gary Lacy and quarterback Neal Jeffrey. At the Hurricane 23 another fourth down came up and the Bears needed three. Jeffrey's pass, intended for tight end Rusty Bundy was incomplete, but Miami was offsides and Baylor had a first down at the 18. Two penalties against Baylor thwarted the drive and Mike Conradt came in and kicked a 44-yard field goal. Baylor led 3-0.

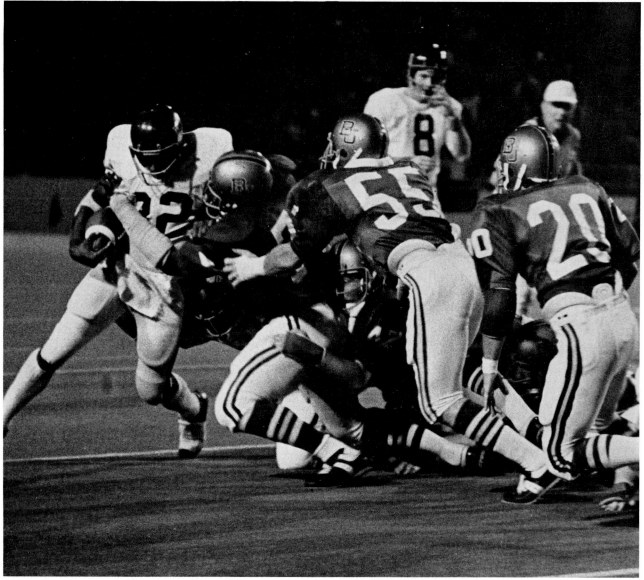

The Bear defense drops Chuck Foreman (32) for a loss. Making the tackle is Millard Neely (78) with Roger Goree (55) and Ricky Duff (20) rushing up to help.

The defense held Miami after the kickoff and following the Hurricane punt the Bears had excellent field position at the 50. On first down Jeffrey fumbled and Rubin Carter recovered for Miami. Hurricane quarterback Ed Carney passed to Phil Corrigan for 12 and to Steve Marcantonio for 14. Chuck Foreman got the needed yardage on the ground as Miami reached the Bear 11. That was the end of the line and on fourth and 16 Burke kicked a 27-yard field goal from the 17. With 10 minutes before halftime the game was tied 3-3.

Baylor came right back and marched 76 yards in eight plays. Three Jeffrey passes were the key ingredients in the drive. He hit Charles Dancer for 12 yards and Kilgore for 26 yards in reaching the Miami 28. On second down and 10 Jeffrey threw long to Dancer in the end zone. Booker Cope, defending on the play, had the ball bounce off his hands and Dancer caught the rebound for a Bear touchdown. Conradt converted and Baylor led 10-3.

There was no more scoring in the first half, in fact there was no more scoring in the game. But the Bear defense was up to the task. In the second half the Hurricane marched to the Baylor 31 where Roger Goree and Paul Savage stopped Foreman for no gain on fourth down and one. At the Baylor nine a Carney pass was intercepted by Tommy Stewart at the goal line. From the 20 Burke missed on a 37-yard field goal attempt. Finally from the Bear 17 Carney was pressured into an incompletion to stop Miami's last threat. The Baylor offense then took the pressure off the defense as they marched to their 45 to run out the clock.

	Miami	Baylor
First downs	19	20
Rushes-yards	47-247	53-208
Yards passing	139	136
Return yards	15	24
Passes	11-30-2	12-16-0
Punts	3-49-0	4-42-1
Fumbles lost	0-0	1-1
Penalties	3-15	4-30

Miami 0   3   0   0— 3
Baylor 3   7   0   0—10
B—FG Conradt 44
M—FG Burke 27
B—Dancer 29 pass from Jeffrey (Conradt kick)
A—35,000

Frog quarterback Kent Marshall (11) is stopped after running for 13 yards. Razorback John Wheat (68) grabs Marshall from behind.

ARKANSAS 27 - TCU 13

For the first time since 1963 the Horned Frogs faced Arkansas unbeaten. This may have seemed promising to the TCU fans among the 42,558 in Amon Carter Stadium. On the other hand TCU has played 144 football games since it last beat the Razorbacks. It looked like that would end through almost three quarters of this game, but a season-long, dormant Arkansas offense chose to awake before all was lost.

TCU kicked off and through each teams first two possessions it looked like they were playing punt, and hope the other team makes a mistake. This eventually paid off for the Frogs as a fumble by Arkansas quarterback Joe Ferguson was recovered by Charlie Davis. The only problem was that the Hogs had driven from their 29 to the Frog 22 before Ferguson fumbled.

After John Moseley returned a TCU punt 55 yards Arkansas tried a field goal at the Frog 29, but Mike Kirkland missed. Two possessions later TCU had the ball on their own four. Nine plays later they were on the Arkansas five. The biggest gain was a 32-yard keeper by quarterback Kent Marshall as every play was a run. Mike Luttrell fumbled on the five and Marshall recovered for the Frogs for no gain. Berl Simmons then kicked a 22-yard field goal with 4:50 left in the first half. TCU led 3-0.

A pass interference penalty cost TCU 44 yards and put the ball on their 24, but on the next play Dickey Morton fumbled and Lyle Blackwood recovered for TCU. Moments later the first half ended.

Early in the third quarter Moseley fumbled a punt return and Ronnie Littleton recovered for TCU at the Arkansas 30. The Horned Frogs picked up a holding penalty and eventually settled for a 41-yard field goal by Simmons. With 11:07 left in the third period TCU led 6-0.

On their next possession TCU went all the way, 76 yards, in 12 plays. Throwing only twice, Marshall stayed on the ground as he ran keepers and handed off to Luttrell

Arkansas quarterback Joe Ferguson (11), who tied a Razorback record by passing for four touchdowns, tries to evade TCU's Ed Robinson (89) on a keeper.

and Ronnie Webb to reach the Razorback two. Billy Sadler ran two yards for the touchdown. Simmons converted and with 5:10 remaining in the third quarter TCU led 13-0.

Then the sleeping giant awoke. On the third play, following the kickoff, Ferguson kept for 23 yards and TCU was penalized 15 yards for a personal foul on the tackle. Walter Nelson replaced Ferguson for one play and then Ferguson came back in and hit Jack Ettinger for 34 yards and a touchdown. Kirkland converted and TCU led 13-7.

Arkansas regained possession as play moved into the fourth quarter. Ferguson literally passed the Razorbacks downfield for a touchdown as not once did he call a running play in the 74-yard drive. He varied his receivers as he hit Richardson, Ettinger and Mike Reppond with completions. Reppond caught the last one for eight yards and the score. Kirkland converted and with 14:01 left Arkansas led for the first time 14-13.

The Razorbacks came right back the next time they got the ball and moved 83 yards to score in seven plays.

Ferguson passes did most of the damage as he hit Hodge for 47 yards, Ettinger for 18 and then back to Hodge for 11 yards and the touchdown. Again Kirkland kicked good and Arkansas led 21-13.

TCU couldn't move and punted to the Razorback 44. Nothing could stop Ferguson now. After reaching the Horned Forg 39 he lost 12 yards and then came back and hit Richardson for 18 and a first down at TCU's 33. A 13-yard pass to Reppond reached the 20 and a 20-yard pass to Hodge reached the end zone. The point after was missed and Arkansas led 27-13.

When the Razorbacks got the ball again they ran out the clock and also the hopes of all the Frog rooters who for a while thought that this might be the year.

	Ark.	TCU
First downs	24	13
Rushes-yards	33-107	53-213
Passing yards	304	57
Return yards	99	3
Passes	20-32-0	7-13-0
Punts	4-44-0	10-42-6
Fumbles lost	5-3	2-0
Penalties yards	8-83	9-117
A—42,558		

Arkansas . . . . 0 0 7 20—27
TCU . . . . 0 3 10 0—13
TCU—FG Simmons 22
TCU—FG Simmons 41
TCU—Sadler 2 run (Simmons kick)
Ark—Ettinger 34 pass from Ferguson (Kirkland kick)
Ark—Reppond 8 pass from Ferguson (Kirkland kick)
Ark—Hodge 47 pass from Ferguson (Kirkland kick)
Ark—Hodge 11 pass from Ferguson (kick failed)

SYNOPSIS

5

TOP TEN

1. Southern Cal
2. Oklahoma
3. Alabama
4. Ohio State
5. Michigan
6. Nebraska
7. Notre Dame
8. LSU
9. Auburn
10. Texas

UPSET OF WEEK:

Florida 42 - Florida State 13

SWC OFFENSIVE PLAYER OF WEEK

Joe Ferguson, Quarterback, Arkansas

SWC DEFENSIVE PLAYER OF WEEK

Deryl McGallion, Linebacker, Houston

FRESHMAN RESULTS

SMU 36 - Baylor 6
Texas Tech 42 - Arkansas 26
Houston 71 - Wichita State 0

SWC TEAM LEADERS FOR SEASON

OFFENSE		AVG.
Rushing	Texas Tech	325 yds.
Passing	Rice	232 yds.
Total	Texas Tech	477 yds.

DEFENSE		AVG.
Rushing	SMU	44 yds.
Passing	Arkansas	127 yds.
Total	SMU	269 yds.

SEASON RECORDS

	W	L	T
Texas	3	0	0
Texas Tech	3	1	0
SMU	3	1	0
Arkansas	3	1	0
Baylor	2	1	0
TCU	2	1	0
Rice	2	1	1
Houston	1	2	1
Texas A&M	1	3	0

CONFERENCE

	W	L	T
Texas	1	0	0
Arkansas	1	0	0
Texas Tech	0	1	0
TCU	0	1	0

Sixth Week
October 14

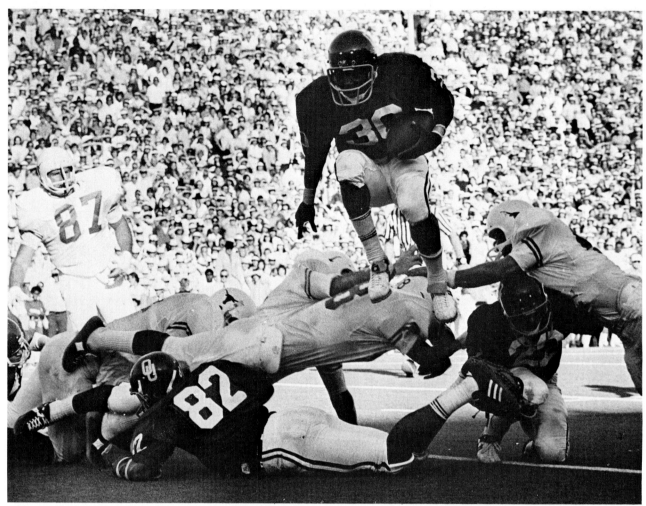

Oklahoma's Greg Pruitt (30) leaps over everyone to score the Sooner's second touchdown. Other identified players are Bill Rutherford (87) of Texas, Albert Chandler (82) of OU and Joe Wylie (22) of OU.

OKLAHOMA 27 - TEXAS 0

A sellout throng filled the Cotton Bowl in Dallas as the Longhorns and Sooners came together for the 67th time. And as usual you can never predict what will happen when these two meet. Oklahoma was first in the nation in rushing, first in total offense and first in scoring. They were going to turn all this loose on the Longhorns. Nearing the end of the third quarter the Sooners had a commanding lead of 3-0. They eventually scored 24 more points, but their defense was the culprit not their offense. The last time the Longhorns failed to score came in the 1963 Cotton Bowl game. Since then they have played 93 regular season games and seven bowl games without having a goose egg thrown on them.

OU kicked off and Texas quarterback Alan Lowry was shaken up on the second play of the game. He sat out only one play and then returned to move Texas out to their 48 where a bad pitchout was fumbled to Oklahoma.

The Sooners quickly moved to a first and goal at the Longhorn six with most of the yardage coming on a 27-yard run by Greg Pruitt. On the next play Joe Wylie fumbled and Malcolm Minnick recovered for Texas at his four. On third down Lowry passed to Jim Moore for 22 yards to the Texas 26. Three plays later Roosevelt Leaks ran for 12 yards to reach the 40 of Texas. On the next play another pitchout was fumbled and Kenith Pope recovered for OU at the UT 33. The Longhorns held at their 20 and Rick Fulcher kicked a 37-yard field goal with 6:01 left in the first quarter. Oklahoma led 3-0.

As the quarter came to a close the Longhorns had moved from their two to the Sooner 45. Leaks reached the 31 on two carries then Pat Kelly dropped a perfectly thrown pass for the second time in the ball game. Two plays later Don Ealey was stopped for no gain on fourth and one at the OU 24.

On their next possession Texas gained the Oklahoma 37 and Mike Dean tried a 54-yard field goal which was short. Following a Sooner punt Leaks ran for 13 yards to the OU 40 on first down, but Tommy Landry fumbled on the next play and lost the ball at the Oklahoma 38. Two possessions later the clock ran out with Texas on their 33.

Early in the third quarter a Lowry pass was deflected by Raymond Hamilton and Rod Shoate intercepted at the

Longhorn Roosevelt Leaks, who gained more than 100 yards rushing, is hauled down on this play by Oklahoma's Lucious Selman (98) and Raymond Hamilton (96). Jon Milstead (49) approaches with help. Others pictured are Travis Roach (66), Bill Wyman (50) and Jerry Sisemore (76) all of Texas.

Texas 28. Pruitt broke through the middle and ran into Randy Braband at the 12, the ball popped loose and Bill Walker recovered for Texas at his 15. Lowry passed 13 yards to Jim Moore and Leaks carried for 17 and then 20 yards. Two plays later Lowry was intercepted by Larry Roach at the OU 28.

On their next possession Texas faced third down 16 at their 25 when Lowry attempted a quick kick. The ball was blocked by Derland Moore and Lucious Selmon fell on it in the end zone for an Oklahoma score. Fulcher converted and with 2:52 left in the third period OU led 10-0.

A fumble by Don Burrisk lost eight yards and Texas was forced to punt on fourth down following the kickoff. Wylie returned 45 yards to the Longhorn 35. On the fourth play of the fourth quarter, Pruitt scored from the six as he leaped over everyone at the goal line. Fulcher converted and OU led 17-0

Following the kickoff Lowry was intercepted on third down by Dan Ruster who returned to the Texas 15. A clip on OU and the Longhorn defense forced a field goal attempt from the 30 which was no good. A Texas clip ruined their next chance after Lonnie Bennett had picked up a first down on a pass reception. Quarterback Dave Robertson then moved the Sooners from their 37 to the

Texas 12. On fourth and eight at that point Fulcher kicked a 29-yard field goal and OU led 20-0.

Pat Padgett returned the kickoff to the 20. On second down Oklahoma's Gary Baccus got between the pitch-back and the intended receiver to bat the ball back into the end zone. Moore recovered the ball for a Sooner touchdown. Fulcher converted and OU led 27-0.

Eleven plays later the game ended when Sooner Wayne Hoffman intercepted quarterback Marty Akins, who had replaced Lowry, at the Texas 45.

The Longhorn defense played beyond expectations as they held OU's 621 yards per game average to just 273 yards. And the Oklahoma defense certainly turned the game around late in the third period. The big difference in the game was the offense. The Sooners lost two fumbles, but the Longhorns lost four fumbles and had four passes intercepted. This not only led to 17 Oklahoma points but it pretty well prevented any Texas points.

	Okla.	Texas
First downs	14	17
Rushes-yards	56-245	41-73
Passing yards	28	186
Return yards	100	0
Passes	3-13-0	11-32-4
Punts	7-34-4	6-32-3
Fumbles lost	2-2	6-4
Penalties-yards	4-60	4-48

Texas . . . . 0 0 0   0— 0
Oklahoma . . . . 3 0 7 17—27
OU—FG Fulcher 37
OU—Selmon recovered blocked punt in end zone (Fulcher kick)
OU—Pruitt 6 run (Fulcher kick)
OU—FG Fulcher 29
OU—Moore recovered fumble in end zone (Fulcher kick)
A—72,030

Four Red Raiders, Gaines Baty (84), Donald Rives (51), Quinton Robinson (54) and Tom Ryan (56) converge on Aggie quarterback Don Dean.

TEXAS TECH 17 - TEXAS A&M 14

The Aggies and Red Raiders were meeting for the 31st time. There has been 17 A & M victories, Tech has had 12 and once they tied. The 34,200 in Kyle Field were watching a ho-hum game until A&M looked up, saw the clock getting down in the short rows, and decided to do something about it since they were behind. Then after they did something about it, Tech had to do something and the game ended in a shower of excitement.

Bubba Dean returned the Tech kickoff 42 yards to the Aggie 48. They reached the Raider 33, when on fourth and three quarterback Don Dean was stopped by Aubrey McCain after one yard.

After forcing a Red Raider punt the Aggies started at their 24 and marched 76 yards for a touchdown in only eight plays. Brad Dusek, playing for the first time since the Nebraska game, went up the middle on a trap and gained 33 yards. Dean passed to Homer May for 18 yards. After Dusek had gained a first down at the 13, Dean pitched out to Bean wide to the right. Mark Green threw a

great block and Bean was stopped at the one. Two plays later Dusek scored. Pat McDermott converted and A & M led 7-0.

Tech took the following kickoff and moved to the Aggie 18, mainly on the running of George Smith. A third down pass failed and Don Grimes kicked a 36-yard field goal, his eighth of the season, to put three points on the board for the Red Raiders. A & M led 7-3 with 2:23 left in the first quarter.

The second quarter was frustrating for both teams and also scoreless. The Aggies moved to the Tech 33, but on the next play Dusek fumbled after gaining seven yards. Steve Van Loozen recovered for Tech.

The Cadets came right back to the Red Raider 23 where they faced a fourth down and three. McCain again saved Tech as he stopped Green after one yard. Then, on the running of Doug McCutchen and quarterback Joe Barnes, Tech moved to the Aggie 41. Smith made eight up the middle, but fumbled and A&M's Paul Hulin recovered.

The Aggies' Carl Roaches (18) returns a Tech punt for good yardage. Tech's Ray Hennig (74) and Tony Green (24) try to cut him off at the pass.

The Red Raiders took the second half kickoff and drove 80 yards in 10 plays to take the lead. George Smith got the ball to midfield on short runs. Barnes kept for 15 yards. A personal foul penalty on A & M put the ball on their 26. McCutchen ran for six and then James Mosley blasted through for the final 20 yards. Grimes converted and Tech led 10-7.

Late in the third quarter the Aggies were threatening. They survived a fumbled pitchout that was recovered by Tech's McCain when the Raiders were offsides. Soon afterwards Dean hit May at the Tech 15. As May struggled toward the end zone he lost the ball and Randy Olson recovered for the Raiders at his four.

Following a Tech punt the Aggies cranked up again at the Raider 43. With Dean, Green and Dusek taking turns at the throttle they moved 40 yards in 11 plays. From the three Dean pitched to Green, the ball hit the turf and bounced right into Green's hands. He scored with 7:50 remaining to play. McDermott converted and A & M led 14-10.

The Red Raiders then began their final push 72 yards away. Things started right when Barnes passed to Andre

Tillman for 24 yards. On third and 12 at the A & M 39, Barnes was thrown for a four-yard loss, but the Aggies were guilty of face mask grabbing. Then on fourth and five Barnes made nine to the 24. He was injured on the play and Jimmy Carmichael came in to replace him. A pass to Tillman was good for nine and Smith ran for eight. At the five McCutchen went in over right tackle. Grimes kicked good and with 1:45 left Tech led 17-14.

Dean brought A & M right back. May tipped a pass and Carl Roaches caught it for 26 yards. Richard Osborne caught one for seven and Dusek ran for 13 on a draw. Osborne reached the Tech 17 with a 24-yard pass. The Aggies' balloon burst on the next play when Greg Waters intercepted Dean at the two and returned to the 10. Three downs, a punt and the game was over.

	Tex. Tech	Tex A&M
First downs	20	18
Rushes-yards	61-243	55-209
Passing yards	40	154
Return yards	12	17
Passes	3-12-0	9-15-2
Punts	7-36	3-50
Fumbles lost	5-1	3-2
Penalties yards	5-35	7-55

Texas Tech .... 3 0 7 7—17
Texas A&M .... 7 0 0 7—14
A&M—Dusek 1 run (McDermott kick)
TT—FG Grimes 36
TT—Mosley 20 run (Grimes kick)
A&M—Green 3 run (McDermott kick)
TT—McCutchen 5 run (Grimes kick)
A—34,200

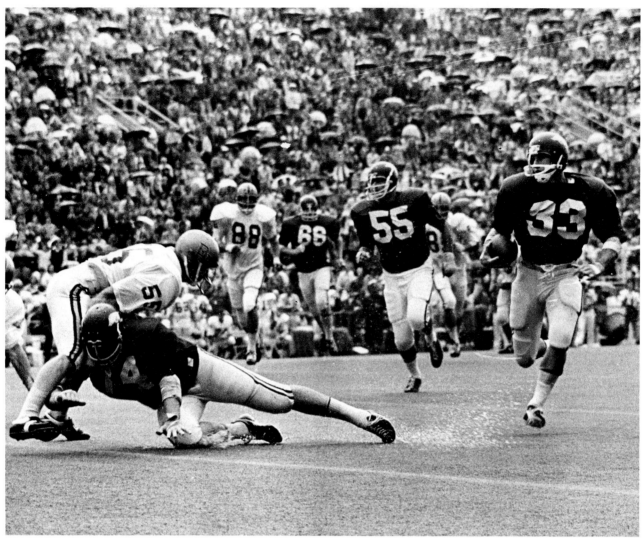

Tom Reed (74) blocks out Roger Goree (55) as Dickey Morton (33), the leading rusher in the game, swings to the left. Arkansas' Mike Griffin (66), John Boozman (55) and Baylor's Mike Black (88) are also pictured.

ARKANSAS 31 - BAYLOR 20

The 41,670 in Razorback Stadium may have been a little apprehensive as they sat in the rain wating for the Baylor-Arkansas game to begin. The last time the Bears beat the Hogs was six years ago. It was in this same stadium and it was raining. The Bears had the rain and Roger Goree going for them. Arkansas had a bunch of thieves playing defense and they recovered three Baylor fumbles and intercepted four of their passes. Goree? Well, all he did was block two Arkansas punts which Baylor turned into touchdowns.

At the start of the game each Baylor punt moved Arkansas closer to the Bear goal. After the first one the Hogs had possession at the Baylor 47. After the second they were on the 24. From there they scored in six plays. Dickey Morton had the big gainer as he ran 11 yards to the two. Mike Saint made one and Morton scored on the next play. Mike Kirkland converted and with 9:23 gone Arkansas led 7-0

When Arkansas got the ball again they were stopped at the Baylor 19 and on the second play of the second quarter Kirkland missed a 36-yard field goal try. On the Razorbacks' next possession he tried again from 42 yards out and missed.

Baylor quarterback Neal Jeffrey, on first down, was intercepted for the first time this year. Louis Campbell made the interception at the Bear 38. After Morton picked up three yards on two running plays, quarterback Joe Ferguson passed to him for 16 yards. Jon Richardson then ran 18 yards to the one. Two plays later Richardson scored. Kirkland converted and Arkansas led 14-0.

Baylor had a golden opportunity just before halftime. John Moseley fumbled a Bear punt and Cary Dorman recovered for Baylor at the Hog 21. Jeffrey passed 15 yards to Charles Dancer at the six. On the next play Campbell had his second interception, this time at his two and he returned to the Arkansas 26. The Razorbacks ran out the clock with one play.

Nobody could hold on to the ball as the second half

The umbrellas in the background are a blur as the Bears' speedy Billy Wilson clears the line of scrimmage with this leap.

started. Campbell recovered a Baylor fumble at the Bear 43. Two plays later Tommy Turnipseede covered an Arkansas fumble at his 29. On the very next play Mark Hollingsworth grabbed a Baylor fumble at their 28. Arkansas ended the exchange game as they scored in five plays with the touchdown coming on a 15-yard pass from Ferguson to Jack Ettinger. Kirkland kicked good and Arkansas led 21-0.

Goree then set up the first Bear score when he blocked Drew Toole's punt and returned to the Hog 21. Six plays later Gary Lacy scored from the three. A two-point conversion failed and Arkansas led 21-6.

On Baylor's next possession Jeffrey lost the ball at his 32 and Danny Rhodes recovered for Arkansas. Morton ran four times and caught one pass on his way to a touchdown. He ran over from the three with 1:26 left in the third quarter. Kirkland converted and the Razorbacks led 28-6.

Robert Armstrong replaced Jeffrey at quarterback and following the kickoff he marched the Bears 71 yards in nine plays. The big play was a pass to Brian Kilgore for 26 yards. He came back to Kilgore for 12 yards and the

touchdown. The two-point conversion failed. With 13:34 left in the game Arkansas led 28-12.

When the Hogs couldn't move following the kickoff, Toole dropped back to punt on fourth down. Goree blocked the punt and recovered the ball on the Arkansas eight. On second down Pat McNeil scored from the seven. Armstrong passed to Dancer for two points and Arkansas led 28-20.

Next time Arkansas had the ball Toole punted on third down. Then Armstrong was intercepted by Hollingsworth and that led to a 23-yard field goal by Kirkland when Baylor held at the five. Arkansas led 31-20.

Any hopes that remained for the Bears were lost when Hollingsworth again intercepted Armstrong.

	Baylor	Arkansas
First downs	11	20
Rushes-yards	44-139	56-259
Passing yards	124	141
Return yards	59	59
Passes	9-21-4	11-28-1
Punts	7-37	6-25
Fumbles lost	3-3	6-2

Baylor ....0 0 6 14—20
Arkansas ....7 7 14 3—31
A—Morton 1 run (Kirkland kick)
A—Richardson 1 run (Kirkland kick)
A—Ettinger 15 pass from Ferguson (Kirkland kick)
B—Lacy—3 run (pass failed)
A—Morton 3 run (Kirkland kick)
B—Kilgore 13 pass from Armstrong (run failed)
B—McNeil 7 run (Dancer pass from Armstrong)
A—FG Kirkland 23
A—41,670

99

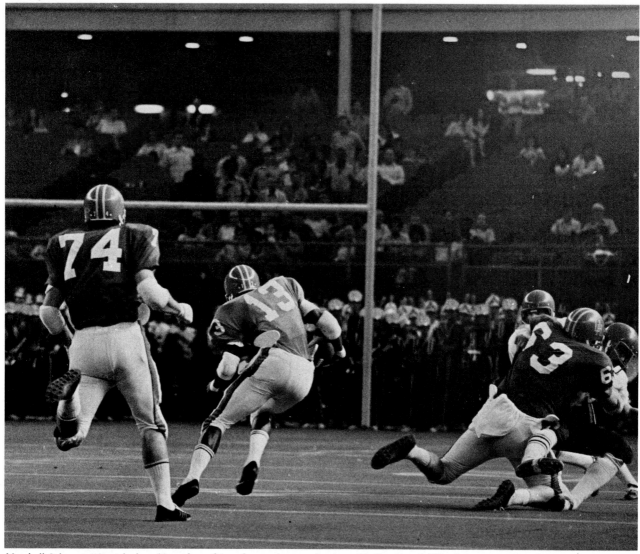

Marshall Johnson (13) picked up 30 yards on this end around run to the Aztec 26. Ken Baugh (63) takes out one defender as Luke Stungis (74) follows Johnson. Two plays later the Cougars scored their fourth touchdown.

HOUSTON 49 - SAN DIEGO STATE 14

The Cougar offense really played offense, the Cougar defense really played defense and they did it all in one game. The Aztecs came to the Astrodome unbeaten in four games. After Houston's first four games Cougar fans never knew what to expect from their unpredictable team. A crowd of 29,891 was on hand for the confrontation.

The Cougars started the avalanche rolling on their first possession as they moved 72 yards in eight plays. The right combination on the drive was quarterback D. C. Nobles passing to Miller Bassler. They connected on three passes of 21, 25 and nine yards, the last one for a touchdown. Ricky Terrell converted and Houston led 7-0.

San Diego State tied it up as they went 70 yards in 12 plays following the kickoff. Quarterbacks Bill Donckers and Jesse Freitas alternated on every play. A seven-yard pass to Harry Benson got the touchdown and Donckers was in at the time. Tim Wulfemeyer's kick tied it at 7-7.

Only 4:04 remained in the first quarter, but Nobles took the Cougars in for two more touchdowns as Houston got off to their best start of the season. First they went 86 yards in 11 plays. The six points came on a pass to Robert Ford good for 24 yards. Terrell converted and Houston led 14-7. Then cornerback Robert Giblin set up their next score when he intercepted Freitas' pass at the Aztecs' 41. Houston scored in five plays. On the fifth play Nobles hit Bryan Willingham cutting across the middle for 25 yards and the touchdown. Terrell kicked good and Houston led at the end of the first quarter 21-7.

Until this game the Aztecs had not been scored on in the first half, but the Cougars dropped another one on them 13 seconds before halftime. It started when Bill George recovered a San Diego fumble at the Cougar 19. The big gainer was an end-around by Marshall Johnson who ran 30 yards to the Aztec 26. Two plays later Nobles hit Ford

The "Mad Dogs" play sack-the-quarterback on this down. Howard Ebow (8) grabs Bill Donckers and Bill Hamrick (41) grabs Ebow. Everett Little (72) and Mack Mitchell (83) are closing fast on the play.

for 26 yards and the fourth touchdown pass for Nobles in the first half. Terrell converted and at the half Houston led 28-7.

The Cougars' fumbled away their first possession of the second half, but moved on the ground to score when they got the ball again. Puddin' Jones scored on a nine-yard run. Terrell kicked good and Houston led 35-7.

Terry Peel replaced Nobles at quarterback and this set the stage for an historic happening. The Cougars were at their one-yard line. On first down Peel found Ford speeding down the sidelines and hit him with a pass at the Cougar 40. Ford won the foot race to the end zone and with Terrell's kick Houston led 42-7. Only five times in history have scores come on 99-yard pass plays. Houston has done it three of those five. Peel and Ford have done it twice. The first one came two years ago against Syracuse. Back in 1966 Bo Burris passed to Warren McVea for 99 yards against Washington State.

With 3:55 remaining in the game Peel scored the Cougars' final touchdown on a 15-yard keeper. Terrell

converted and Houston led the Aztecs 49-7.

San Diego State scored its second touchdown with three seconds left. Fred Hight ran over from one yard out. Wulfemeyer's kick made the final score 49-14 in the Cougars favor.

The Houston offense rolled up a total of 601 yards against a team that had allowed an average of 194 yards in its first four games. The "Mad Dog" defense intercepted four passes and recovered one fumble.

	San Diego	Houston
First downs	21	25
Rushes-yards	51-228	38-247
Passing yards	191	354
Return yards	158	76
Passes	18-30-4	17-31-0
Punts	15-43	4-41
Fumbles lost	2-1	2-1
Penalties yards	7-53	11-126

San Diego State ....7 0 0 7—14
Houston ....21 7 14 7—49
UH—Bassler 8 pass from Nobles (Terrell kick)
SDS—Benson 7 pass from Donckers (Wulfemeyer kick)
UH—Roberts 24 pass from Nobles (Terrell kick)
UH—Willingham 25 pass from Nobles (Terrell kick)
UH—Ford 26 pass from Nobles (Terrell kick)
UH—Jones 9 run (Terrell kick)
UH—Ford 99 pass from Peel (Terrell kick)
UH—Peel 15 run (Terrell kick)
SDS—Hight 1 run (Wulfemeyer kick)
A—29,891

TCU's Billy Sadler (33) wings his way into the Tulsa end zone for the Horned Frogs first touchdown of the game. Al Humphrey (99) grabs for Sadler's leg and George Haynes (43) prepares to ground the high flying Frog.

TCU 35 - TULSA 9

The Horned Frogs last met the Hurricane 31 years ago and hold a 7-2 edge in victories. For Tulsa, this was their last shot at a win over a SWC team for 1972. They had previously lost to Houston, Arkansas and Texas Tech. A crowd of 18,500 was on hand in Skelly Stadium for their last night game of the year. TCU quarterback Kent Marshall was lost for the remainder of the season when he suffered a broken collarbone late in the first quarter.

On the Frogs' first possession Marshall fumbled at his 17 when hit by Arthur Moore. The Hurricane scored in five plays with Ed White going in from the six-yard line. Chad Utley tipped Sam Henry's conversion attempt and it was no good. Tulsa led 6-0.

The lead was short lived as TCU scored in three plays after starting from their 25 following the kickoff. On second down, at the 31, Mike Luttrell exploded through right tackle and was hauled down 66 yards later at the Tulsa three. Billy Sadler dove over on the next play and with Berl Simmons' conversion TCU led 7-6.

Marshall was injured on the next TCU series and was replaced by Perry Senn. Ronnie Webb ran for nine and four yards on two carries. Then Senn passed three times in a row to tight end Lane Bowen, good for 16, nine and 11 yards. Senn capped off the 68-yard drive on an 11-yard keeper, around left end, for the touchdown. Simmons converted and early in the second quarter the Horned Frogs led 14-6.

Lyle Blackwood returned a Tulsa punt to the TCU 46, but a Frog fumble was recovered by the Hurricane at the TCU 39. Quarterback Todd Starks hit Leonard Isabell with passes twice to reach the 19, but the Frogs stiffened and Henry kicked a 33-yard field goal. TCU led 14-9.

With 5:40 left before halftime the Horned Frogs started a 69-yard prolonged march for another touchdown. Senn got things started with a 12-yard keeper. Tulsa was penalized for grabbing Larry Harris' face mask. On fourth and one at the Tulsa 24, Ronnie Littleton ran for 10 yards. Fourth and one came up again at the five and

102

Ed Robinson (89) grabs an old teammate Raymond Rhodes (21). Rhodes is one of the former Horned Frogs now playing for Tulsa. Dede Terveen (55) dives in to help out.

Webb crunched out two to the three. TCU was penalized, back to the nine, but Luttrell then ran it back to the three. Luttrell scored from there with 46 seconds left. Simmons added the extra point and TCU led 21-9.

Tulsa, with the aid of a roughing penalty, came back to the Frog 25, but Henry missed on a 42-yard field goal effort.

Early in the third quarter Utley gave TCU excellent field position when he blocked a Tulsa punt. Ken Steel fell on the ball at the Hurricane 15. Simmons kicked a field goal but Tulsa was offsides. Instead of fourth down and six it would bring up fourth down and inches. The Frogs passed up the three points and Webb ran for the first down. A motion penalty stopped the Purple and Simmons missed on the field goal.

Steve Bowling, who had replaced Starks, took Tulsa to the Frog 16, but TCU held and took over there. A TCU drive was stalled, early in the fourth quarter, by a clipping penalty after reaching the Hurricane 32.

The teams then started trading interceptions. Blackwood intercepted Starks, who had replaced Bowling, at the Tulsa 30. On second down Senn was intercepted by Arthur Calloway at the 25. Starks was then intercepted by Gary Whitman at the Frog 39. After an exchange of punts TCU started at their 25. Luttrell and Littleton skirted the ends with running plays to reach the Tulsa 22. Then Luttrell crossed up the Hurricane by throwing a halfback pass to Sadler at the four. On fourth down Luttrell scored from the one. Simmons converted and TCU led 28-9.

Less than a minute remained when the Frogs kicked off. Whitman intercepted Starks again and TCU had possession at the Hurricane 20. They scored in two plays. Luttrell threw another halfback pass to Sadler for 13 yards and then Senn hit Bowen for seven and the touchdown. Simmons tacked on the point. TCU led 35-9 and three seconds later it was all over.

	TCU	Tulsa
First downs	19	19
Rushes yards	59-289	46-157
Passing yards	88	120
Return yards	81	8
Passes	7-15-1	8-25-3
Punts	4-33	7-25
Fumbles lost	2-2	0-0
Penalties yards	10-84	7-90

TCU .... 7 14 0 14—35
Tulsa .... 6 3 0 0—9
Tulsa—White 6 run (kick failed)
TCU—Sadler 3 run (Simmons kick)
TCU—Senn 11 run (Simmons kick)
Tulsa—FG Henry 33
TCU—Luttrell 3 run (Simmons kick)
TCU—Luttrell 1 run (Simmons kick)
TCU—Senn 7 pass to Bowen (Simmons kick)
A—18,500

SYNOPSIS

TOP TEN

1. Southern Cal
2. Oklahoma
3. Alabama
4. Ohio State
5. Nebraska
6. Michigan
7. LSU
8. Notre Dame
9. Colorado
10. Tennessee

UPSET OF WEEK:

None

SWC OFFENSIVE PLAYER OF WEEK

Dickey Morton, Tailback, Arkansas

SWC DEFENSIVE PLAYER OF WEEK

Roger Goree, End, Baylor

FRESHMAN RESULTS

Arkansas 28 - Oklahoma State 21
Texas Tech 45 - Houston 34
Texas 42 - Baylor 7
Rice 37 - SMU 28
Texas A & M 42 - TCU 27

SWC TEAM LEADERS FOR SEASON

OFFENSE	AVG.	DEFENSE	AVG.
Rushing .... Texas Tech	308 yds.	Rushing .... SMU	44 yds.
Passing .... Rice	230 yds.	Passing .... Texas A & M	122 yds.
Total .... Texas Tech	438 yds.	Total .... SMU	269 yds.

SEASON RECORDS

	W	L	T
Texas Tech	4	1	0
Arkansas	4	1	0
Texas	3	1	0
TCU	3	1	0
SMU	3	1	0
Rice	2	1	1
Baylor	2	2	0
Houston	2	2	1
Texas A & M	1	4	0

CONFERENCE

	W	L	T
Arkansas	2	0	0
Texas	1	0	0
Texas Tech	1	1	0
TCU	0	1	0
Baylor	0	1	0
Texas A& M	0	1	0

Seventh Week
October 21

The Mustang pass rush buries Rice quarterback Bruce Gadd. Ed Johnson (66) and Louis Kelcher (72) do the damage as Leonard Carey (31) and Randy Savage (63) zero in if needed.

SMU 29 - RICE 14

This was the first conference game of the season for the Owls and Mustangs. An umbrella-laden crowd of 20,398 sat in the Cotton Bowl. A steady rain peppered the artificial turf of this regionally televised game. A close game became just the opposite when a Rice fumble halted their go ahead drive and the Mustangs turned to the pass to take the game safely out of reach.

Rice kicked off and SMU drove to the Owl 23 before being halted by Rice defenders. Clint Hackney tried a 40-yard field goal which was no good.

The next time the Mustangs got the ball they marched 80 yards to score in nine plays. Wayne Morris had runs of 18 and 11 yards. Quarterback Keith Bobo ran for 19 yards and hit on two passes. Both were for eight yards, the first to Rory Best and the second to Alvin Maxson for the touchdown. Hackney converted and SMU led 7-0.

Early in the second quarter a Mark Williams punt was downed at the SMU six. The Mustangs were forced to

punt and Bruce Henley returned 30 yards to the Mustang 34. On second down quarterback Bruce Gadd was intercepted by Bobby White at the SMU 14. Bobo was thrown for a seven-yard loss on second down and Sam McLarty punted to his 42 on third down. Two passes later Rice had six points. Gadd hit Edwin Collins at the eight for 34 yards, then Gary Butler for eight and the touchdown. Williams converted and with 9:18 left it was 7-7.

SMU took the kickoff and moved from their 26 to the Rice 23 before being halted. There, Hackney kicked a 41-yard field goal. SMU led 10-7. White's second interception of Gadd came three plays after the Mustang kickoff. SMU had the ball at the Rice 31. On fourth down five at the 15, Hackney kicked a 32-yard field goal. With one minute left in the first half SMU led 13-7.

On the Mustangs' first possession of the second half Hackney took up where he left off in the first half. At the

On fourth down and two at the SMU 39 the Owls go for it. Gary Ferguson (21) swung wide to escape Robert Smith (45) and the onrushing Mustangs. He made 37 yards to the two-yard line.

Rice 13, on fourth and four, he kicked a 30-yard field goal and SMU led 16-7.

The next time SMU got the ball they drove to the Owl 27 where Morris fumbled and Richard Hollas recovered for Rice. As play moved into the fourth quarter the Owls soon faced a fourth down and two at the SMU 39. They went for it as Gary Ferguson swung wide and ran all the way to the Mustang two. Ferguson scored on a wide pitch to the right on third down. Williams converted and SMU led 16-14 with 11:59 to play.

Rice held SMU following the kickoff and were held in turn by the Mustangs. Williams punted and Doug Berg fumbled the ball to Rice's Ron Arceneaux at the SMU 27. After picking up a first down at the 17, easily within field goal range for Williams if needed, Gadd fumbled the ball on the snap and Cleve Whitener recovered for the Mustangs at his 14.

After gaining a first down at their 29, the ponies faced a third down and nine at their 30. Following a time out Kenny Harrison took off on a fly pattern, caught Bobo's pass at the Rice 48, and scampered down the right

sideline for a touchdown. Hackney's kick was no good and SMU led 22-14.

Three plays later Gadd fumbled and Louie Kelcher recovered for SMU at the Rice 40. The Mustangs scored in five plays. The payoff came on a screen pass to Harrison who got a clearing block from Don Deweber and scored from the 26. Hackney kicked good and with 3:07 left SMU led 29-14.

The Owls came back, with Bill McCabe at quarterback, to reach the Mustang 13. On the next play Robert Popelka intercepted McCabe in the end zone. With 1:56 remaining SMU, with the aid of two successive roughing the kicker penalties, ran out the clock.

	Rice	SMU
First downs	17	22
Rushes-yards	35-139	57-216
Passing yards	189	229
Return yards	42	12
Passes	14-32-3	13-18-0
Punts	5-40	3-41-6
Fumbles lost	2-1	8-2
Penalties yards	7-61	6-69

Rice .... 0 7 0 7—14
SMU .... 7 6 3 13—29
SMU—Maxson 8 pass from Bobo (Hackney kick)
R—Butler 8 pass from Gadd (Williams kick)
SMU—FG Hackney 40
SMU—FG Hackney 33
SMU—FG Hackney 30
R—Ferguson 2 run (Williams kick)
SMU—Harrison 69 pass from Bobo (kick failed)
SMU—Harrison 26 pass from Bobo (Hackney kick)
A—20,398

107

Roosevelt Leaks (46) finds a hole in the middle on this run. Jim Benton (87) watches as Danny Rhodes (56) tries to get in position to stop Leaks.

TEXAS 35 - ARKANSAS 15

The annual showdown between the Razorbacks and Longhorns was being played before a record crowd of 80,844, the largest ever for a Southwest Conference game. A national television audience was also viewing the contest. This was a rainy Saturday for most of Texas and Memorial Stadium in Austin was receiving more than its share. A closely fought battle see-sawed back and forth until a bad center-snap on a punting situation changed the character of the game completely. Texas continued its season-long knack of losing the ball. They lost five of eight fumbles and had one pass intercepted.

Arkansas kicked off and Texas started scrimmage at their 20. On first down Don Burrisk fumbled and David Reavis recovered for Arkansas at the 24. The Razorbacks reached the 12, but on third down quarterback Joe Ferguson was penalized for intentionally grounding the ball. With the ball moved back to the 24 Mike Kirkland came in and missed on a field goal attempt.

Texas again started at their 20 and almost like an instant replay Burrisk again fumbled on first down.

Danny Rhodes recovered for Arkansas at the 22. On fourth and five at the 17 Kirkland kicked a 34-yard field goal. Arkansas led 3-0.

The Longhorns took the ensuing kickoff and marched 73 yards, all on the ground, to score in 15 plays. Roosevelt Leaks carried 10 times including the last five in a row as he scored from the four. Billy Schott converted and with 6:37 left in the first quarter Texas led 7-3.

After an exchange of punts the Razorbacks moved from their 42 to the Texas 19 in 10 plays. Needing eight yards on fourth down, Kirkland kicked a 36-yard field goal. Texas led 7-6.

Early in the second quarter Mike Dean attempted a 52-yard field goal for Texas which was no good. Mike Rowan gave the Longhorns possession again when he intercepted Ferguson at the Texas 31. On fourth down at the 40, Lowry punted out of bounds on the Arkansas six. The Razorbacks took the lead with nine seconds left before halftime. In 17 plays they stubbornly moved to the Texas 20. A 16-yard Ferguson to Mike Reppond pass was

Arkansas' John Wheat (68) drops Longhorn quarterback Alan Lowry (15) for a loss as teammates Louis Campbell (37) and Danny Rhodes (56) prepare to help if needed. Texas' Bruce Hebert (54) looks on.

the longest gain in the drive. Kirkland kicked good from 37 yards for the go-ahead field goal. Arkansas led 9-7.

As the second half got underway Tommy Harris intercepted Lowry at the Hog 46. Stymied at the Texas 43, Drew Toole watched the punt-snap go over his head. He recovered at his own 18, but Texas took over. On second and goal at the five, Lowry fumbled the ball forward out of the end zone just before he crossed the goal. Instead of a Texas touchdown Arkansas had possession on their 20.

On the Longhorns' next series Leaks fumbled at the Hog 25 and Jon Rhiddlehoover recovered for Arkansas. Following a Toole punt Texas finally put one away using only five plays. From their 49 Lowry ran for seven, Leaks made 12, Lowry kept for 18, Leaks again for eight and Lowry for six and the touchdown. Donald Ealey ran over the conversion and Texas led 15-9 with less than 30 second left in the third quarter.

Dean's kickoff was caught by the wind and took a reverse bounce when it came down. Tommy Landry caught it on the first bounce and ran it down to the Arkansas 26. Leaks and Lowry went to work again. Leaks gained nine yards on first and second down. Lowry gained 16 on third down and ran across from the one on

the next play. A pass failed on the conversion and with 13:56 left Texas led 21-9.

Lowry and Leaks did it again when Texas got the ball back on their 44. Leaks made five, Lowry 13 and seven, Leaks 25, five and one for the score. Schott converted and Texas led 28-9. Next Malcom Minnick grabbed a Ferguson screen pass and returned to his 46. The Longhorns, five plays later, crossed up the Hogs by giving the ball to Ealey. He went 26 yards down the right sideline for the touchdown. Schott converted and Texas led 35-15.

With time expiring fast the Hogs took the kickoff and scored in 11 plays. A 37-yard pass to Reppond got almost half of the 80 yards and a four-yard pass to Reppond got the touchdown. A conversion pass failed and Texas led 35-15.

An Arkansas on-side kick failed to travel the necessary 10 yards and Texas ran out the clock.

	Ark.	Texas
First downs	20	22
Rushes-yards	40-81	68-394
Passing yards	143	14
Return yards	0	51
Passes	14-38-2	1-3-1
Punts	5-39-4	2-38
Fumbles lost	1-1	8-5
Penalties yards	4-55	3-35
A—80,844		

Arkansas . . . . 6 3 0 6—15
Texas . . . . 7 0 8 20—35
Ark—FG Kirkland 30
Tex—Leaks 4 run (Schott kick)
Ark—FG Kirkland 36
Ark—FG Kirkland 37
Tex—Lowry 6 run (Ealey run)
Tex—Lowry 1 run (pass failed)
Tex—Leaks 1 run (Schott kick)
Tex—Ealey 26 run (Schott kick)
Ark—Reppond 5 pass from Ferguson (pass failed)

The "Mad Dogs" close in. Bill Stohler grabs Miami quarterback Ed Carney (11) for a loss. Tom Smith (39) was preparing to lead interference. Other Cougars pictured are Gerald Hill (60), Bubba Broussard (2) and Robert Giblin (24).

MIAMI 33 - HOUSTON 13

With the Cougars heavily favored only 17,860 came to the Orange Bowl to view the slaughter. Instead they saw the Hurricane play their finest game of the season and Houston vice versa. Miami hogged the ball and when they did have to punt they had Mike Burke who averaged 50.3 per kick.

Miami received the opening kickoff, ran off 15 plays, used up half of the first quarter and climaxed it all with a 30-yard field goal by Mike Burke. The Hurricane led 3-0.

The Cougars ran off three plays and punted to the Miami 39. The Hurricane then kept the ball five minutes plus and drove to the Houston 13. There, on fourth down, Burke kicked another 30-yard field goal and Miami led 6-0.

Houston again couldn't move and an offensive pass interference penalty had Hal Roberts punting from his end zone. Miami got possession at the Cougar 48. On third down four at the 42 quarterback Ed Carney faked to

Chuck Foreman and handed off to Mike Latimer on the flanker-around. Latimer went the distance for a touchdown. A two-point conversion pass failed and Miami, early in the second quarter, led 12-0.

On their third possession the Cougars made their first first down and continued on to cover 72 yards in seven plays. After a run of Reggie Cherry's had gained 20 yards to the Miami 38, the Hurricanes were guilty of piling on and the ball was moved to the 23. Quarterback D. C. Nobles kept on third down and made it to the 10, fumbling and recovering on the play. On the next play Nobles passed complete to Bryan Willingham who barely came down in bounds after a leaping catch in the end zone. Ricky Terrell converted and Miami led 12-7.

Near the end of the first half Miami got a break when Robert Ford fumbled a punt and Johnny Williams recovered for the Hurricane at the Houston 21. After a

Quarterback Terry Peel (9) pitches wide to Puddin' Jones (30) on this play. Jones was the leading rusher in the game with 83 yards.

penalty advanced the ball to the 16 the "Mad Dogs" held for three downs. Then, they blitzed, and Foreman got the ball on a draw play to score standing. Another conversion pass failed and with 3:58 left Miami led 18-7.

Midway through the third period an exchange of interceptions led to another Miami touchdown. the Cougars' Howard Ebow grabbed a Carney pass at the Houston one and returned to the six. On the next play Terry Peel, who had replaced Nobles at quarterback, was intercepted by Paul Horschel. He returned to the Cougar three. Carney scored on a keeper and Burke converted. Miami led 25-7.

Foreman then returned an earlier Houston favor when he fumbled Roberts' punt. David Bourquin recovered for Houston on the Miami 15. On first down Peel passed to Marty Watts for a touchdown. Terrell's kick was blocked and Miami led 25-13.

As play moved into the fourth quarter the Cougars had opportunities they couldn't cash in. They reached the Hurricane 10 and then had a backfield foul up on a fourth down and two play. Later Burl Fuller recovered a Miami fumble at the Hurricane 18, but they ended up on the 32.

Late in the game Nobles, who had returned as quarterback, overthrew Del Stanley in the flat and Horschel intercepted on the run and ran 27 yards for the touchdown. Carney passed to Witt Beckman for two points and with 2:22 remaining Miami led 33-13.

Puddin' Jones was the leading rusher, beating Foreman by one yard at 83-82. The Cougars passing was way off completing only eight of 25 and their two interceptions led to two touchdowns for Miami.

	Hou.	Mia.
First downs	15	13
Rushes-yards	42-162	51-182
Passing yards	87	73
Return yards	29	52
Passes	8-25-2	6-14-1
Punts	6-36-5	6-50-3
Fumbles lost	3-1	4-2
Penalties yards	7-63	8-88

Houston . . . . .0 7 6 0—13
Miami . . . . .6 12 7 8—33
M—FG 30 Burke
M—FG 30 Burke
M—Latimer 42 run (pass failed)
UH—Nobles 6 pass to Willingham (Terrell kick)
M—Foreman 16 run (pass failed)
M—Carney 4 run (Burke kick)
UH—Peel 16 pass to Watts (kick failed)
M—Horschel 27 pass interception (Carney pass to Beckman)
A—17,860

Frog quarterback Perry Senn beats the rush of Max Bird (87) and passes to wide open John Ott (83) for a 29-yard gain. Ronnie Webb (30) hits the turf as Guy Morriss (68) and Jerry Wauson (74) hold off A & M's Bill Wiebold (61).

TCU 13 - TEXAS A&M 10

College Station was one of the few places in Central Texas that was dry on Saturday night. A crowd of 28,770 was on hand to see whether the Cadets or the Horned Frogs would suffer their second SWC defeat of the season. It was another one of those games which could have gone either way. Perhaps the difference was in turnovers as A & M continued its season-long habit by losing five of seven fumbles. That, TCU and the clock slapped another loss on the hard luck Aggies.

A & M started being benevolent on the opening kick-off. Bubba Bean fumbled to TCU's Frankie Grimmet. The Cadet's defense held and Berl Simmons' 45-yard field goal try was wide to the left. Simmons got another chance after an exchange of punts. Mike Luttrell set it up as he took a pitchout at his 37 and ran the right sideline to the A & M 16. Three more Luttrell carries only gained six yards, so Simmons came in and kicked a 27-yard field goal.

The Cadets were repeatedly thwarted by the Horned Frog defense and their own ability to lose the ball. Terry

Drennan recovered an Aggie fumble at the TCU 17, then Ed Robinson latched on to a Skip Walker fumble at the Frog 32. Early in the second quarter A & M reached the TCU 11, but quarterback Don Dean fumbled and Tookie Berry recovered for TCU.

On their next possession A & M held on to the ball for 58 yards and six plays to score. Brad Dusek gained 20 yards rushing and a Dean pass to Homer May, which was tipped by May, came down into the hands of Carl Roaches for a 26-yard gain to the Frog 30. After reaching the TCU 10, Dean passed to Roaches at the one and he scored. Pat McDermott converted and with 3:51 left in the first half the Cadets led 7-3.

Moments later A & M had the ball again when Greg Anderson punted to Roaches. The Frogs got penalized for a late hit when Roaches was tackled on the return. A scrambling run by Dean and his pass to Richard Osborne helped the Cadets reach the TCU 30 with time rapidly running out in the first half. McDermott came in and

Brad Dusek carries for the Aggies on this play. The Frogs' Ken Steel (73) is blocked out, but Rusty Putt (85) presents a problem. Lee Ray (89) is shown behind Dusek. Also pictured for A & M are Homer May (80) and Ralph Sacra (76).

kicked a 47-yard field goal with 30 seconds left on the clock. At the half A & M led 10-3.

After picking up only two first downs in the first half the Frogs' offense hatched in the second 30 minutes. They drove to the Aggie 25, but were stopped when Ed Simonini dropped Luttrell for a loss on fourth down and inches. They came back to get three points before the third quarter ended. From their 20 quarterback Perry Senn, starting in place of the injured Kent Marshall, passed to John Ott for 29 yards, to Lane Bowen for 11 and to Steve Patterson for seven. Luttrell ran up the middle for 17. Senn was dropped for a four-yard loss to blunt the drive and Simmons kicked a 32-yard field goal. A & M led 10-6.

Then late in the fourth quarter the Frogs put the winning drive in motion from their 47. Twice they came up with clutch plays on fourth down. On fourth and inches Luttrell threw a halfback pass to Ronnie Littleton for seven yards. Later on, facing fourth and three at the Aggie 28, Senn passed to Bowen for seven yards. Three running plays reached the nine and then Luttrell pulled his pass play to Littleton again for the touchdown. Simmons

kicked good and TCU led, with 1:33 remaining, 13-10.

The Aggies came fighting back and the clock was the one thing they couldn't overcome. Dean passed to Osborne for 14 yards, to Roaches for 16 and to Roaches again for 25. This put the ball on TCU's 30. With 11 seconds left a pass interference call moved the Cadets to the 24 and an unsportsmanlike conduct penalty gained half the distance to the 12. Osborne caught an 11-yard pass and went out of bounds at the one with five second left. Dusek was stopped short of the goal and the Aggies were offsides, moving the ball back to the six. Two seconds were left and McDermott tried a 23 yard field goal which missed, but the officials had signaled the end of the game before the play.

The crowd was standing as though stunned for quite a few moments, it was that kind of an ending.

	TCU	A&M
First downs	11	22
Rushes-yards	51-178	50-140
Passing yardage	147	224
Return yardage	4	23
Passes	11-17-0	15-24-0
Punts	8-41-4	7-34-9
Fumbles lost	3-1	7-5
Penalties yards	5-70	2-10

TCU	3	0	3	7—13
A&M	0	10	0	0—10

TCU—FG Simmons 27
TCU—Roaches 10 pass from Dean (McDermott kick)
A&M—FG McDermott 47
TCU—FG Simmons 32
TCU—Littleton 9 pass from Luttrell (Simmons kick)
A—28,770

113

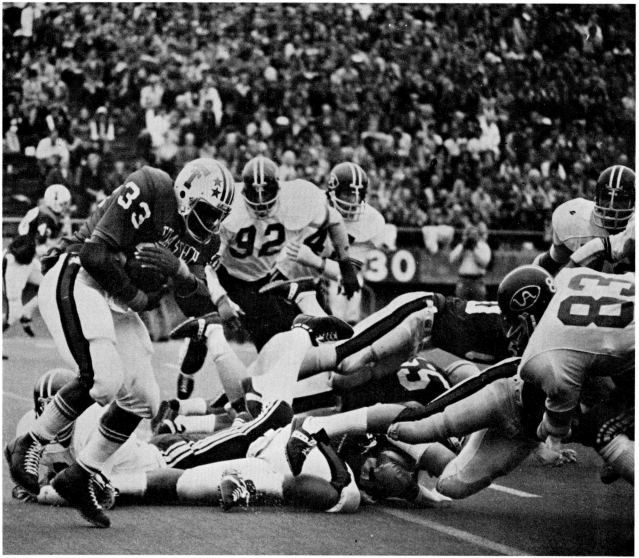

Tech's Junior Fullback James Mosley looks for daylight on this run. Mosley scored two touchdowns in the game, each one from the one-yard line.

TEXAS TECH 35 - ARIZONA 10

The Wildcats and Red Raiders used to play every year, but when Tech joined the Southwest Conference Arizona ceased to be an annual foe. You wonder why when you consider that the Red Raiders have won 19 out of 22 games with the Wildcats. A crowd of 33,320 came to Jones Stadium and saw Tech put the game safely away before a rain storm sent most of them scurrying for cover.

The Wildcats started out on the right foot. On their first possession they marched 76 yards in seven plays. Two plays were the big gainers. One was a run of 29 yards by Bob McCall and the other was a 17-yard pass from quarterback Bill Demory to tight end John Muller. The latter was good for a touchdown. Charlie Gorham converted and Arizona led 7-0.

Just past the midway point of the first quarter Tech put the ball in play at the Wildcat 46. A penalty set them back to their 39. Quarterback Joe Barnes went to the air and

found George Smith open down the left sideline. Smith ran to the Arizona three for a 58-yard gain. Doug McCutchen scored from the three, but an offsides infraction put the ball back to the eight. McCutchen had to run a little farther as he scored from the eight. Don Grimes kicked good and the game was tied at 7-7.

Late in the quarter Tech gained possession at its 24 following an Arizona punt. The Raiders dropped the ball twice as they drove downfield and fortunately recovered them both. The second one, Barnes fumbled and Tillman recovered, resulted in a 12-yard gain to the Wildcat 23. Tillman then caught a pass for 22 yards for a first and goal at the one. James Mosley made the final yard and Grimes converted. With 29 seconds gone in the second quarter Tech led 14-7.

Following the kickoff Arizona drove to the Red Raider 14 in eight plays. They had to settle for a 31-yard field goal

Split end Andre Tillman sets up Tech's second touchdown as he runs to the Arizona one after catching a pass from Joe Barnes. The Wildcats' Roussell Williams makes the stop on Tillman.

by Gorham. The Red Raiders led 14-10.

As halftime approached the Red Raiders continued their successful "fumble forward" offense. Barnes got off a run of 37 yards and fumbled but Tech maintained possession at the Wildcat 27. Barnes was shaken up and Jimmy Carmichael replaced him at quarterback. Smith ran around left end, fumbled, and Ronnie Samford recovered at the 12. After McCutchen made three Smith went left again, held on to the ball, and scored. Grimes kicked good and Tech led 21-10 with 2:21 left before the half.

In the second half the Red Raiders got on the scoreboard once in each quarter while shutting out the Wildcats. Their first score came about when Arizona's Demory lost the ball and Gaines Baty recovered for Tech at the Wildcat 23. The Raiders scored in five plays with the help of a pass interference penalty. Barnes made the final yard for the score. Grimes converted, but Tech was penalized 15 yards for holding. Grimes then kicked a 36-yard extra point and the Red Raiders led 28-10.

In the fourth quarter Lawrence Williams returned an Arizona punt 38 yards to the Wildcat 11. Carmichael came in and directed the final touchdown. Cliff Hoskins reached the one on three carries and Mosley dove over left tackle for the score. Grimes kicked the point after, his 36th in a row, and Tech led 35-10.

Arizona's Bob McCall caused the Raiders fits in the first half as he rushed for 100 yards on 14 carries. In the second half Tech's defense defensed him pretty good as he had a net of 21 yards. With a 5-1 record the Red Raiders now return to conference warfare playing SMU next week.

	Ariz.	Tex.Tech
First downs	15	18
Rushes yards	53	172
Passing yards	46	214
Return yards	25	70
Passes	9-25-0	7-14-2
Punts	7-43	6-35
Fumbles lost	3-2	4-0
Penalties yards	6-46	11-118

Arizona .... 7 3 0 0—10
Texas Tech .... 7 14 7 7—35
A—Muller 17 pass from Demory (Gorham kick)
TT—McCutchen 8 run (Grimes kick)
TT—Mosley 1 run (Grimes kick)
A—FG Gorham 31
TT—Smith 9 run (Grimes kick)
TT—Barnes 1 run (Grimes kick)
TT—Mosley 1 run (Grimes kick)
A—33,320

With the rain coming down hard Baylor quarterback Neal Jeffrey (11) hands off to Wayne Prescher on this running play. Bear blockers are Cary Dorman (51) and Richard Mason (66).

OKLAHOMA STATE 20 - BAYLOR 7

Saturday in Stillwater's Lewis Stadium it rained on Baylor's parade. They unbelievably fumbled 15 times and lost the ball seven times. They had three passes intercepted, one returned for a touchdown. They had a 16-yard gain ignored by offsetting confusion on the part of the officials. They had a snap, fumbled by the punter, lead to the go ahead touchdown. They had a net gain of 115 yards rushing in the first half and ended up with 107 at the end of the game. All was not lost though as the defense again gave an outstanding performance. A homecoming crowd of 39,000 braved the elements.

There was no scoring in the first quarter thanks to the Bear defense. And there was no scoring for the Cowboys in the first half with the Bear defense again being the culprit. Gene Wilson lost a fumble at his 32 in the first quarter and Baylor held. In the second quarter a bad pitch-out by quarterback Neal Jeffrey was lost at the Bear 30 and later Wayne Prescher lost the ball at his 25. Both Cowboy opportunities went nowhere because of the "Jolly Green Giants."

Meanwhile the Bear offense did hold onto the ball long enough to put some points on the scoreboard. Starting at their 15 they moved to the 33 where Rusty Parrott punted on fourth down. The Cowboys were guilty of roughing Parrott and Baylor had new life at their 48. They drove the remaining 52 yards in 14 plays. Most of it came on the running of Prescher who carried six times and reached the OSU one on his final carry. Gary Lacy scored from there and Mike Conradt converted to give Baylor a 7-0 lead with 11 minutes left in the first half.

The fumble lost by Prescher, mentioned earlier, came with two minutes left and gave the Bears an opportunity to perform a goal line stand. The Cowboys gained a first and goal at the two with 49 second left. Joe Johnson dropped Tony Boxell for no gain, Derrel Luce stopped OSU quarterback Brent Blackman for no gain on a sweep and Johnson swamped Blackman for a seven-yard loss on third down. Time ran out before the Cowboys could line up for a field goal.

The second half was a nightmare for Baylor as mistakes

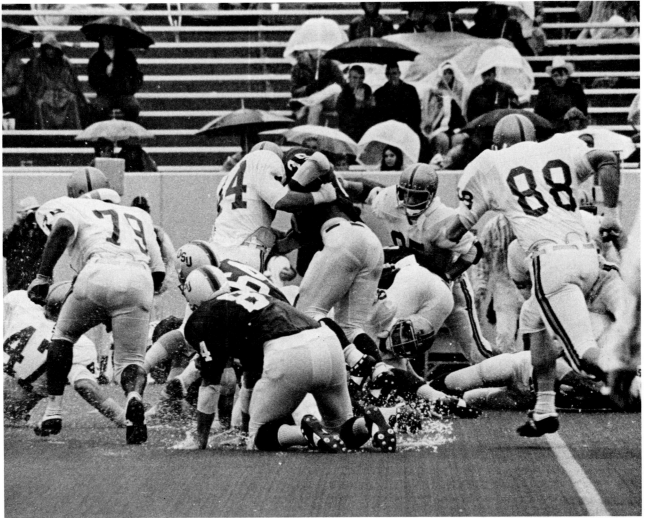

The Bear defense jams a cowboy drive. Ed Taylor (44) grabs George Palmer (35) for no gain. Other Baylor defenders are Paul Savage (47), Joe Johnson (79), Coy Zunkey (85) and Mike Black (88).

set up all three State touchdowns. About midway in the third quarter a Jeffrey pass was intercepted when Lee Stover batted the ball up at the line then grabbed it and ran 59 yards for a touchdown. Eddie Garrett converted and the game was tied at 7-7.

Baylor took the kickoff back to their 38 where Jeffrey passed to Charles Dancer for 14 yards. A Bear penalty and two incomplete passes killed the drive and then Parrott fumbled the punt snap and chased the ball back to his 21 where OSU took over. They scored in five plays. George Palmer scored from one yard out and with Garrett's conversion OSU led 14-7. One minute was left in the third quarter.

Midway through the fourth quarter Brian Kilgore picked up 16 yards on a reverse. He fumbled and the ball was batted out of bounds by a Cowboy, but he didn't have possession. First the officials gave the ball to OSU. Coach Grant Teaff protested and they gave the ball back to Baylor. Then Cowboy coach Dave Smith protested. The officials huddled in the middle of the field and then put the ball back at the 31, wiping out the gain, and ruled no play. Figure that one out.

Three plays later Jeffrey was intercepted by Elvin

Brown. Tack on a clipping penalty against Baylor and the Cowboys were on the Bear 27. Blackman passed to Charlie Beall for 27 yards and a touchdown. Garrett missed the extra point and OSU led 20-7.

Robert Armstrong replaced Jeffrey, but nothing changed. He took the Bears to the Cowboy 27 and then fumbled. On Baylor's last possession Armstrong gained seven yards on a keeper and fumbled. Naturally both fumbles were lost. To top it all off it rained so hard halftime festivities were cancelled. Stillwater ran deep.

The 15 fumbles is a new SWC record. The old record of 12 was held by Arkansas against these same Cowboys in 1957.

	Baylor	OSU
First downs	14	12
Rushes-yards	57-107	66-195
Passing yards	112	27
Return yards	9	77
Passes	10-21-3	1-5-0
Punts	6-38-3	8-33-0
Fumbles lost	15-7	7-4
Penalties yards	7-51	5-39

Baylor .... 0 7 0 0—7
Okla State............ 0 0 14 6—20
B—Lacy 1 run (Conradt kick)
OSU—Stover 59 pass interception (Garrett kick)
OSU—Palmer 1 run (Garrett kick)
OSU—Beall 27 pass from Blackman (kick failed)
A—39,000

SYNOPSIS

TOP TEN

1. Southern Cal
2. Alabama
3. Nebraska
4. Ohio State
5. Michigan
6. LSU
7. Colorado
8. Oklahoma
9. UCLA
10. Texas

SWC OFFENSIVE PLAYER OF WEEK

Keith Bobo, Quarterback, SMU

SWC DEFENSIVE PLAYER OF WEEK

Ed Simonini, Linebacker, Texas A & M

FRESHMAN RESULTS

LSU 44 - Houston 10
Texas A & M 42 - Baylor 7

UPSET OF WEEK: (Tie)

Missouri 30 - Notre Dame 26
Colorado 20 - Oklahoma 14

SWC TEAM LEADERS FOR SEASON

OFFENSE	AVG.
Rushing	Texas Tech 285 yds.
Passing	Rice 222 yds.
Total	Texas Tech 429 yds.

DEFENSE	AVG.
Rushing	SMU 63 yds.
Passing	Arkansas 108 yds.
Total	SMU 281 yds.

SEASON RECORDS

	W	L	T
Texas Tech	5	1	0
SMU	4	1	0
Texas	4	1	0
TCU	4	1	0
Arkansas	4	2	0
Rice	2	2	1
Baylor	2	3	0
Houston	2	3	1
Texas A & M	1	5	0

CONFERENCE

	W	L	T
Texas	2	0	0
SMU	1	0	0
Arkansas	2	1	0
Texas Tech	1	1	0
TCU	1	1	0
Baylor	0	1	0
Rice	0	1	0
Texas A & M	0	2	0

Eighth Week
October 28

39 YEARS AGO
OCTOBER 28, 1933
Arkansas 3 - SMU 0
Texas A&M 14 - Baylor 7
Texas 18 - Rice 0
TCU 0 - Centenary 0
Texas Tech 26 - Haskell 6

Quarterback Perry Senn (19) keeps inside the block of Billy Sadler (33) for short yardage. Tom Freistroffer (96) the Irish defensive end is the object of Sadler's blocking.

NOTRE DAME 21 - TCU 0

Last week the unbeaten Irish was blindsided by Missouri and fell from the all-victorious list. They were fully prepared for the Horned Frogs, but their mistakes kept them from breathing easy until the fourth quarter. Both teams had identical 4-1 records as 59,075 came to South Bend to watch Notre Dame and TCU meet for the first time. A heavy rain stopped minutes before the kickoff and this attributed to the sloppy play.

During the first half the Irish were running up and down the field like a grass fire, but they kept losing the ball. Fortunately for TCU, they couldn't score without it. They had three lost fumbles and an intercepted pass in the first two quarters. Horned Frog David McGinnis stopped two drives when he recovered fumbles at the TCU 29 and 20. Terry Drennan covered the other fumble at the TCU 42. The Irish had gained 279 yards in the first half while TCU managed only 55.

The Frogs were having their problems too. Their first possession was their longest drive. Quarterback Perry Senn, who alternated throughout the game with Ronnie Littleton, passed to Lane Bowen for a first down at the Frog 40. Littleton ran a keeper for nine yards, but the big Notre Dame defense formed a wall which shut off the drive. Later TCU did get into Irish territory as a Senn to Billy Sadler pass carried to the Notre Dame 47. Two plays later Senn was intercepted by Mike Townsend.

Another Senn interception, this one by Ken Schlezes, led to a second quarter touchdown by Notre Dame. Starting at their 49 they scored in six plays. After gaining a first down at the Frog 35 the Irish sprung Andy Huff for another first and 10 at the 16. Quarterback Tom Clements ran two keepers to reach the 11. On third and five he found end Jim Roolf alone at the goal line and hit him with an 11-yard pass for a touchdown. Bob Thomas converted and Notre Dame led 7-0.

The Irish almost reached the Horned Frog end zone

TCU's Lane Bowen (82) grabs this first quarter pass from Perry Senn for 11 yards and a first down. Making the stop is Notre Dame's Jim Zlock (37.)

again before halftime. A Clements to Mike Creaney pass carried 41 yards to the TCU 15. Lyle Blackwood ended the threat three plays later when he intercepted Clements in the end zone with less than a minute left.

In the third quarter the Christians moved to midfield when a pass intended for Sadler was tipped into Freddie Pouncy's hands by Notre Dame's Mike Townsend. Mike Luttrell had a run to the Irish 39, but a clipping penalty on TCU brought the ball back to their 46 and killed the drive.

Meanwhile the Irish managed to get another seven points in the third quarter when the Frog defense was up tight on a third and one at the Notre Dame 43. Art Best ran outside right tackle, burst into the secondary, faked out David McGinnis at the TCU 20 and sped into the end zone. Thomas converted and Notre Dame led 14-0.

Early in the fourth quarter the Horned Frogs made their deepest penetration of the game and with a little luck should have had a touchdown. Luttrell, who had completed seven out of seven halfback passes this year, lofted one to Littleton. The quarterback dropped the ball and he was behind the Notre Dame secondary. Senn then passed

complete to John Ott for a first down at the Irish 35. That was the end of the line as Notre Dame held and the Frogs were forced to punt.

The final Irish touchdown covered 51 yards in three plays and was set up by Roolf who went 35 yards on an end around run. Eric Penick, the leading rusher in the game with 158 yards, scored from the 11. Thomas converted and the Fighting Irish led 21-0 with 3:59 left in the game.

The "Purple Gang" played tough on defense and never let up even though they spent a lot of time on the field. Tackle Charlie Davis was singled out for praise by Irish coach Ara Parseghian who said, "He played a super game, he's tough to handle."

	TCU	ND
First downs	8	22
Rushes yards	46-70	63-432
Passing yards	62	88
Return yards	0	70
Passes	6-16-3	5-16-1
Punts	10-40-4	5-35
Fumbles lost	3-1	6-4
Penalties yards	5-55	4-60

Texas Christian........0 0 0 0— 0
Notre Dame ....0 7 7 7—21
ND—Roolf 11 pass from Clements (Thomas kick)
ND—Best 57 run (Thomas kick)
ND—Penick 11 run (Thomas kick)
A—59,075

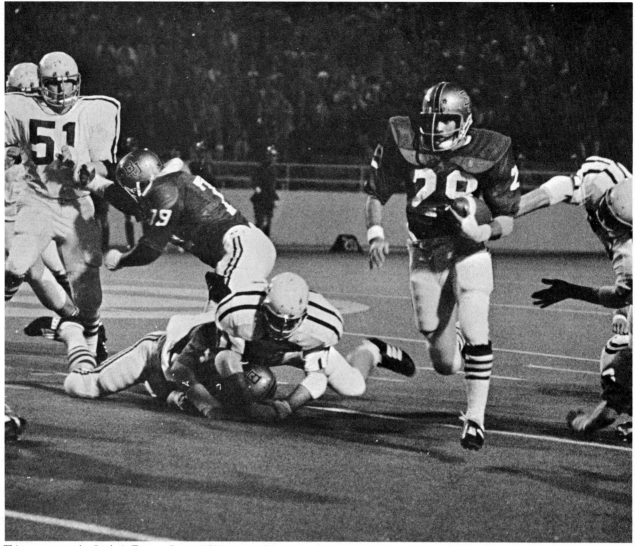

This punt return by Baylor's Tommy Stewart (29) was good for 21 yards to the A & M 31 and set up the Bears' first touchdown. Baylor tackle Joe Johnson is number 79 and the Aggies' 51 is center Skip Kuehn.

BAYLOR 15 - TEXAS A&M 13

A homecoming crowd of 40,000, third largest in Baylor Stadium history, sat through intermittent rain to watch the Bears and Cadets meet for the 69th time. Last year A&M won 10-9 when Mike Conradt missed an extra point attempt. This year he started off on the wrong foot as he missed the conversion after Baylor's first quarter touchdown. He more than redeemed himself as he came back later to kick three field goals to provide the margin of victory. The Aggies' late charge again fell short. They have lost their last three games by three, three and two points.

The Bears first drew blood midway through the first quarter. Tommy Stewart returned an Aggie punt 21 yards to the A & M 31. Quarterback Neal Jeffrey passed to Charles Dancer on a crossing pattern. Dancer caught the ball and was downed at the five, a 26-yard gain. Billy Wilson carried into the middle twice and scored from the two on his second carry. Conradt missed his first

conversion of the year and with 7:32 left in the first period Baylor led 6-0.

Early in the second quarter Baylor had possession at their 19 following an Aggie punt. Jeffrey passed to Brian Kilgore for 10 yards. A pass interference penalty on A&M helped keep the Bears moving. Gene Wilson got loose up the middle for a 15-yard run. The Cadets halted things at their 23 and Conradt came in for a 40-yard field goal attempt. His kick hit an upright, dropped to the crossbar and fell over for three points. Baylor led 9-0.

The Aggies came right back following the Bear kickoff. Quarterback Don Dean hit tight end Homer May for 27 yards and next passed to Richard Osborne for eight more. Baylor then stiffened at their 38 and when fourth down came up the Cadets were back on their 45. After the A&M punt a Baylor drive was halted when Robert Murski intercepted Jeffrey at the Aggie 12. Lex James then replaced Don Dean at quarterback and was intercepted

Neal Jeffrey (11) looks back after making the handoff to Billy Wilson (30). Wilson scores the first Baylor touchdown on this play as Grady Hoermann (31) and Dwight LaBauve (43) arrive too late for the Aggies.

by Ira Dean who returned to the A & M 16. The Bears reached the five, on an 11-yard completion to Kilgore, and Conradt kicked a 21-yard field goal with 14 seconds remaining.

After Baylor's kickoff Brad Dusek ran to the Bear 37 on a draw play and Pat McDermott tried a 54-yard goal which was short. Baylor led at the half 12-0.

Things got better for the Cadets in the second half, but not before they got worse. On their first scrimmage play in the third quarter they fumbled and Keith Stone recovered for Baylor at his 47. The Bears moved to the A & M 11 in 10 plays, mainly on the running of Billy and Gene Wilson and Kilgore. The Aggies held and Conradt kicked a 28-yard field goal to put Baylor ahead 15-0.

After an Aggie interception at the Bear 46 the Baylor defense held and when the Bears couldn't move Rusty Parrott punted from his own five. The punt carried to the Aggie 39 where Carl Roaches hauled it in, behind a clearing block by Corky Sheffield, broke clear and ran 61 yards for an A & M touchdown. The two-point conversion run failed and with 3:06 left in the third

quarter Baylor led 15-6.

Early in the final period Conradt missed on a 52-yard field goal attempt. The Aggies started at their 20 and moved 80 yards in eight plays. The barn-burner was a run of 54 yards by Bubba Bean. He was pushed out of bounds at the Baylor 14 by Ira Dean. Don Dean kept for seven and Bean ran for five to the two. Two plays later Dusek scored from the one. McDermott converted and with 7:59 left Baylor led 15-13.

The Aggies had three more possessions, but could not advance beyond their 31 as the "Jolly Green Giants" would not let them get into field goal range. The game ended with the Bears still owning their two-point margin. For Baylor, it was their first conference win in two years.

	A&M	Baylor
First downs	10	13
Rushes-yards	41-130	56-156
Passing yards	113	77
Return yards	61	68
Passes	8-24-2	6-16-2
Punts	10-36-3	9-34-7
Fumbles lost	2-1	2-0
Penalties yards	5-45	1-5

Texas A & M .... 0 0 6 7—13
Baylor ....6 6 3 0—15
B—Wilson 2 run (kick failed)
B—FG Conradt 40
B—FG Conradt 21
B—FG Conradt 28
A&M—Roaches 61 punt return (run failed)
A&M—Dusek 1 run (McDermott kick)
A—40,000

Texas backs peel off in formation on this run. Left to right are Don Burrisk (25), Donald Ealey (34) and Steve Fleming (24). Peering over Ealey's shoulder is reserve quarterback Marty Akins.

TEXAS 45 - RICE 9

The Owls and Longhorns first met in 1914 and have never missed a year since. Their 58th meeting was homecoming for Rice and 65,000 fans were on hand for the occasion. A cool night was just right for football and the Longhorns made the most of it.

Texas kicked off and Rice couldn't move. Mark Williams punted to the Longhorn 38. Texas marched 68 yards in twelve plays. Roosevelt Leaks gave a preview of things to come when he bolted 14 yards up the middle on first down. A penalty rubbed out the run, but it only delayed the inevitable. Leaks gained most of his yardage up the middle as he ran for 28 yards total. Quarterback Alan Lowry threw only one pass, but it was a big one. On third and 11 he hit Pat Kelly for 18 yards to keep the drive alive. Donald Ealey scored from the one when Rice was keyed on Leaks. Billy Schott converted and Texas led 7-0 with eight minutes left in the first quarter.

Following the Longhorn kickoff the Owls faced a third down and three needed at their 33. Quarterback Bruce Gadd lofted a safety valve pass to Gary Ferguson, but

Texas linebacker Randy Braband picked off the ball in mid-flight and returned 34 yards for a touchdown. With Schott's kick Texas led 14-0.

Two possessions later the Owls' Ferguson caught a Gadd pass, but fumbled when hit and Doug English recovered for Texas at the Rice 36. Leaks burst through for 26 yards on first down only to have a clipping penalty wipe out all but two yards of the gain. Next an illegal procedure penalty set Texas back five more to the Owl 39. Leaks came back with the same play that was wiped out earlier and ran 39 yards for the score. Schott kicked good and with 2:19 remaining in the first stanza Texas led 21-0.

As play moved into the second period Rice moved into Texas territory reaching the 28. Gadd was then thrown for a 13-yard loss and Williams, on the next play, dropped a beautiful punt out of bounds at the Longhorn two. Lowry dropped back to pass on first down. Steve Pruitt and Richard Hollas blitzed through and planted Lowry in the end zone for a Rice safety. Texas led 21-2.

Kerry Cooper returned the free kick 21 yards to the

A Mark Williams punt which went out of bounds at the Texas two led to this safety for Rice. Steve Pruitt (65) and Richard Hollas (53) blew in to drop quarterback Alan Lowry in the end zone.

Rice 47. Gadd then moved the Owls 53 yards in 10 plays. He passed complete to Ron Arceneaux for 18 yards and to Ferguson for 14 to reach the Texas 20. On fourth down two at the 12 Gadd passed nine yards to Edwin Collins. Gaining at a one yard per play clip the Owls scored in three plays. The payoff came on a one-yard pass to Ferguson. Williams converted and Texas led 21-9.

Texas turned Leaks loose and came roaring back. In seven plays that covered 80 yards Leaks gained 57 yards on four carries. His last carry was 26 yards and a touchdown. Schott converted and Texas led 28-9.

With three seconds left in the first half Mike Dean kicked a 50-yard field goal for Texas which gave the Longhorns a 31-9 lead at intermission.

With Leaks on the bench to stay Texas took the kickoff and drove 80 yards in 11 plays with Don Burrisk scoring from two yards out. The big gainer in the series was a 37-yard pass that Lowry threw to Kelly on a fly pattern. Schott was successful and Texas led 38-9.

The Steers final touchdown was put on the platter by Glenn Gaspard who intercepted Gadd at the Texas 23 and returned 47 yards to the Rice 30. Marty Akins replaced Lowry at quarterback. Steve Fleming ran for 15 yards and Akins followed that with a 13-yard keeper. On a third down play Tom Landry scored from the one. With Schott's conversion Texas led 45-9.

In the last quarter mistakes stopped three Longhorn scoring sorties. Akins passed to Rick Davis for a touchdown which was called back because of an illegal receiver downfield. Later, after Adrian Ford and Greg Dahlberg had intercepted Gadd's replacement, Bill McCabe, two fumbles stopped Texas. Fleming fumbled at the Owl six and Lonnie Bennett at the five.

If you have to stop Lowry and Leaks to beat Texas then Rice was 50 percent successful. Lowry made 20 yards on eight carries. Leaks ran for 154 yards in 15 tries and his understudy Fleming added 110 more on 19 attempts. Gadd hit on 21 of 30 passes for 192 yards, but suffered two costly interceptions.

	Texas	Rice
First downs	27	9
Rushes-yards	78-468	23-30
Passing yardage	55	284
Return yards	106	0
Passes	2-9-0	28-47-4
Punts	1-25	5-38-8
Fumbles lost	2-2	2-2
Penalties-yards	10-80	5-45

Texas .... 21 10 14 0—45
Rice .... 0 9 0 0— 9
UT—Ealey 1 run (Schott kick)
UT—Braband 34 pass interception (Schott kick)
UT—Leaks 39 run (Schott kick)
Rice—Safety, Lowry tackled in end zone
Rice—Ferguson 1 pass from Gadd (Williams kick)
UT—Leaks 27 run (Schott kick)
UT—FG Dean 50
UT—Burrisk 2 run (Schott kick)
UT—Landry 1 run (Schott kick)
A—65,000

Tech's George Smith (38) escapes the grasp of SMU's Louie Kelcher (72), but has another problem, Mike Leitko (74), coming up.

TEXAS TECH 17 - SMU 3

It was SMU homecoming in the Cotton Bowl. A crowd of 35,953 was there to watch the Red Raiders (who led conference teams in rushing and total offense) meet the Mustangs (who led the nation in rushing defense and the conference in total defense). Overall defense won out, but it was the Tech defense. They shut down Alvin Maxson and Wayne Morris (the first time this year) and forced quarterback Keith Bobo to scramble out of the pocket time after time during the game. Meanwhile the Mustangs were coughing up the ball on four turnovers and two of them led to scores for the Red Raiders.

Their first bit of charity came on the fifth play of the game. Morris fumbled at his 43 and Greg Waters recovered for Tech. The Mustangs held at their 26 and Don Grimes, whose toe has been busy this season, kicked a 43-yard field goal. With less than five minutes elapsed Tech led 3-0.

SMU received the kickoff and drove 74 yards in 19 plays. A Bobo pass of 29 yards to Kenny Harrison was the big play in the drive. Bobo also got in a big run of 16 yards which put the ball on the Tech 10. The Raider defense dropped Bobo for a 10-yard loss. Two plays later, Clint Hackney kicked a 38-yard field goal.With 2:30 left in the first period the score was tied 3-3.

Another turnover ended a promising move by Mustangs early in the second quarter. Bobo retreated into his own end zone and let fly far upfield to speedster Rufus Shaw. Randy Olson saved a 93-yard touchdown when he caught Shaw on a shoestring tackle at the Tech 41. The play covered 52 yards. The turnover came three plays later when Maxson, attempting a halfback pass, was intercepted by Davis Corley who returned to midfield.

On SMU's next possession Quintin Robinson caught a scrambling Bobo and the ball popped loose. Baty

The Mustang's Wayne Morris (25) is caught in flight by Red Raider Donald Rives (51) as Davis Corley (70) comes underneath. Bill Thomas (57) blocks Quinton Robinson (54) as Aubrey McCain (80) comes rushing on the scene. In the background is Tech's Randy Olson (20).

recovered for Tech on the Mustang 31. The Red Raiders scored in seven plays. Quarterback Joe Barnes got 15 on a keeper and George Smith gained a first down at the one. Two plays later James Mosley scored and with Grimes' kick Tech led 10-3.

Before the first half ended the Mustangs got close enough for Hackney to attempt a 46-yard field goal which was wide to the right.

Neither team could score in the third quarter although the Raiders had an excellent opportunity late in the period. At his 20 Barnes went left on a keeper, cut back across field, and ran 71 yards to the SMU nine. Three plays later, from the six, Barnes hit Calvin Jones in the end zone. An offensive pass interference penalty nullified the touchdown. On the next play Ted Thompson intercepted Barnes to snuff out the threat.

It looked like it would end at 10-3 as both teams just couldn't get their offense untracked and the minutes kept ticking off the scoreboard clock. With about four minutes left in the game Tech moved from their 37 to the Mustang

42, just picking up first downs and using up time. Then on a third down and three play Jones ran a deep pattern down the sidelines and Barnes hit him, over the outstretched arms of Andy Duvall, at the SMU 15. Jones trotted in for the touchdown which ended any hopes that the Mustangs might have harbored. Grimes kicked the extra point and Tech led 17-3 with 1:34 left.

The game ended when Waters intercepted Bobo with eight seconds on the clock. This was the final turnover in a game that for SMU was full of frustrations. Barnes was the leading rusher with 129 yards on 20 carries.

	Texas Tech	SMU
First downs	11	17
Rushes-yards	48-190	46-83
Passing yards	98	210
Return yards	24	22
Passes	8-14-1	13-31-2
Punts	9-35	7-38
Fumbles lost	3-0	4-2
Penalties yards	4-40	6-44

Texas Tech	3	7	0	7	17
SMU	3	0	0	0	3

TT—FG Grimes 43
SMU—FG Hackney 38
TT—Mosley 1 run (Grimes kick)
TT—Jones 42 pass from Barnes (Grimes kick)
A—35,953

Reggie Cherry (27) picks up yardage around right end on this play. Cherry scored Houston's second touchdown in the fourth quarter. On the ground is Marty Watts (16) and Puddin' Jones (30) is in the background.

MISSISSIPPI STATE 27 - HOUSTON 13

A Starkville homecoming crowd of 29,000 was on hand to watch their Bulldogs confront the Cougars of Houston. Missed opportunities plagued Houston, a pattern they have followed all season. When it was all over the Bulldog's bite was worse than their bark.

Late in the first quarter State opened the scoring by marching 68 yards in eight plays. Quarterback Rockey Felker dominated the drive as he gained 20 yards on two keepers and passed twice for 41 yards. The second aerial went to Bill Buckley for 13 yards and a touchdown. Glenn Ellis kicked the extra point and Mississippi State led 7-0 with 3:35 left in the first quarter.

Puddin' Jones returned the State kickoff 45 yards to the Bulldog 44. Two plays gained three yards, but on third down quarterback D. C. Nobles passed to tight end Marty Watts for 24 yards to the 17. On second down Jones burst through the middle for 13 yards and a

touchdown. Ricky Terrell converted and with 1:59 remaining in the first period it was a standoff at 7-7.

The Cougars missed on two opportunities in the second quarter and were bailed out when State threatened, by Howard Ebow's interception at the Houston three. First they moved 49 yards to the Bulldog 20 where on fourth and three they failed to pick up the first down. Then later Tommy Kaiser intercepted a deflected pass at the Houston 20 and returned to the Cougar 47. Houston moved to a first and goal at the Bulldog three. Two passes gained most of the yardage. Mike Welch caught one for 16 yards, on a third down play, and Jones gathered one in for 15 yards. On first and goal Nobles found Watts wide open in the end zone, but Watts dropped the pass. On second and goal Nobles threw into a crowd and John Calhoun intercepted for State and ran it out to his 18.

The missed opportunities carried over into the third

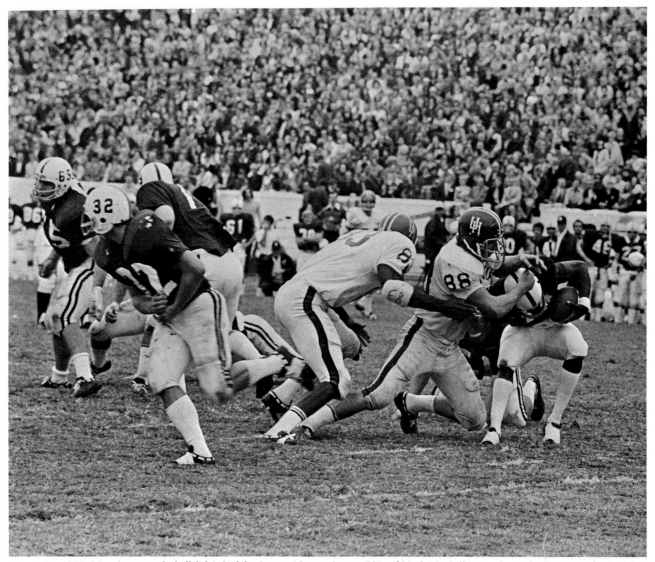

Wayne Jones'(32) fake of carrying the ball didn't fool the Cougars' Steven George (88) and Mack Mitchell (83) as they sack State quarterback Melvin Barkum for a loss.

quarter. The Cougars took the second half kickoff from their 34 to the Bulldog 19, but a screen pass failed on third and three. Harold Evans gave Houston another chance when he intercepted a pass and returned it 16 yards to the State 35. The Cougars drove to a first and goal at the seven. On fourth down at the two Nobles dropped back, stumbled, and fell down at the eight.

Early in the fourth quarter Gerald Hill recovered a State fumble at the Bulldog 35. The Cougars finally crashed one in with Reggie Cherry getting the touchdown from the five. Calhoun blocked Terrell's kick and with 13:04 remaining Houston led 13-7.

The Bulldogs then got a break when a Hal Roberts' punt went only 29 yards and was returned 13 to the Cougar 32. Felker directed them to a touchdown in eight plays. On the State possession before this the Cougars stopped the Bulldogs at the seven on fourth and one, but there was no stopping them this time. A four-yard pass from Felker to Buckley got the tying score with 5:44 to go. It remained that way when Ellis missed the extra point.

Four scrimmage plays later the Bulldogs had the ball at the Houston 45 following another Roberts punt of 29 yards. A holding penalty on third down gave State a first down at the 28. Lewis Grubbs ran for seven and the Cougars were assessed 11 yards for a personal foul. From the 10 Felker scored on a keeper with 2:10 left. Ellis converted and State led 20-13.

On the second play following the kickoff Terry Peel was intercepted by Billy Southward and returned to the Cougar 22. Houston was penalized to the seven for piling on. Wayne Jones scored from the two with five seconds on the clock. Ellis' conversion made the final score: Bulldogs 27 - Cougars 13.

	Houston	Miss. State
First downs	14	21
Rushes yards	46-174	54-171
Passing yards	110	176
Return yards	94	53
Passes	8-18-3	15-24-4
Punts	5-34	3-43
Fumbles lost	3-1	2-1
Penalties yards	4-32	1-5

Houston ....7 0 0 6—13
Miss. State ....7 0 0 20—27
MSU—Buckley 13 pass from Felker (Ellis kick)
UH—Jones 13 run (Terrell kick)
UH—Cherry 5 run (kick blocked)
MSU—Bucklay 4 pass from Felker (kick failed)
MSU—Felker 10 run (Ellis kick)
MSU—Jones 1 run (Ellis kick)
A—29,000

129

High-stepping Hog Dickey Morton (33) makes good yardage on this carry. Jon Richardson (24) helps open the hole as Joe Ferguson (11) looks on.

ARKANSAS 42 - NORTH TEXAS 16

The threat of rain held the attendance down to an estimated 30,000 in Little Rock's War Memorial Stadium. For the first time in three weeks it failed to rain on the Razorbacks and those rain-shy folks missed one of Arkansas' best games of the year. It was certainly a balanced attack for the offense minded Hogs as they gained 256 yards rushing and 256 yards passing. The defense covered two Eagle fumbles and intercepted three of their passes. None of the Arkansas scores were cheap as the closest they started to the State goal was the Eagle 43.

The Razorbacks got moving on their second possession. From their 28 they moved the 72 yards in 16 plays which included two offside penalties on North Texas. Dickey Morton and Jon Richardson picked up most of the yardage on short runs. Quarterback Joe Ferguson passed only once and it went to Jim Hodge for 14 yards. Richardson scored from the one and Mike Kirkland converted for a 7-0 lead for the Hogs.

Arkansas scored once more in the first quarter and it

came on their next possession. This drive covered 60 yards and took only three plays. Morton ran for three and grabbed a short pass for two. On third down Ferguson found Mike Reppond open down the middle. Reppond caught the ball at the State 40 and ran it over covering 55 yards in all. Kirkland kicked good and Arkansas led 14-0.

It was again on their second possession that the Razorbacks moved for a touchdown. This drive of 54 yards featured the passing of Ferguson. He hit on three out of three. One of 10 yards to Steve Hedgepeth, then to Reppond for 12 and to Hodge for 17 and a first and goal at State's seven. Morton ran seven for the score on the next play. Kirkland was on target and the Hogs led 21-0.

The Razorbacks scored again on their last possession of the first half. Once more Morton and Richardson shared the load on running plays and Ferguson threw twice. Hodge caught one for 19 yards and Hedgepeth the other for 13 yards. Richardson scored from two yards out and Kirkland converted. Arkansas led 28-0.

On this keeper Arkansas quarterback Joe Ferguson (11) is surrounded by Eagles. Offensive guard Mike Griffin (66) tries to block Ferguson free.

In the third quarter an Eagle fumble recovered by Ed Rownd and a pass interception by Mark Hollingsworth killed any good intentions State harbored. Late in the quarter Arkansas gained control at the Eagle 47 and scored in seven plays. Marsh White had a run of 18 yards for the big gainer. Ferguson passed six yards to Hedgepeth for the touchdown. Kirkland kicked the extra point and Arkansas led 35-0.

North Texas scored on the last play of the third quarter. A fumbled punt by John Moseley gave them possession at the Razorback 38. On third and seven quarterback Rick Shaw passed to David Kervin for 35 yards and a touchdown. Going for two points Shaw pitched out to Charlie Johnson, but the ball was missed and bounced back upfield. Shaw ran back, picked it up and threw a 25-yard pass to Kervin alone in the end zone. Getting two points the hard way made the score 35-8 favor of Arkansas.

Walter Nelson, who has backed up Bill Montgomery and Joe Ferguson at quarterback, entered the game in the fourth quarter and directed the Hogs 73 yards in six plays. After White and Mike Saint had run for 10 yards Nelson

passed to Matt Morrison for 17 yards. On the next play he faked a run and passed deep for Reggie Craig who caught the ball at the State two. White ran it over on the following play. Kirkland made it a perfect night and Arkansas led 42-8 with almost eight minutes left.

The Eagles squeezed in another score before the end when Nelson was intercepted by Sheldon Pendarves who returned to the Hog 40. Johnson ran for five, Shaw passed to David Yaege for 26 yards, Shaw kept for four and Johnson scored from the five. Johnson also ran over for the two point conversion. Final score: Arkansas 42 - North Texas 16.

	NTSU	Ark
First downs	16	25
Rushes-yards	37-90	61-256
Passing yards	251	256
Return yards	46	9
Passes	14-40-3	15-21-1
Punts	6-37	5-29
Fumbles lost	3-2	2-2
Penalties-yards	3-24	2-19

North Texas . . . . 0 0 8 8—16
Arkansas . . . . .14 14 7 7—42
A—Richardson 1 run (Kirkland kick)
A—Reppond 55 pass from Ferguson (Kirkland kick)
A—Morton 7 run (Kirkland kick)
A—Richardson 2 run (Kirkland kick)
A—Hedgepeth 6 pass from Ferguson (Kirkland kick)
NTS—Kervin 35 pass from Shaw (Kervin pass from Shaw)
A—White 2 run (Kirkland kick)
NTS—Johnson 5 run (Johnson run)
A—30,000

SYNOPSIS

TOP TEN
1. Southern Cal
2. Alabama
3. Nebraska
4. Michigan
5. Ohio State
6. LSU
7. Oklahoma
8. UCLA
9. Texas
10. Penn State

SWC OFFENSIVE PLAYER OF WEEK
Roosevelt Leaks, Fullback, Texas

SWC DEFENSIVE PLAYER OF WEEK
Donald Rives, Guard, Texas Tech

FRESHMAN RESULTS
Texas Tech 42 - Oklahoma 21
TCU 18 - Baylor 0
Texas 45 - Rice 14

UPSET OF WEEK
Missouri 20 - Colorado 17

SWC TEAM LEADERS FOR SEASON

OFFENSE		AVG.	DEFENSE		AVG.
Rushing	Texas	293 yds.	Rushing	SMU	84 yds.
Passing	Rice	233 yds.	Passing	Baylor	111 yds.
Total	Texas Tech	406 yds.	Total	SMU	282 yds.

SEASON RECORDS

	W	L	T
Texas Tech	6	1	0
Texas	5	1	0
Arkansas	5	2	0
SMU	4	2	0
TCU	4	2	0
Baylor	3	3	1
Rice	2	3	1
Houston	2	4	1
Texas A & M	1	6	0

CONFERENCE

	W	L	T
Texas	3	0	0
Texas Tech	2	1	0
Arkansas	2	1	0
TCU	1	1	0
SMU	1	1	0
Baylor	1	1	0
Rice	0	2	0
Texas A & M	0	3	0

Ninth Week
November 4

39 YEARS AGO
NOVEMBER 4, 1933
Texas Tech 12 - Texas Western 0
Baylor 7 - TCU 0
Centenary 20 - Texas A&M 0
Texas 10 - SMU 0
Santa Clara 13 - Rice 0
Arkansas open date

Houston's leading rusher, Puddin' Jones (30), makes short yardage behind the block of Luke Stungis (74) on Buzzy Lewis (38). Jones scored two touchdowns from one yard out.

HOUSTON 31 - FLORIDA STATE 27

The Cougars, the Jekyll-Hyde team, came into Tallahassee a 10-point underdog and ruined Florida State's bowl hopes before 29,482 fans. The Seminoles were never in it although they closed the gap to four points at the end. Houston presented a new defensive wrinkle for State quarterback Gary Huff. Since Huff, because of his quick release, had not been sacked many times this season, the Cougars rushed only three men which gave them additional coverage on Huff's receivers. It worked so well that despite rushing only three men they dumped Huff five times. You can't throw the ball when there is no one open. Couple this with an offense which gained 345 ground yards and the ingredients for victory were present and accounted for.

Houston's first score followed a short Seminole punt in the opening period. Robert Ford returned to the State 22. The Florida State defense stopped the Cougars at the eight and Ricky Terrell kicked a 25-yard field goal, his first of the year. Houston led 3-0 with 11:11 elapsed.

Mack Mitchell's fumble recovery gave Houston possession at the Seminole 36. This led to a 52-yard field goal attempt by Sandy McCrea which was short. Huff's fumble at his 10, recovered by Bubba Broussard, gave Terrell another shot at a field goal. From the State 29 his kick fell short.

Time was fast running out in the first half when a punt rush produced another short kick for State that rolled dead at their 38. Puddin' Jones ran for two and on second down quarterback D. C. Nobles kept inside left end and was finally run down at the State one yard line. Jones scored from there and with Terrell's conversion the Cougars led 10-0. They took their 10-point lead to the dressing room at halftime.

Robert Ford returned the second half kickoff 49 yards to the 50. Houston scored in eight plays. Marshall Johnson, shifted to running back, had runs of 13 and two yards and Reggie Cherry carried twice for 17 and 12 yards. On third down at the eight Nobles passed down the

The Cougars' Del Stanley (19), with Seminole Ron Ratliff (42) hanging on, makes a reception in the State end zone. The Touchdown throw, from D. C. Nobles, covered eight yards.

middle to Del Stanley in the end zone for the touchdown. Terrell converted and Houston led 17-0.

The "Mad Dogs" stopped State on fourth and one at the Houston 23. The Seminoles got the ball right back as Nobles suffered his only pass interference of the day. The throw was deflected at the line and Larry Strickland intercepted at the Houston 31. On fourth and six at the 27 Huff passed complete to Gary Parris who went all the way for a Seminole touchdown. Ahmet Askin kicked good and with 5:19 left in the third period the Cougars led 17-7.

Following Florida State's kickoff the Cougars started at their 20. On first down Johnson found a huge hole at left tackle and ran 80 yards for a touchdown. Terrell converted and Houston led 24-7.

The Seminoles scored once more before time ran out in the third quarter. Huff passed to Barry Smith for 19 and 34 yards in reaching the Houston 14. Fred Miller scored from the three and Askin converted to narrow the gap to 10 points at 24-14.

Midway through the fourth quarter the Cougars found the Seminole end zone again. A short punt gave Houston possession at the State 34. The pressure was mounting

against Huff and the Seminoles as Jones scored on fourth down from the two. Terrell converted and with 7:30 left Houston led 31-14.

State marched 76 yards to score converting two fourth down plays along the way. The touchdown came on a Huff to Miller pass of four yards. Askin kicked the point and with 4:19 remaining Houston led 31-21.

The Seminoles came back to score again as Mike Davidson went across on third down at the one. Broussard threw Huff for a loss on the two-point conversion try and with 24 seconds left Houston led 31-27.

Luke Stungis covered the onside kick attempt and Houston ran out the clock. With three home games remaining the Cougars stand 3-4-1 for the season.

	Houston	Fla. St.
First downs	12	22
Rushes-yards	58-345	33-49
Passing yards	24	409
Return yards	64	49
Passes	3-11-1	27-51-2
Punts	7-40	6-33
Fumbles lost	0-0	4-2
Penalties yards	5-60	1-15

Houston . . . . .3 7 14 7—31
Florida State . . . . .0 0 14 13—27
H—FG Terrell 25
H—Jones 1 run (Terrell kick)
H—Stanley 8 pass from Nobles (Terrell kick)
FSU—Parris 27 pass from Huff (Askin kick)
H—M. Johnson 80 run (Terrell kick)
FSU—F. Miller 3 run (Askin kick)
H—Jones 1 run (Terrell kick)
FSU—F. Miller 4 pass from Huff (Askin kick)
FSU—Davidson 1 run (run failed)
A—29,482

A & M linebacker Ed Simonini (77) grabs Hog quarterback Joe Ferguson before he can release the ball. Coming to help Simonini are Max Bird (87) and Al Thurmond (29).

TEXAS A&M 10 - ARKANSAS 7

What a historic day for the Aggies. They finally came out on the long end of a close game. They beat Arkansas at Kyle Field for the first time since 1956. They gave coach Emory Bellard his first ever conference victory. The crowd of 36,700 saw a bruising defensive struggle between the Razorbacks and Cadets which was decided, as most close games are, by turnovers. The Aggies intercepted Hog quarterback Joe Ferguson six times and recovered a Razorback fumble while losing two interceptions to Arkansas. For the Razorbacks it was another bitter pill in a season that has gone sour after such pre-season promise. A & M knows that feeling very well.

Arkansas got a break on the Aggies' first possession, but it was short lived. Louis Campbell intercepted Cadet quarterback Don Dean's pass and returned 29 yards. Arkansas was penalized for clipping on the return and the ball was moved back to the A & M 41. On third down Ferguson was intercepted by Robert Murski who returned to the Aggie 35.

On the Razorbacks' next possession Dickey Morton gained 30 yards running and caught a seven-yard pass in helping Arkansas move from their 29 to the Aggie 27. There, on fourth and three, Mike Kirkland attempted a 44-yard field goal which failed.

Late in the first quarter the Cadets began a drive at their 20 which would eventually produce three points as play moved into the second quarter. Bubba Bean started things with a 22-yard run. Dean connected on three passes. One of 16 yards to Richard Osborne moved the ball into Arkansas territory. Homer May caught one of eight yards and two plays later Dean hit Osborne again for 15 yards to the Hog 16. At the nine a fourth down needing three came up and Pat McDermott entered to kick a 26-yard field goal. A & M led 3-0.

The Aggies got the ball right back as Morton fumbled on first down following the kickoff. Bill Wiebold recovered at the Arkansas 24. Upon reaching the five A & M forsook the field goal on fourth down four and

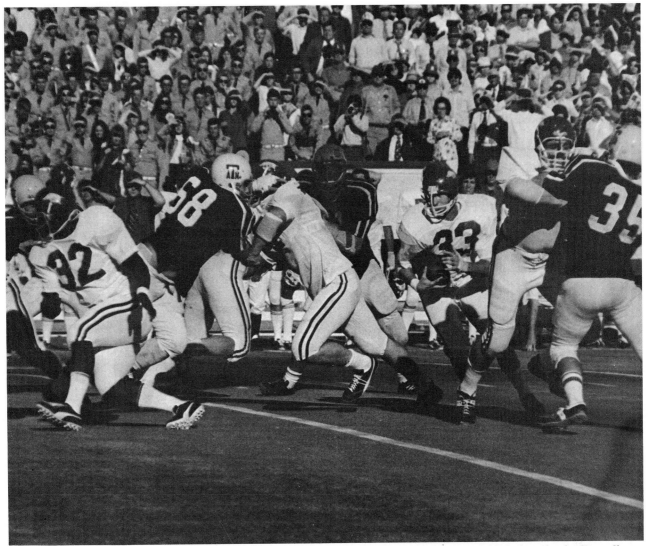

Razorback Dickey Morton (33) finds a nice hole as Aggies' Boice Best (68) and Paul Hulin (35) are blocked out by the Hog offensive line. Leading interference for Morton is Marsh White (32).

Skip Walker was thrown for a five-yard loss by John Wheat.

Later a Mark Hollingsworth interception and 27-yard return gave the Razorbacks excellent field position at A&M's 29. Three plays gained nothing and Kirkland tried a 46-yard field goal which was no good. Shortly the first half ended with the Aggies clinging to their three-point lead.

On Arkansas' first two possessions of the second half Ferguson was intercepted. The second one led to the Aggies' only touchdown. Larry Ellis returned his theft 26 yards to the Hog 26. The Cadets scored in eight plays with Dean gaining 20 yards on four keepers. Brad Dusek scored from the two and McDermott converted. A & M led 10-0 with 5:27 remaining in the third quarter.

As the fourth period was fast approaching the Razorbacks started their only payoff drive of the game. They covered 76 yards in 11 plays. Morton had 19 yards on four carries and Ferguson had two complete passes to Steve Hedgepeth, first for 18 yards and two plays later a 15 yarder. Marsh White, besides having a 14 yard run, got

the touchdown on a run of two yards. Kirkland converted and with 13:30 left in the game A & M led 10-7.

On their last three possessions the Hogs lost the ball on an interception, ran out of downs at the A & M 37 and again suffered an interception. The Aggies took over at their own 49 following Al Thurman's interception and ran out the clock.

The Razorback defense, despite seven turnovers by the offense, held the Cadets to one touchdown and a field goal. On the other side of the field the Aggie defense got those seven turnovers. For both teams it was a great defensive effort.

	Arkansas	A&M
First downs	16	12
Rushes-yards	44-161	57-140
Passing yards	115	77
Return yards	55	64
Passes	9-26-6	5-11-2
Punts	3-37	9-41
Fumbles lost	1-3	0
Penalties-yards	4-44	6-30

Arkansas . . . . .0 0 0 7— 7
Texas A&M. . . . . .0 3 7 0—10
A&M—FG McDermott 26
A&M—Dusek 2 run (McDermott kick)
ARK—White 2 run (Kirkland kick)
A—36,700

Donald Ealey (34) is tripped up at the line of scrimmage after receiving a handoff from Texas quarterback Alan Lowry (15). Andy Duvall (16) and Robert Popelka (43) are defending for the Mustangs.

TEXAS 17 - SMU 9

In a showdown defensive struggle the Longhorns bested the Mustangs. A crowd of 72,500 was on hand in Memorial Stadium to see if SMU was to be the team to sidetrack the Texas drive for a fifth straight SWC crown. The Longhorn rooters weren't able to relax until Glenn Gaspard recovered a disputed fumble on the Texas 34 with only 1:35 remaining in the game.

The first quarter was scoreless which may have been expected. SMU was the SWC leader in rushing defense and total defense while Texas was second in rushing defense and first in scoring defense.

Early in the second quarter Texas started from their 25. Roosevelt Leaks, in succession, ran for 12, 17, one, 14, 12 and four. This placed the ball on the Mustang 15. On the next play Leaks was stopped, but quarterback Alan Lowry had handed off to Don Burrisk who ran up the middle for 15 yards and a touchdown. Billy Schott converted and with 11:37 remaining in the first half Texas led 7-0.

Following an exchange of punts the Mustangs had possession on their 39 and quickly moved to the Longhorn 12. The key play was a pass thrown by quarterback Keith Bobo, tipped by Texas' Mike Bayer and caught by SMU's Kenny Harrison. The play covered 49 yards to the 12. Bobo was thrown for losses totaling 13 yards on the next two downs. On third down Wayne Morris got seven yards back reaching the 18. Clint Hackney came in and kicked a 35-yard field goal. With 4:40 to go in the half Texas led 7-3.

SMU received good field position, after holding the Longhorns, taking the Texas punt at the UT 49. After an incomplete pass a screen pass to Harrison lost two yards. On third down Bobo fired a pass intended for Harrison, but Mike Rowan intercepted on the dead run and returned 35 yards to the SMU 23. Leaks carried for five yards then followed a Jerry Sisemore block for 12 yards on second down. He picked up three on first and goal. Lowry kept for two and on the next play followed a Leaks

Robert Popelka (43) slows up Texas' Don Burrisk (25) on this run. Coming to help secure the tackle is No. 48 of the Mustangs who is not listed on the SMU roster. Looking back is Randy Savage (63).

block across the goal. Schott kicked good and with 1:16 left before halftime Texas led 14-3.

The Longhorns had trouble holding onto the ball in the third period. Early in the quarter Leaks lost the ball at the Mustang 43 and later Lowry fumbled at the SMU 47. Louis Kelcher recovered Lowry's bobble at his 49. The Mustangs marched the 51 yards in nine plays. The big play came on a run of 15 yards by Alvin Maxson. He started around left end, reversed his field back to the right and was brought down on the Texas 10. Three plays later Morris scored from the three around left end. A two point conversion attempt failed and with 3:46 left in the third quarter Texas led 14-9.

Early in the fourth quarter the Longhorns had an opportunity to pull away when Doug English recovered a Morris fumble at the SMU 26. They drove to the seven where Leaks fumbled and Robert Popelka recovered for the Mustangs.

When they got the ball again the Longhorns marched from their 46 to the Mustang 16 where SMU held and Schott kicked a 33-yard field goal. With 3:15 to play Texas led 17-9.

The Mustangs kept the Texas rooters from relaxing as they took possession at their 24 following the kickoff and moved steadily downfield. On fourth down and nine at the Texas 49 Maxson weaved his way 15 yards to the Longhorn 34, but fumbled when tackled and Gaspard recovered. Maxson claimed he was down before losing the ball, but the officials ruled differently. With a little over one minute left Texas took over and ran out the clock.

Leaks gained 175 yards on 33 carries to lead all rushers. It was his third game in a row to gain over 150 yards. The Mustangs shut out Texas in the passing department as Lowry missed all six of his attempts.

	SMU	Texas
First downs	12	17
Rushes-yards	47-105	64-308
Passing yards	118	0
Return yards	53	45
Passes	8-17-2	0-6-0
Punts	8-40	8-39
Fumbles lost	2-2	3-3
Penalties yards	3-15	3-32

SMU .... 0 3 6 0— 9
Texas .... 0 14 0 3—17

T—Burrisk 15 run (Schott kick)
SMU—FG Hackney 35
T—Lowry 1 run (Schott kick)
SMU—Morris 3 run (pass failed)
T—FG Schott 33
A—72,500

Gary Lacy (23) waits for this 23-yard pass, over the outstretched hand of the Frogs' Tookie Berry (54). This completion came during the Bears first touchdown drive. Also pictured is Dede Terveen (55).

BAYLOR 42 - TCU 9

The saga of the resurrection of the Baylor Bears continued in Fort Worth before a homecoming crowd of 22,925. For the first time in nine years they defeated the Horned Frogs. And for the first time since 1954 they did it at TCU - Amon Carter field.

The game started out like most Bear-Frog games with TCU scoring first. In the past that was enought to send Baylor reeling. Times have changed and TCU realized this before the first half ended.

In the first quarter a bad pitchout from Bear quarterback Neal Jeffrey to Billy Wilson was recovered by TCU's Ed Robinson at the Baylor 25. Billy Sadler scooted 16 yards to the nine and two plays later Mike Luttrell scored from the three. Berl Simmons kicked the extra point and TCU led 7-0.

In the second quarter the Frog's Larry Harris fumbled and Paul Savage recovered for the Bears at his 49. Jeffrey passed to Gene Wilson for 11 yards, to Charles Dancer for 23 and to Brian Kilgore for 15. This set the ball on the

TCU two. Two plays later Gary Lacy scored from the one. Mike Conradt converted and with 3:37 left in the first half the score was tied at 7-7.

Following a TCU punt the Bears started at their 20 and were now confronted by the clock as well as the Horned Frogs. Billy Wilson got runs of 14, four and five yards as the Bears reached their 45. Jeffrey then connected on five straight passes to reach the TCU two. The first one, for 38 yards to Dancer, was called back because of a motion penalty. This didn't faze Jeffrey as he came right back to hit Lester Ealey for 21 yards, Dancer for 15 yards, Kilgore for 16 yards and Dancer again for six yards. Two plays later he had his sixth in a row as he tossed a one yarder to Ken Townsend for the touchdown with 39 seconds left. Conradt kicked good and at the half Baylor led 14-7.

The first time they got the ball in the second half Baylor scored again. Lacy started off the 66-yard drive with a 13-yard run and Kilgore set up the touchdown with a 12-yard reverse to the TCU three. In between those plays Jeffrey

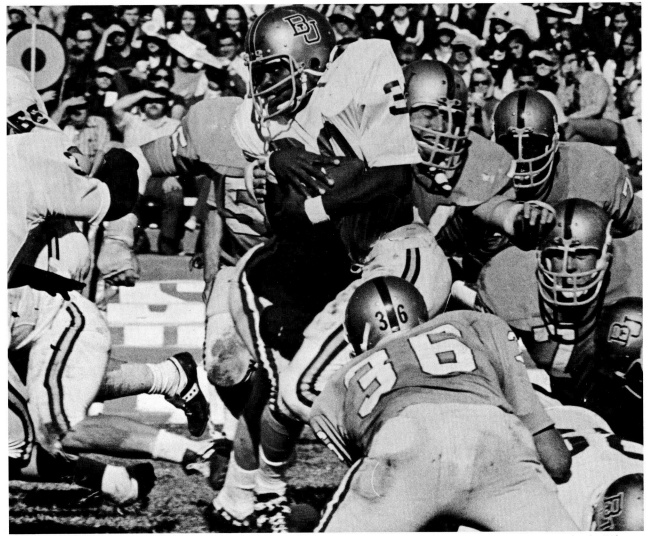

Baylor's Billy Wilson (30), who scored the Bears' third touchdown, makes seven yards on this second quarter run. Tookie Berry reaches for Wilson as Gary Whitman (36) is blocked out of the play by Rusty Bundy (89).

passed complete to Ealey, Lacy and Kilgore for a total of 38 yards. Billy Wilson scored from the three. Conradt kicked good and Baylor led 21-7.

Four plays following the kickoff Greg Anderson got off a tremendous punt of 61 yards. Tommy Stewart tried to field the ball over his head, but fumbled into the end zone. He ran back and covered the ball and TCU was given a safety. Baylor led 21-9.

Ronnie Littleton returned the Bear free kick to their 46. A personal foul on Baylor tacked on another 15 yards. On first down at the 31 Sadler fumbled when hit by Keith Stone and Mike Black recovered for Baylor. Dede Terveen got the ball back for TCU when he recovered a Bear fumble at his 44. Baylor held, but following a Frog punt Jeffrey passed to Ealey who lost the ball when hit by Gary Whitman. David McGinnis caught the ball in mid-air and Gene Wilson saved a score when he downed him at the Baylor 37. The "Jolly Green Giants" held and TCU punted from the 41.

The Bears scored three touchdowns in the fourth quarter and all were set up on intercepted passes. Stewart got the first one when he grabbed a Perry Senn pass at the

TCU 36 and returned 32 yards to the four. Lacy scored from the two with 11:03 left. Baylor led 28-9.

Darrel Luce intercepted Senn next, at the Horned Frog 19, and he was dropped at the one on his return. Randy Cavender, who had replaced Jeffrey, scored on a keeper and Baylor led 35-9.

Bill Walter replaced Senn at quarterback and was intercepted by Don Drake at the TCU 34. The Bears scored in five plays with most of the yardage coming on a Cavender pass to Karl Ray for 26 yards. Ray Harper scored from the two with 40 seconds on the clock. Conradt converted after all three fourth quarter touchdowns and the Bears ended on top of a 42-9 score.

Next week it's "Showdown at the Waco Corral" with the Texas Longhorns and a cast of fifty thousand.

	Baylor	TCU
First downs	21	6
Rushes-yards	56-169	45-109
Yards passing	232	44
Return yardage	112	40
Passes	16-27-2	6-19-6
Punts	5-43-2	10-41-7
Fumbles lost	6-3	2-2
Penalties yards	5-49	6-35

Baylor .... 0 14 7 21—42
TCU .... 7 0 2 0— 9
TCU—Luttrell 3 run (Simmons kick)
B—Lacy 1 run (Conradt kick)
B—Townsend 1 pass from Jeffrey (Conradt kick)
B—B. Wilson 3 run (Conradt kick)
TCU—Safety, Stewart killed fumbled punt in end zone
B—Lacy 2 run (Conradt kick)
B—Cavender 1 run (Conradt kick)
B—Harper 2 run (Conradt kick)
A—22,925

141

Punter John Garner (35), subbing for the injured George Smith, gained 43 yards on six carries. Owls pictured are Cornelius Walker (76) and the Medford boys, Larry (73) and Jody (52).

TEXAS TECH 10 - RICE 6

The Owls and the Red Raiders, for some reason, just cannot generate enought scoring when they meet to keep the scoreboard operator awake. In 1970 Tech won 3-0 and last year Rice prevailed 9-7. Counting this year's game the Owls, in three years, have punched out five field goals, all by Mark Williams. The Red Raiders have totaled up two touchdowns and two field goals. The Owls have yet to score a touchdown on a Jim Carlen coached team. The 20,000 in Rice Stadium had trouble staying awake.

Rice opened the scoring with 6:21 left in the first quarter. They drove 60 yards in nine plays. Quarterback Bruce Gadd passed to Edwin Collins for 30 yards, half of which was lost on a clipping penalty, and then to Collins again for 17 yards. Gary Ferguson's run of 17 yards put the ball on the Red Raider 19, but the Owls could get no further. Williams came in and kicked a 37-yard field goal. Rice led 3-0.

After an exchange of punts Tech started a scoring drive at their 46 and punched the ball across in seven plays.

Doug McCutchen caught a pass for nine yards and then ran for seven yards. John Garner had a run of 13 yards and quarterback Joe Barnes gained 14 and 11 on keepers. The latter was for the touchdown. Don Grimes kicked the extra point and Tech led 7-3 with only 28 seconds left in the opening period.

Following the Tech kickoff Tom Ryan intercepted Gadd on a pass that was deflected by Tim Schaffner. From the Rice 47 the Red Raiders drove to the 14, but then an ineligible receiver downfield set them back to the 29. On the next play Richard Hollas intercepted Joe Barnes and returned 41 yards to the Tech 41. On fourth down and six Williams was wide to the right on a 55-yard field goal attempt.

Later Jimmy Carmichael relieved Joe Barnes who was shaken up on a tackle. A handoff was bobbled and Hollas recovered for Rice at the Raider 17. Three plays later Danny Willis intercepted Gadd at the Tech eight.

Rice held and the Raiders punted to their 48. The Owls

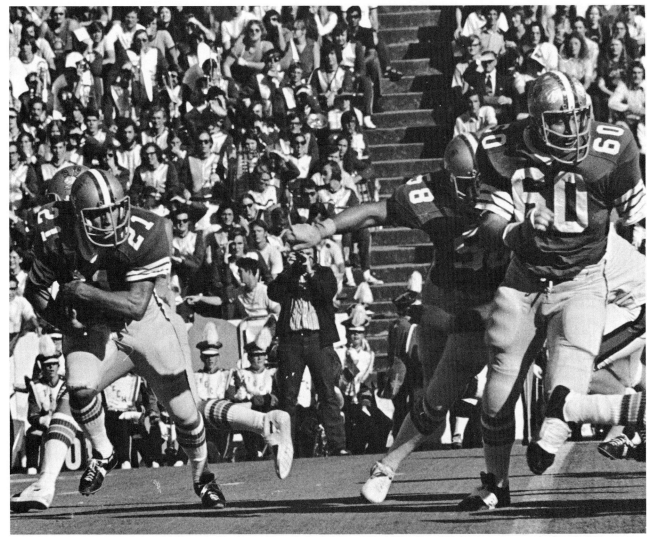

Gary Ferguson (21) starts left and follows the blocking of Bart Goforth (60) and David Vandiver (58). Ferguson became the first Owl this season to rush for over 100 yards in a game. He gained 111 yards on 20 carries.

marched to the Tech two mainly on the running of John Coleman and Ferguson plus a 12-yard interference penalty. On third down Ferguson, on a halfback pass, overthrew a lonesome Gary Butler in the end zone. With 2:09 left in the first half Williams kicked a 20-yard field goal. Tech led at the half 7-6.

In the third period the Rice defense held Tech in check and their offense had a threatening march of 53 yards. From their 19 they drove to the Raiders 23 with the big plays coming on a run of 18 yards by Ferguson and a Gadd to Collins pass for 14 yards. The threat ended when Williams missed a 40-yard field goal.

As play moved into the fourth quarter the Owls were moving again, but a bad pitch at Tech's 39 was recovered by the Raider's Randy Lancaster way back at the Rice 49. Tech reached the Rice 23 mainly on a 21-yard run by McCutchen, but Barnes was dropped for a 12-yard loss and Grimes missed on a 47-yard field goal attempt.

The Owls started at their 20 and marched to the Red Raider 26 before calling on Williams again. This came about when Danny Willis stopped Rice on a third and three play. He knocked down a Gadd to Butler pass to end the threat. Williams missed from 43 yards and 6:48 remained.

Staying on the ground and using McCutchen to blast out yardage the Red Raiders drove 75 yards to the Owl five-yard line. A 28-yard run by McCutchen reached the Rice 10, but three plays gained only five yards and Grimes came in on fourth down and booted a 22-yard field goal. With 1:05 on the clock Tech led 10-6.

Gadd brought the Owls back for one last chance starting at his 22. A pass to Collins covered 18 yards to the 40. Ferguson caught a pass for seven and then a personal foul on Tech covered 20 yards to the Red Raiders 32. Gadd passed to John Coleman for eight yards to the 24. Rice called time with 17 seconds left. On the next play Butler was over thrown in the end zone corner and Greg Waters intercepted for Tech with 10 seconds remaining.

	Tech	Rice
First downs	17	17
Rushes-yards	57-273	41-160
Passing yards	21	148
Return yards	25	41
Passes	4-11-1	12-23-3
Punts	5-32	2-42
Fumbles lost	3-1	1-1
Penalties-yards	6-65	5-45

Texas Tech	7	0	0	3—10
Rice	3	3	0	0— 6

Rice—FG Williams 37
Tech—Barnes 11 run (Grimes kick)
Rice—FG Williams 20
Tech—FG Grimes 22
A—20,000

SYNOPSIS

TOP TEN

1. Southern Cal
2. Alabama
3. Nebraska
4. Michigan
5. Ohio State
6. LSU
7. Oklahoma
8. UCLA
9. Texas
10. Penn State

SWC OFFENSIVE PLAYER OF WEEK

Neal Jeffrey, Quarterback Baylor

SWC DEFENSIVE PLAYER OF WEEK

Robert Murski, Cornerback, Texas A&M

FRESHMAN RESULTS:

Texas 52 - SMU 6

UPSET OF WEEK:

Texas A & M 10 - Arkansas 7

SWC TEAM LEADERS FOR SEASON

OFFENSE	AVG.	DEFENSE	AVG.
Rushing	Texas 295 yds.	Rushing	SMU 116 yds.
Passing	Rice 221 yds.	Passing	Baylor 101 yds.
Total	Texas Tech 392 yds.	Total	Baylor 274 yds.

SEASON RECORDS

	W	L	T
Texas Tech	7	1	0
Texas	6	1	0
Arkansas	5	3	0
Baylor	4	3	0
TCU	4	3	0
SMU	4	3	0
Houston	3	4	1
Rice	2	4	1
Texas A&M	2	6	0

CONFERENCE

	W	L	T
Texas	4	0	0
Texas Tech	3	1	0
Baylor	2	1	0
Arkansas	2	2	0
TCU	1	2	0
SMU	1	2	0
Texas A & M	1	3	0
Rice	0	3	0

Tenth Week
November 11

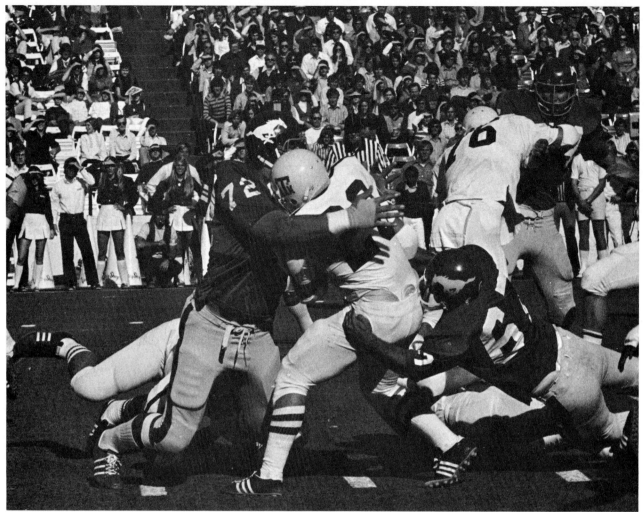

Skip Walker (23), who scored two first quarter touchdowns, is halted on this run by Mustang's Louie Kelcher (72) and Don Randell (67). In the background A & M's Ralph Sacra (76) blocks SMU's Mike Leitko (74).

TEXAS A&M 27 - SMU 17

The Aggies, on the bottom most of the year, have turned around. On the way up they passed the Mustangs on the way down. Three weeks ago SMU was 4-1. Now they stand 4-4 as they dropped their third game in a row. A crowd of 32,109 was on hand in the Cotton Bowl for the SWC game.

Rufus Shaw juggled A & M's kickoff in the end zone, then decided to run it out and was downed at the 11. Following the SMU punt the Aggies started at their 45. The Mustangs held at their 37. With the aid of a 14 mph wind Pat McDermott kicked a 54-yard field goal. This bettered his school record by one yard. The Cadets led 3-0.

Shaw returned the ensuing kickoff to the Mustang 10. Again SMU couldn't move and Carl Roaches returned Sam McLarty's punt 13 yards to the Pony 35. The Aggies scored in three plays. On the third play Skip Walker took a pitchout from quarterback Don Dean and skirted left end for 24 yards and a touchdown. McDermott kicked good and A & M led 10-0.

On their third possession the Mustangs still couldn't move the ball and McLarty punted from the shadow of his own goal to the Aggie 42. A five-yard penalty put the ball back to the 37, from where the Cadets marched 63 yards in seven plays. A Dean pass over the middle was complete to Roaches, for 31 yards, to start things rolling. From the eight Walker again found a hole on the left side and scored standing. McDermott converted and A & M led 17-0 with over three minutes remaining in the first quarter.

The Mustangs got good field position when the Cadets were penalized to their 43 when they interferred with a Mustang fair catch. SMU had not picked up a first down yet and play was now in the second quarter. Quarterback Keith Bobo dropped back and fired long to Kenny Harrison at the Aggie goal line. Harrison leaped in front of defender Robert Murski and hauled in the touchdown pass. Clint Hackney kicked wide on the conversion and A & M led 17-6.

The Mustangs later moved to the Aggie 16, but facing a fourth down four they went the field goal route.

146

In this fourth quarter action Aggie linebacker Ed Simonini (77) drops Alvin Maxson (28) for a two yard loss. The Mustangs had to settle for a field goal. Ken Harrison (15), SMU's split end is shown in the background and A&M's Boice Best (68) is rushing to give help if needed.

Hackney's attempt was off target. The first half ended with no change on the scoreboard.

The Aggie offense, which had a great first quarter, was dormant through the second and third periods. The Mustangs threatened in the third quarter when Bobo ran a keeper for 26 yards to the Cadet 23, but a holding penalty wiped out the run.

Late in the period the Mustangs again found poor field position at their three. With a drive that ended in the fourth quarter SMU went 97 yards for a touchdown. Wayne Morris got the drive started with a 17-yard run to the 20. Later Bobo kept for 15 yards and reached the A&M 28. Going to the air Bobo passed to Oscar Roan who was downed at the 13. Four plays later Bobo scored from the one. A pass to Roan picked up a two-point conversion and A & M led 17-14.

With the Pony offense coming to life, the defense stiffened and forced a Cadet punt. SMU had the ball again at their 30. Staying on the ground Bobo, Morris and Alvin Maxson moved the ball to the Aggie 20.

On one 12-yard run Bobo dropped the ball and had it bounce right back into his hands. On second and seven from the 20 Maxson was dropped at the 22 by Ed Simonini. After an incomplete pass Hackney kicked a 39-yard field goal to knot the game at 17-17. Only 6:10 remained.

The Aggies woke up in time and came right back to take the lead. From their 16 they used up precious Mustang minutes to reach the SMU 20. That is where the Ponies finally hauled down Homer May after a 41-yard pass play. Unable to move further McDermott came in and kicked a 37-yard field goal. With 2:12 left the Cadets had regained the lead 20-17.

Disaster then struck SMU before they could strike back. Mike Bruton hit Bobo who was dropping back to pass and Kent Finley recovered at the Mustang three. Three plays later Ronnie Hubby scored from the two and when McDermott's conversion made it 27-17 it was all over for the Mustangs.

	A&M	SMU
First downs	8	18
Rushes-yards	57-188	46-137
Passing yards	90	142
Return yards	47	9
Passes	4-6-0	11-19-1
Punts	7-38	7-41
Fumbles lost	2-1	3-1
Penalties-yards	10-103	8-79

SMU .... 0 6 0 11—17
A&M .... 17 0 0 10—27
A&M—FG McDermott 54
A&M—Walker 24 run (McDermott kick)
A&M—Walker 8 run (McDermott kick)
SMU—Harrison 43 pass from Bobo (kick failed)
SMU—Bobo 1 run (Roan pass from Bobo)
SMU—FG Hackney 39
A&M—FG McDermott 37
A&M—Hubby 2 run (McDermott kick)
A—32,109

147

Safety coming up as TCU's Charlie Davis (71) grabs quarterback Joe Barnes (12) on the goal line and Rusty Putt (85) makes a frontal attack. Tech's Tom Furgerson (79) approaches from the rear.

TCU 31 - TEXAS TECH 7

Last week TCU's homecoming was spoiled by Baylor. This time they were the spoiler and Texas Tech was the surprised victim. Before a Jones Stadium homecoming crowd of 40,120, a regional television audience and bowl scouts the Frogs put a damper on the Red Raiders SWC hopes and possible post season play.

Terry Drennan was pulled from the TCU secondary and installed as quarterback for the Frogs. Not since six games ago had Drennan played quarterback and then only briefly in the closing moments of a TCU victory. He and a choking TCU defense were the cause of the about face. It was their first victory in Lubbock since 1963.

TCU didn't hide their intentions long as they held Tech after the kickoff and on their first possession moved 56 yards in 13 plays for a touchdown. On a fourth down and one play at the Tech 20, Drennan kept inside and twirled out of tackles to reach the 11. Three plays later he kept left and tossed a six-yard scoring pass to a lonesome Steve Patterson in the end zone. Berl Simmons kicked good and

the Horned Frogs led 7-0.

Tech was guilty of clipping on the kickoff which went out of the end zone. This put the ball on their 10. On second down quarterback Joe Barnes dropped back to pass. Charlie Davis and Rusty Putt dropped Barnes in the end zone and with the safety TCU led 9-0.

Following the Red Raiders free kick TCU started at their 36. Ronnie Webb, Mike Luttrell and Billy Sadler moved the ball on the ground to the Tech 37. There Drennan passed to Patterson for 12 yards to the 25. Facing a fourth down three at the 18 Simmons came in for a field goal attempt. Perry Senn, the holder, took the snap and passed to Luttrell in the flat. Luttrell romped in for the touchdown. Simmons' extra point try was blocked and TCU led 15-0.

Tech took the ensuing kickoff and moved from their 20 to the 44. On a first down play a Barnes pass was tipped by Andre Tillman, tipped again by Lyle Blackwood and intercepted by Dede Terveen at his 42. Moving on the

Frog quarterback Terry Drennan (13), who was listed as safety in the game program, passes to Steve Patterson for TCU's first touchdown. Tech defenders are Donald Rives (51), Davis Corley (70), George Herro (50) and Quinton Robinson (54). Frogs shown are Lloyd Draper (75), Guy Morriss (68), Billy Sadler (33) and Ronnie Peoples (60).

ground again the Horned Frogs pounded to the Tech two but the Raiders held and Simmons kicked a 19-yard field goal. During the drive Sadler had a 19-yard run which was the big play. TCU led 18-0 with 13:51 left in the first half.

After halftime activities the Horned Frogs wasted no time as they moved 54 yards in nine plays on their first possession. At the Tech 26 Simmons kicked a 43-yard field goal and TCU led 21-0.

The Tech offense finally came to life and moved, after the kickoff, 74 yards in 12 plays. Barnes, Doug McCutchen and James Mosley took turns running the ball. McCutchen scored from less than one yard out. Don Grimes converted and with 5:50 left in the third quarter TCU led 21-7.

Tech came right back after a TCU punt. From their 28 Barnes passed to John Garner for 23 yards. Later, on a third down, Barnes passed to Tillman for 16 yards and a first down and McCutchen converted a fourth down into a first moments later. At the TCU nine Barnes' pass to Lawrence Williams in the end zone was dropped. He came back to Williams and again the ball was dropped. A pass to Garner gained to the six and a TCU holding penalty gave Tech a first down. McCutchen gained two, Barnes lost three, a pass was incomplete and Ed Robinson dropped Barnes at the 13. The Purple Gang had lowered the boom on Tech and they never again threatened.

In the fourth quarter TCU scored twice more. First Simmons kicked a 49-yard field goal to make it 24 to 7. Then later a fourth down gamble by Tech at their 39 failed and TCU scored in two plays. Webb ran 19 yards and Luttrell, on second down, went in from the 20. Simmons converted and TCU led 31-7.

	TCU	Tech
First downs	21	19
Rushes-yards	77-358	39-53
Passing yards	42	144
Return yards	8	8
Passes	4-5-0	13-26-1
Punts	4-42	3-43
Fumbles lost	1-0	1-1
Penalties yards	5-43	2-34

TCU ....15 3 3 10—31
Texas Tech ....0 0 7 0— 7
TCU—Patterson 6 pass from Drennan (Simmons kick)
TCU—Safety, Barnes tackled in end zone
TCU—Luttrell 18 pass from Senn (kick failed)
TCU—FG Simmons 19
TCU—FG Simmons 43
Tech—McCutchen 2 run (Grimes kick)
TCU—FG Simmons 49
TCU—Luttrell 20 run (Simmons kick)
A—40,120

Former fullback Scott Binnion (36), now a linebacker, makes the stop on Rice fullback John Coleman (44). John Wheat (68) prepares to help if needed.

RICE 23 - ARKANSAS 20

In 1948 Little Rock's War Memorial Stadium was dedicated. The last time Rice defeated Arkansas in Little Rock was 1948. Last year in Houston Arkansas' Bill McClard kicked a tying field goal with two seconds remaining. This year both teams were coming off a loss which had eliminated them from the SWC title chase. A crowd of 51,475 saw the Razorbacks fall behind with one second left on the clock.

Freshman Roland Boyce handled the ball first for Rice as he returned the opening kickoff to the Owl 28. Later he would be the handler on Rice's last play of the game. On first down split end Edwin Collins took a pitchout from quarterback Bruce Gadd on a reverse. Collins pulled up and threw back across the field to flanker Ron Arceneaux who was hauled down at the Arkansas 29 after a 43-yard gain. Gary Ferguson picked up a first down at the 19 on two running plays. The Razorbacks held and Mark Williams missed a 35-yard field goal.

Arkansas couldn't move from their 20 and Rice got excellent field position when Bruce Henley returned the

Hog punt 52 yards to the Razorback 11. Gadd was thrown for a nine-yard loss on second down which led to a 29-yard field goal by Williams. Rice led 3-0.

Jon Richardson fumbled the Owl kickoff and Johnny Peterson recovered for Rice on the Arkansas 20. A holding penalty set the Owls back to the 35. John Coleman ran for five, Gadd passed to Collins for 15, then found Collins open again for 13 to the two. Boyce scored on the next play. Williams converted and Rice led 10-0.

The teams then exchanged punts until Rice's second possession of the second quarter. Gadd was then intercepted by Billy Burns at the Arkansas 29. The Razorbacks scored in nine snaps. The big plays were Marsh White's 20-yard run and quarterback Joe Ferguson's pass to Mike Reppond for 18 yards. Joe Ferguson scored from the nine on a keeper. Mike Kirkland converted and Rice led 10-7.

Two possessions later Arkansas reached the Owl 18 and Kirkland kicked a 35-yard field goal. With 26 seconds left in the first half the score was tied 10-10.

A scrambling Joe Ferguson (11) is chased by a trio of Owls. Cornelius Walker (76), David Snelling (50) and John Kelly (89) close in on their target.

Williams missed a 38-yard field goal which was set up when Richardson fumbled the second half kickoff at his 29. Later in the period he got another chance when Rodrigo Barnes recovered a Joe Ferguson fumble at the Hog 31. This time he connected on a 48-yard effort and Rice led 13-10.

Arkansas received the kickoff and scored in four plays. On third down four play Joe Ferguson ran a keeper for 27 yards to the Rice 39. On the following play Dickey Morton bolted through on the left and hot footed it 39 yards for a touchdown. Kirkland converted and Arkansas led 17-13.

Mike Davis returned an Owl punt 36 yards to the Rice 15 to set up the next Hog score. On a third and seven play Joe Ferguson lost nine which brought in Kirkland who kicked a 38-yard field goal. Arkansas led 20-13.

Rice got a break as the third quarter was coming to an end. Arkansas had forced an Owl punt at their 49, but Williams was roughed on the kick and Rice retained possession at the Hog 34. Gary Ferguson reached the 14 on three carries. Four plays later Williams kicked a 32-yard field goal with three seconds left in the third period. Arkansas led 20-16.

Early in the final quarter Williams missed a 48-yard field goal. Two possessions later Gadd was intercepted by Jim Irwin at the Arkansas five. Drew Toole punted on third down and Henley returned 13 yards to the Hog 39.

After picking up a first down the Owls floundered and needed 22 yards on fourth down. Gadd passed to Gary Butler, on a post pattern, for 27 yards to the 13. One minute remained in the game. Gadd passed to Gary Ferguson for five yards and Rice used its last time out with 0:47 left. Gadd ran for four, then followed that with a pass to Arceneaux for a first down at the one. Coleman was held for no gain. Skipping a huddle Gadd took the snap and threw out of bounds. Rice was guilty of grounding the ball, but Arkansas was offsides so the play was run over. Boyce scored on the next play with 0:01 on the clock. Williams converted and Rice had won 23-20.

	Rice	Arkansas
First downs	12	11
Rushes-yards	50-121	52-204
Passing yards	159	37
Return yards	104	39
Passes	10-26-2	3-12-0
Punts	6-35	10-36
Fumbles-lost	1-0	5-3
Penalties-yards	4-58	2-25

Rice ....10 0 6 7—23
Arkansas ....0 10 10 0—20
Rice—FG Williams 29
Rice—Boyce 2 run (Williams kick)
Ark—Ferguson 9 run (Kirkland kick)
Ark—FG Kirkland 35
Rice—FG Williams 48
Ark—Morton 39 run (Kirkland kick)
Ark—FG Kirkland 38
Rice—FG Williams 32
Rice—Boyce 1 run (Williams kick)
A—51,475

151

Robert Giblin (24) has just intercepted a State pass and begun his 51-yard journey for a Cougar touchdown. Bubba Broussard (2) and Randy Peacock (31) come running to help.

HOUSTON 48 - COLORADO STATE 13

It was homecoming for the Houston Cougars and a crowd of 23,143 was on hand in the Astrodome. Also showing up were the Colorado State Rams who, after eight straight losses, were looking for their first victory of the season. They now have lost nine straight.

The first quarter was rather lackadaisical as both teams seemed to be going nowhere. The Cougars did move to the Rams nine-yard line, but a fourth down running play failed. Only seven seconds remained in the opening period when lightening struck. Facing a third down two at the State 47 quarterback D. C. Nobles dropped back and hit Bryan Willingham for a touchdown. Willingham caught the ball at the 10 going full blast. Ricky Terrell converted and Houston led 7-0.

Having broken the scoring ice the Cougars put 21 points on the board in the second quarter. Two of the scores were the end result of pass interceptions. Deryl McGallion intercepted Ram quarterback Pat Juliana

and returned six yards to the State 49. The Rams were guilty of piling on McGallion and this moved the ball to the 34. After reaching the nine in eight plays, Nobles passed to Puddin' Jones in the left flat. Jones ran it in for the touchdown and with Terrell's kick Houston led 14-0.

Robert Giblin brought the Cougars right back. He intercepted Juliana at the Houston 49 and went down the sideline for 51 yards and a touchdown. Terrell kicked good and Houston led 21-0.

When the Cougars kicked off the Ram's Johnny Square, formerly of Houston Yates, gathered the ball in at his four. Heading upfield he broke through at his 35 and outran the pursuing Cougars for a State touchdown. Wade Smylie converted and Houston led 21-7.

Houston punched across once more before halftime. Robert Ford returned the Rams kickoff 37 yards to his 44. The Cougars moved 56 yards in seven plays, the big gainer being a Nobles pass to tight end Marty Watts for

Marshall Johnson (13) evades a bunch of Rams as he scores Houston's final touchdown from the seven. Other Cougars shown are Wayne Johnson (29) and Walker Westerlage (71).

17 yards. Nobles scored from the six on a keeper around tight end. Terrell converted and Houston led at the half 28-7.

Early in the third period another interception led to a Cougar touchdown. Jeff Bouche grabbed this one and returned 15 yards to the Ram 41. Seven plays later Nobles flipped over the goal from the one. Terrell kicked the extra point and Houston led 35-7.

When Houston got the ball again Terry Peel replaced Nobles at quarterback. He moved the Cougars 55 yards in eight plays. The big gainer came on a 24-yard pass from Peel to Ford. Milton Ward got the touchdown from the one. Terrell's kick was good and Houston led 42-7.

The Rams came back and drove to the Houston one, but failed to score. Under a heavy State rush Hal Roberts punt was short and the Rams were successful on this possession. After reaching the Cougar 22 Juliana rolled left on a keeper, cut back to the middle and ran all the way to the Houston end zone. A two-point pass attempt failed and with 13:09 left in the game Houston led 42-13.

Bouche's second interception set up the final Cougar

touchdown. He returned his theft 44 yards to the Ram 35. Freshman quarterback Lester Saucier came in and took Houston the 35 yards. His pass of 22 yards to Wayne Johnson got most of the needed yardage. Marshall Johnson scored on a weaving run from the seven. A pass for two points failed and with 45 seconds left Houston led 48-13.

Puddin' Jones was the leading rusher getting 103 yards on 20 carries. The only bright spot for Colorado was their kickoff returns. Square returned four for 151 yards and Noah Palmer ran back three for 94 yards. The "Mad Dogs" Houston defense intercepted four passes and recovered one Ram fumble.

	CSU	Hou
First downs	9	19
Rushes-yards	46-135	63-252
Passing yardage	37	129
Return yardage	12	138
Passes	5-17-4	6-13-0
Punts	6-43-5	5-34-2
Fumbles lost	1-1	4-2
Penalties-yards	2-30	3-31

Colorado State	....	0 7 0 6—13
Houston	....	7 21 14 6—48

UH—Willingham 47 pass from Nobles (Terrell kick)
UH—Jones 9 pass from Nobles (Terrell kick)
UH—Giblin 51 pass interception (Terrell kick)
CSU—Square 96 kickoff return (Smylie kick)
UH—Nobles 6 run (Terrell kick)
UH—Nobles 1 run (Terrell kick)
UH—Ward 1 run (Terrell kick)
CSU—Juliana 22 run (pass failed)
UH—Johnson 7 run (pass failed)
A—23,143

153

Gary Lacy (23) goes for short yardage to gain a Baylor first down in the second quarter. Blocking for Lacy are Kenny Townsend (90), Gene Wilson (37), Harold Rodgers (50) and Richard Mason (66). Longhorns shown are Jay Arnold (41) and Tommy Lee (45).

TEXAS 17 - BAYLOR 3

The Baylor Bears, the doormat of the SWC in recent years and a unanimous choice for the cellar this year, must be doing something right. Before a record crowd of 48,394 they had a chance to derail the Longhorn Conference Championship Express and in the process gain a tie for the league lead. In addition to all that they had a shot at that elusive Cotton Bowl berth which they have yet to experience.

What happens when an irresistable force meets an immovable object? After a little over 45 minutes the immovable object gives a little and the irresistible force just keeps right on pounding away. Going into the fourth quarter the Longhorns had managed only four first downs and fullback Roosevelt Leaks had 56 yards on 12 carries. Fifteen minutes later Texas had 16 first downs and Leaks had amassed 162 yards and two touchdowns. For their last quarter surge the Longhorns used two tight ends on offense and ran, and ran, and ran. Not once did the ball get over four feet off the ground.

The Bear defense must share some of their glory with the Texas defense who, in the fourth quarter, held Baylor to one first down. In the first half when the Longhorn offense couldn't move, the defense again and again stopped the Baylor offense and set up the only points that Texas made in the first 30 minutes.

Baylor kicked off and the Longhorns lost Don Burrisk to a knee injury on their first series. When forced to punt quarterback-punter Alan Lowry shanked one out of bounds at the Baylor 45, a punt of 17 yards. The Bears reached the Texas 25 mainly on a 21-yard run by Gary Lacey. On fourth down three at the 18 Mike Conradt kicked a 35-yard field goal. With less than five minutes elapsed the Bears led 3-0.

The Longhorns best first half effort came early in the second quarter when they moved from their 20 to the Baylor 43. It ended when Donald Ealey fumbled when hit hard and Tommy Turnipseede recovered for Baylor.

Later Lowry quick-kicked 82 yards to the Bear 16, but

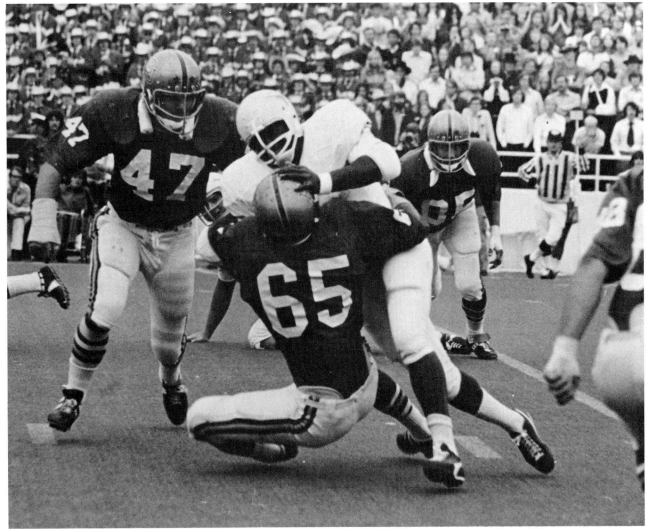

Mike Wilder (65) makes the stop on Roosevelt Leaks on this first quarter play. Paul Savage (47) prepares to help Wilder. For three quarters the Bears held Leaks in check, but in the fourth quarter it was a different story.

Baylor brought the ball back out of danger before punting at the Texas 40. Then with 1:25 left Jeffrey fumbled at his 13 and Bruce Cannon recovered for Texas at the Bear five. Lowry ran over on first down, but Texas was offside. From the 10 Lowry was dumped for a five-yard loss by Roger Goree. After two incomplete passes Billy Schott kicked a 32-yard field goal. At the half it was a 3-3 standoff.

To start the third quarter the Bears had their best drive of the game, but it was all for naught. Lacey and Brian Kilgore did most of the damage. Kilgore caught two Jeffrey passes. One for 13 and another for 15. Longhorn pass interference put the ball at the Texas 19. Kilgore ran for four and on second down Jeffrey tried to hit Charles Dancer in the end zone. Mike Rowan intercepted for Texas.

Late in the third quarter Jeffrey fumbled at his 35 and Bill Rutherford recovered for Texas. On fourth and one at the 26 the Longhorns shunned the field goal and went for the first down. Goree and Tommy Stewart dropped Lowry for no gain. The noise from the Baylor partisans was deafening.

Following a Baylor punt Texas started at their 30 as the fourth quarter opened. Staying on the ground it was all Leaks and Lowry. Lowry set up the touchdown on a 24-yard keeper to the Baylor two. Two plays later Leaks scored and with Schott's conversion Texas led 10-3.

Goree stopped Texas on their next possession with a fumble recovery and when the Longhorns got the ball again it was at their 15 with 6:15 to play. They marched 85 yards in 6:05 and probably would not have scored, but Baylor used all their timeouts to stop the clock in hopes that they could get the ball back. Leaks carried 12 times and gained 59 of the 85 yards. He scored from the one with 10 seconds left and Schott made it 17-3 with his conversion.

	Texas	Baylor
First downs	16	15
Rushes-yards	58-263	52-141
Passing yards	33	87
Return yards	4	13
Passes	3-14-0	7-20-2
Punts	8-40	8-36
Fumbles lost	4-2	2-2
Penalties-yards	3-36	5-46

Texas ....0 3 0 14—17
Baylor ....3 0 0 0— 3
Bay—FG Conradt 35
UT—FG Schott 32
UT—Leaks 1 run (Schott kick)
UT—Leaks 2 run (Schott kick)
A—48,394

SYNOPSIS

10

TOP TEN

1. Southern Cal
2. Alabama
3. Michigan
4. Oklahoma
5. Nebraska
6. Penn State
7. Texas
8. LSU
9. Ohio State
10. Notre Dame

UPSET OF WEEK:

Michigan State 19 - Ohio State 12

SWC OFFENSIVE PLAYER OF WEEK

Jerry Sisemore, Tackle, Texas
Travis Roach, Guard, Texas

SWC DEFENSIVE PLAYER OF WEEK

Charles Davis, Tackle, TCU

FRESHMAN RESULTS

Arkansas 22 - Tulsa 19
Baylor 10 - Rice 6
Texas 23 - TCU 21
Texas Tech 28 - Texas A&M 13

SWC TEAM LEADERS FOR SEASON

OFFENSE	AVG.
Rushing	Texas 291 yds.
Passing	Rice 213 yds.
Total	Houston 381 yds.

DEFENSE	AVG.
Rushing	SMU 119 yds.
Passing	Baylor 93 yds.
Total	Baylor 272 yds.

SEASON RECORDS

	W	L	T
Texas	7	1	0
Texas Tech	7	2	0
TCU	5	3	0
Arkansas	5	4	0
SMU	4	4	0
Baylor	4	4	0
Houston	4	4	1
Rice	3	4	1
Texas A & M	3	6	0

CONFERENCE

	W	L	T
Texas	5	0	0
Texas Tech	3	2	0
Baylor	2	2	0
TCU	2	2	0
Arkansas	2	3	0
Texas A & M	2	3	0
Rice	1	3	0
SMU	1	3	0

Eleventh Week
November 18

39 YEARS AGO
NOVEMBER 18, 1933
Arkansas 63 - Hendrix 0
Texas Tech 13 - Baylor 0
Texas A&M 27 - Rice 0
Centenary 7 - SMU 0
TCU 30 - Texas 0

Lyle Blackwood (25) fumbled Texas' first punt at his 40-yard line. The ball bounces behind David McGinnis (27) and Tommy Landry (22). Lonnie Bennett (33), approaching from the right, recovered for Texas at the TCU 39.

TEXAS 27 - TCU 0

The sky was gray and the field wet when the Frogs and Longhorns met in Amon-Carter field before 33,536. It was a miserable display of ball handling as both teams fumbled 15 times and lost four apiece. Fortunately for Texas they scored three times before playing give away with the ball. As for scoring, the Horned Frogs had not scored on Texas in two and one-half games and they added four more quarters to their string.

TCU held Texas on their first possession and quarterback Alan Lowry punted to Lyle Blackwood. Running forward Blackwood fumbled the punt and Lonnie Bennett recovered for Texas at the Frog 39. On fourth and one at the 30 Roosevelt Leaks burst through for 11 yards to the 19. Tommy Landry ran for nine to the 10 and on the next play picked up another nine to the one. Lowry sneaked in from there and Billy Schott converted to make it 7-0 for Texas with 4:35 used up on the clock.

Following the Texas kickoff Ronnie Webb, on first down, ran for 18 yards. A motion penalty nulified the run.

Two plays later quarterback Terry Drennan fumbled when hit and Bruce Cannon recovered for Texas at the TCU 27. Leaks and Landry gained the seven, then Lowry ran three straight keepers. He scored from the one on the third carry. Schott converted and Texas led 14-0 with six minutes left in the first quarter.

After the kickoff TCU proceeded to move to the Texas 41 before punting. As play moved into the second quarter a Longhorn punt from the end zone gave TCU possession at the Texas 47. Mike Luttrell fumbled on first down and Sherman Lee covered the ball for Texas at his 44. A 22-yard pass from Lowry to Jimmy Moore gained most of the yardage in reaching the Frog 30. Lowry kept and ran 14 to the 16. Then Leaks and Lowry took turns carrying to move to the TCU three. Lowry found a huge hole and scored standing. Schott kicked good and Texas led 21-0.

For the rest of the first half Texas tried to catch up with TCU in the fumble department. Donald Ealey fumbled at the Frog 37 and Ed Robinson recovered for TCU. Then

Longhorn quarterback Alan Lowry (15)is brought down to earth (and mud) by Frogs' Gary Whitman (36) and Tookie Berry (54).

later, Leaks fumbled at the end of a run which put him over 1,000 yards gained for the season. Blackwood recovered for the Horned Frogs at his 15.

If you were late getting back to your seat after halftime you didn't miss much. Both teams failed to pick up one first down in the third quarter. TCU did threaten when a Longhorn fumble gave them possession at the Texas 25. On fourth down at the 21 Bill Rutherford sacked Drennan for an eight yard loss and the punt-filled quarter ended. Also crowded into the third period was another Longhorn fumble and a Lowry quick-kick which was fair caught by Blackwood at the Texas 39.

In the fourth quarter the Frogs reached the Texas 48, but then a Drennan pass was tipped by intended receiver Webb and intercepted by Tommy Keel of Texas.

Approaching the midway point in the quarter TCU's Greg Anderson punted from his 18 to Jimmy Moore at the Texas 40. Following the sideline Moore broke into the clear downfield, but lost his balance and fell at the Frog 18. Marty Akins replaced Lowry at quarterback and the Longhorns scored in four plays. Bennett ran for eight yards and Dan Steakley barreled eight more to the two.

Two plays later Akins scored from the two. The last Texas fumble occurred when the snap for extra point was fumbled and the attempt failed. Texas led 27-0.

Drennan moved the Frogs 62 yards to the Texas 11, but a pass intended for Lane Bowen was tipped by Adrian Ford and intercepted by Gary Yeoman in the end zone. A short Lowry punt and a late hit penalty put TCU back on the Texas 33. Drennan, Ronnie Littleton and Larry Harris moved the ball to the two. Drennan lost a yard and on fourth down the shutout was preserved when Harris was stopped at the two with 29 seconds remaining.

Texas won its fifth straight SWC crown and a Cotton Bowl berth New Years Day. An oddity in the game occurred when all four touchdowns came on quarterback sneaks.

	Texas	TCU
First downs	12	12
Rushes-yards	62-205	58-172
Passing yards	48	44
Return yards	0	1
Passes	3-10-0	6-13-2
Punts	10-37	10-33
Fumbles lost	7-4	8-4
Penalties-yards	4-31	5-45

Texas	14	7	0	6—27
TCU	0	0	0	0—0

Tex—Lowry 1 run (Schott kick)
Tex—Lowry 1 run (Schott kick)
Tex—Lowry 3 run (Schott kick)
Tex—Akins 2 run (kick failed)
A—33,536

159

SMU quarterback Keith Bobo (19) hands off to Wayne Morris (25) as Alvin Maxson (28) leads interference. Maxson scored two of the Mustang touchdowns and Bobo passed for the other.

SMU 22 - ARKANSAS 7

It was snowing, it was 34 degrees, it was Arkansas' 50th homecoming. The weather matched the results as far as the Razorback rooters were concerned. A crowd of 38,342 braved the elements in Razorback Stadium to watch the Mustangs and Hogs meet for the 48th time.

The game was another bitter pill for the Razorbacks in a season that has been full of bitter pills. Their main trouble was six lost fumbles, two pass interceptions and SMU tackle Louie Kelcher, not necessarily in that order. Kelcher made 14 tackles, recovered two fumbles and caused another. One bright spot for Arkansas came when Dickey Morton became the first Razorback to ever rush for more than 1,000 yards in one season. It was a sweet victory for the Mustangs as they had not defeated Arkansas in Arkansas since 1954.

Jon Richardson returned SMU's opening kickoff to his 23. Walter Nelson started at quarterback. This was the first varsity game the senior had ever started. On second down he recovered a fumble and on third down he lost a fumble to Kelcher. SMU had possession on the Arkansas 22. Three plays gained only two yards. Clint Hackney came in and kicked a 37-yard field goal. SMU led 3-0.

The teams then settled down and exchanged punts until late in the period when Arkansas started moving from their 48. Nelson passed to Matt Morrison for 11 yards, then came back to hit Steve Hedgepeth. The pass-run combination covered 34 yards to the Mustang seven. Three plays later Morton went over from the three. Mike Kirkland converted and Arkansas led 7-3.

Early in the second quarter Richardson fumbled a Mustang punt and Oscar Roan recovered for SMU at the Arkansas 28. The Mustangs regained the lead in six plays. Alvin Maxson gained to the 17 on two runs. On a third down and 10 quarterback Keith Bobo kept for nine yards to the eight. On fourth and one Bobo passed to Rory Best for the touchdown. The extra point was no good and SMU led 9-7.

Richardson fumbled the kickoff and Robert Gibson

Dickey Morton (33) is grabbed here by Leonard Carey (31), but during the game he went over 1,000 yards rushing for the season to become the first Razorback in history to do so. Marsh White (32) blocks Kris Silverthorn (85). To the far right is Mustang Mike Leitko (74).

recovered for SMU at the Razorback 23. Three running plays and the Mustangs were back in the Arkansas end zone again. Wayne Morris ran for three, Maxson for 7 and Maxson again for 13 and the touchdown. Hackney kicked good and SMU led 16-7

Joe Ferguson entered the game at quarterback late in the second quarter. The Razorbacks moved to the SMU 12 mainly on two Ferguson to Mike Reppond passes good for 16 and 19 yards. Ferguson was dropped by Kelcher for a 10-yard loss and Kirkland tried a 39-yard field goal with seven second left. The kick was wide.

Neither team could score in the third quarter as penalties plagued both sides. As the quarter was coming to a close Ferguson was intercepted by Jim Ryan at the Hog 40 and returned to the 25. Morris ran for nine and two plays later Bobo passed to Best for 12 yards to the three. On the second play of the fourth quarter Maxson scored from the one. The two-point conversion failed and SMU led 22-7.

The remainder of the quarter was a nightmare for both teams It went something like this: Ferguson fumbled and Don Randell recovered at the SMU 26. Two plays later

Morris fumbled and Doug Yoder recovered at the SMU 29. Six plays later Ferguson lost five yards and fumbled to Leonard Carey at the SMU 20. After reaching the Hog 41 SMU was penalized 15 yards for a personal foul. Sam McLarty punted and the Mustangs were penalized for interfering with the fair catch. Ferguson threw two incompletions, then was intercepted by Ryan at the SMU 46. Morris lost 14 yards on third down and McLarty punted. Scott Bull came in at quarterback for Arkansas and six plays later fumbled the snap to Mack Rogers at the SMU 22. Four running plays ran out the clock. By then most of the crowd had left.

	SMU	Ark.
First downs	11	16
Rushes-yards	59-164	41-115
Passing yards	181	161
Return yards	56	32
Passes	3-8-0	11-22-2
Punts	9-36	6-40
Fumbles lost	4-2	9-6
Penalties-yards	6-51	1-20

SMU ....3 13 0 6—22
Arkansas ....7 0 0 0— 7
SMU—FG Hackney 37
Ark—Morton 3 run (Kirkland kick)
SMU—Best 8 pass from Bobo (kick failed)
SMU—Maxson 13 run (Hackney kick)
SMU—Maxson 1 run (run failed)
A—38,342

Tommy Turnipseede (33) stops Lawrence Williams (42) on this play, but Williams returned the opening kickoff 67 yards which led to Tech's first score. The two Bears getting ready to pounce are Keith Stone (48) and Dale Lechler (80).

TEXAS TECH 13 - BAYLOR 7

The Red Raiders and Bears, once in the thick of the SWC race, met in a game which would have bearing on who the conference runner-up would be. There were 18,000 on hand in Baylor Stadium who watched both teams threaten, all through the game, to beat themselves. Baylor carried out its threat. They fumbled and lost their first kickoff, had their first pass intercepted, their first punt was partially blocked and they fumbled away the reception on Tech's first punt. In all they fumbled six times, lost five and had two passes intercepted. The Red Raiders didn't exactly have glue on their fingers as they lost four of five fumbles. They had a secret weapon lurking on the sideline however. Cliff Hoskins had gained only 167 yards this year in seeing limited action. When Doug McCutchen was injured in the first quarter Hoskins replaced him and rushed for a total of 204 yards.

Baylor's kickoff opened the game. Lawrence Williams returned 67 yards before Robert Weygandt brought him down at the Bear 33. McCutchen and James Mosley gained on the ground to the Baylor four before the Bears held. Don Grimes came in and kicked a 21-yard field goal. With 5:20 gone Tech led 3-0.

Pat McNeil fumbled the Red Raider kickoff and Tech's David Knaus recovered at the Baylor 29. Moments later McCutchen lost the ball when hit and Darrel Luce covered it for the Bears at his 18. McCutchen was injured on this play. The Raiders came right back when Kenneth Wallace intercepted Neal Jeffrey at the Baylor 44. Rufus Myers fumbled at the Bear 31 and Coy Zunker recovered for Baylor. Myers was replaced by Hoskins on the next Tech possession.

This came shortly when Tommy Stewart "all thumbed" a punt at his 23. Williams recovered for Tech. Roger Goree forced a field goal attempt when he dumped quarterback Joe Barnes for a four yard loss. Grimes kicked good from 34 yards and with 30 seconds left in the first quarter Tech led 6-0.

Billy Wilson returned the Raider kickoff 33 yards to his

Bear fullback Gene Wilson (37) gets good yardage on this run during the Baylor touchdown drive. Tim Mills (63) helped open the hole as Billy Wilson (30) carries out his fake in the background. Tech defenders are Donald Rives (51) and Danny Willis (23).

42. Jeffrey, using mostly Brian Kilgore and Pat McNeil, drove the Bears to the Tech 10 in nine plays. There Jeffrey fumbled the snap and Donald Rives got the ball for Tech. The Red Raiders, before halftime, got all of their fumbles out of their system by fumbling twice more.

A major penalty halted the first Baylor drive of the third quarter, but they came downfield again, upon regaining possession, to reach the Tech 37. There a handoff was lost and Tom Ryan recovered for Tech. The next time they got the ball another fumble, this one on a pitchout, was recovered by Gaines Baty at his 41. The Red Raiders scored in six plays. The big gainer was a 31-yard run by Hoskins. He also scored the touchdown from the three with 2:33 left in the third period. Grimes converted and Tech led 13-0.

The Bears took the kickoff and drove 76 yards to score. The drive was kept alive on a roughing the kicker penalty at the Tech 45. With the ball at the 30 Baylor scored in six more plays. The payoff came on a Jeffrey pass to Kilgore from the 15. Kilgore caught the ball and was literally knocked into the end zone. Mike Conradt kicked good and with 12:14 left Tech led 13-7.

The Red Raiders then played ball control and when Baylor got the ball again only 6:45 remained. Unable to move the Bears had to punt the ball away. Using Hoskins again and again the Raiders drove from their 39 to the Baylor three. There a Grimes field goal attempt was blocked by Luce which gave the Bears one last chance.

The chance was short lived as Jeffrey was intercepted by Danny Willis at the Bear 34. The Red Raiders then ran out the clock.

Tech received word before the game that they had been invited to the Sun Bowl to meet North Carolina. Hoskins was presented the game ball by his teammates.

	Tech	Baylor
First downs	20	19
Rushes-yards	72-329	47-213
Passing yards	18	60
Return yards	0	0
Passes	1-6-0	5-16-2
Punts	4-25	4-33
Fumbles	4-5	5-6
Penalties-yards	4-40	6-34

Texas Tech ....6 0 7 0—13
Baylor ....0 0 0 7— 7
Tech—FG Grimes 21
Tech—FG Grimes 34
Tech—Hoskins 3 run (Grimes kick)
Bay—Kilgore 15 pass from Jeffrey (Conradt kick)
A—18,000

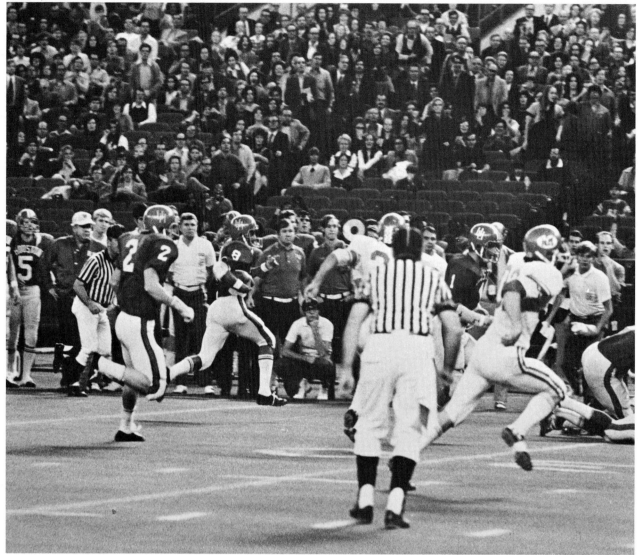

Howard Ebow (8) heads upfield after grabbing Houston's only interception of the game. Leading interference for Ebow is Deryl McGallion (1) and Bubba Broussard (2).

HOUSTON 33 - NEW MEXICO 14

The Cougars jumped above .500 for the first time this season and in accomplishing this they beat New Mexico soundly. An Astrodome crowd of 20,366 was on hand as Houston's offense rolled up a total of 27 first downs and 553 yards. Fullback Nat "Puddin" Jones, a Brady senior, blasted forth for 184 yards to put him over 1,000 yards for the season. He scored three touchdowns. This was the first ever meeting between Houston and the Lobos from Albuquerque.

New Mexico scored first as they took the opening kickoff and moved 51 yards in four plays. Ben Turner's 39 yard return set the Lobos up on their 49. On the fourth play quarterback Bruce Boone went left, stumbled, found his footing and ran 33 yards down the sideline for a touchdown. Keith McDonald converted and with 1:41 elapsed New Mexico led 7-0.

Houston wasted no time in tying it up. Following the

kickoff they drove 83 yards in 13 plays. Jones gained 40 of the needed yards which included a 15-yard run. Quarterback D. C. Nobles threw in a run of 17 yards. Jones got the last five over left guard. Ricky Terrell converted and the score was tied at 7-7.

The next time the Cougars came away empty handed as Nobles was stopped for no gain on a fourth down play at the New Mexico four. One play later, Houston had the ball back, Boone fumbled when hit by Howard Ebow and Jeff Bouche fell on the ball at the four. On his third straight carry over right tackle Jones scored. A bad center snap foiled the extra point. With 1:37 left in the first quarter Houston led 13-7.

The previous Lobo fumble cost them a Cougar touchdown. Their next one cost them a New Mexico touchdown. Mainly on a 41-yard run up the middle by Fred Henry, the Lobos reached the Houston 10. Two

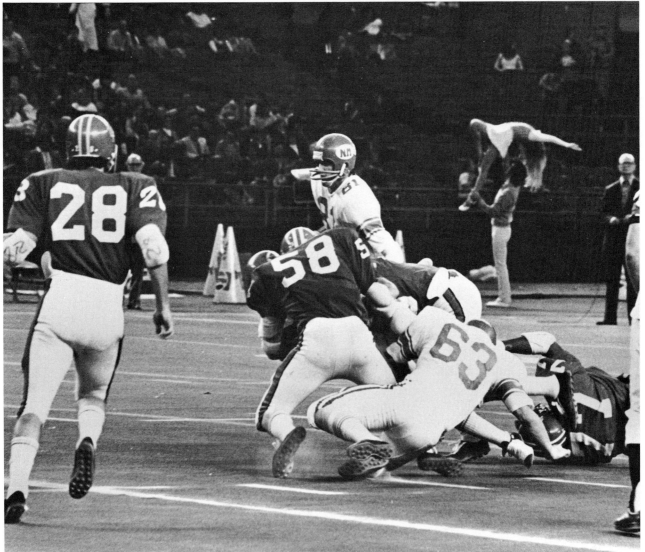

While cheerleaders performed in the background the "Mad Dog" defense was playing "sack the quarterback." Bill Jones (58) helps Everett Little (77) and an unidentified Cougar bring down Eddie Dunaway of New Mexico. Tommy Kaiser (28) rushes in to help.

plays later, at the seven, Boone lost the snap and Bill Stohler recovered for the Cougars at his eight.

Eight plays covered 92 yards and Houston had another touchdown. Jones carried for 20 yards. Nobles passed to Marty Watts for 18 yards and a 25-yard pass to Robert Ford reached the Lobo 25. Jones blasted his way for 12 to the 13. He then found a hole up the middle to score from the 13. A two-point pass play failed and at the half Houston led 19-7.

Robert Ford started and ended the next Houston drive. He returned the second half kickoff 29 yards to his 36. Seven plays later he caught a 23-yard Nobles pass for the touchdown. Nobles also had a 20 yarder to Watts during the drive. Terrell kicked good and Houston led 26-7.

Less than four minutes later Nobles again burned the Lobos with his passing. The Cougars drove 47 yards in four plays. The fourth play was a 32-yard pass to flanker Del Stanley. The perfectly thrown pass settled into Stanley's arms just as he crossed the New Mexico goal line going full steam. Terrell kicked the extra point and

with a little over eight minutes remaining in the third period Houston led 33-7.

Late in the game the Lobos closed out the scoring. Halfback Henry passed to tight end Ken Smith for nine yards and a New Mexico touchdown. A Boone pass to Paul Labarerre covered 36 yards and helped set up the score. McDonald converted and with 1:26 on the clock Houston led 33-14.

Nobles hit on 15 of 19 passes for 221 yards and two touchdowns. In the last two games he has directed the Cougars into the enemy end zone 10 times.

	New Mexico	Houston
First downs	10	27
Rushes-yards	42-158	67-332
Passing yards	158	221
Return yards	51	80
Passes	8-15-1	15-26-1
Punts	9-43	6-42
Fumbles lost	5-2	1-1
Penalties yards	5-50	9-100

New Mexico ....7 0 0 7—14
Houston ....13 6 14 0—33
NM—Boone 33 run (McDonald kick)
UH—Jones 5 run (Terrell kick)
UH—Jones 1 run (kick failed)
UH—Jones 13 run (pass failed)
UH—Ford 23 pass from Nobles (Terrell kick)
UH—Stanley 32 pass from Nobles (Terrell kick)
NM—Smith 9 pass from Henry (McDonald kick)
A—20,366

Early in the fourth quarter the Cadets reached the Owl 11-yard line, but there Ronnie Hubby (28) fumbled and John Kelly (not shown) recovered for Rice. Owls pictured are Preston Anderson (40), David Snellings (50), Larry Walling (80) and Rodney Norton (59).

RICE 20 - TEXAS A&M 14

Both teams were coming off big wins. The Owls over Arkansas and the Aggies over SMU. A crowd of 28,231 sat huddled in the cold at Kyle Field to watch the 57th meeting between the Owls and Cadets.

In the first quarter both teams had shots at a field goal and that is all. First, Rice moved from their 19 to the A&M 30 and when the drive stopped there Mark Williams attempted a 47-yard field goal which missed. Five minutes later the Aggies gave Pat McDermott the same opportunity from the same distance and he missed.

Early in the second quarter, following a Williams punt, the Aggies had possession at their 35. A & M stormed 65 yards in 12 plays. Quarterback Don Dean and fullback Brad Dusek carried the load. Dean had runs of 12 and eight yards and Dusek had 13 and nine. Skip Walker ran around the left side for 11 yards and an apparent touchdown, but it was ruled he stepped out of bounds at

the three. A disgusted Walker slammed the ball to the ground and the Cadets were penalized 15 yards for spiking. The Aggies overcame that setback as moments later Dean passed five yards to Richard Osborne for the score. McDermott converted and with 9:13 gone in the second period A & M led 7-0.

Rice received the kickoff and couldn't move. Williams punted 51 yards to Carl Roaches at the Aggie 16. Roaches broke through a crowd at his 45 and was off to the races. The 84-yard return along with McDermott's extra point put A&M ahead 14-0 with five minutes left until the half.

The Aggies had an opportunity to leave the Owls floundering when Ed Simonini tipped a pass thrown by Owl quarterback Bruce Gadd and Grady Hoermann intercepted at the Rice 28. Hoermann was charged with throwing the ball in the air and that cost the Aggies 15 yards. Rice held and regained possession at their 14.

John Coleman (44) is stopped on the A & M one by the Aggie defense. Those identified are Grady Hoermann (31), Al Thurmond (29) and Larry Ellis (46) Owls pictured are Bruce Gadd (10), Roland Boyce (36) and Gary Butler (81). Boyce scored on the next play.

Gadd went to the air and moved the Owls 86 yards in just six plays, all passes. He hit Gary Butler for 25 and then passed to John Coleman for three. He came back to Butler for 29 yards. His next pass was incomplete, but he regained his touch as he fired to Edwin Collins for 17 to the Aggie 12. Collins also caught the next pass, this one for 12 and the touchdown. Williams converted and A&M led 14-7 with one minute left before halftime.

On Rice's second possession of the third quarter, Gadd took the Owls 91 yards in 10 plays. Two big plays were passes to Collins and Butler for 32 and 27 yards respectively. After reaching the Aggie 27 the Owls stayed on the ground and five plays later Roland Boyce wedged in for the touchdown from the one. Williams converted and with 5:58 left in the period it was a 14-14 standoff.

As the fourth quarter approached, a Robert Murski punt got a good bounce and carried to the Owl four. Four downs later Williams punted to the Rice 41. The Aggies drove to the Owl 11 as the final period opened, there Ronnie Hubby fumbled and John Kelly recovered for

Rice. The Owls drove to the Aggie 27 where Williams kicked a 44-yard field goal and Rice led 17-14.

Following the Owl kickoff Bruce Henley intercepted a Don Dean third down pass and returned the ball 26 yards to the A & M 22. The Cadets held and on fourth down Williams connected on a 35-yard field goal. Rice led 20-14 with 6:10 on the clock.

On the Cadets' next possession Dean was again intercepted by Henley. Williams missed a 26-yard field goal try. Moments later Bubba Bean fumbled a Dean pitchout and after a wild scramble Larry Walling recovered for Rice at the A & M three. With 1:19 remaining the Owls ran out the clock on three plays.

	Rice	A & M
First downs	22	14
Rushes-yards	45-120	47-189
Passing yards	271	62
Return yards	70	100
Passes	16-29-1	8-13-2
Punts	6-39	5-39
Fumbles-lost	0-1	2-5
Penalties-yards	4-36	7-55

Rice ....0 7 7 6—20
Texas A&M...........0 14 0 0—14
A&M—Osborne 5 pass from Dean (McDermott kick)
A&M—Roaches 84 punt return (McDermott kick)
R—Collins 12 pass from Gadd (Williams kick)
R—Boyce 1 run (Williams kick)
R—FG 44 Williams
R—FG 35 Williams
A—28,231

SYNOPSIS

TOP TEN

1. Southern Cal
2. Alabama
3. Michigan
4. Oklahoma
5. Nebraska
6. Penn State
7. Texas
8. LSU
9. Ohio State
10. Auburn

SWC OFFENSIVE PLAYER OF WEEK

Cliff Hoskins, Tailback, Texas Tech

SWC DEFENSIVE PLAYER OF WEEK

Louis Kelcher, Tackle, SMU

FRESHMAN RESULTS:

Texas A & M 10 - Texas 8
Air Force 38 - Houston 25

UPSET OF WEEK:

South Carolina 24 - Florida State 21

SWC TEAM LEADERS FOR SEASON

OFFENSE	AVG.	DEFENSE	AVG.
Rushing..........................Texas 281 yds.		Rushing..........................SMU 119 yds.	
Passing...........................Rice 220 yds.		Passing...........................Baylor 83 yds.	
Total...........................Houston 398 yds.		Total...........................SMU 278 yds.	

SEASON RECORDS	W	L	T
Texas.............................	8	1	0
Texas Tech........................	8	2	0
TCU..............................	5	4	0
SMU..............................	5	4	0
Houston...........................	5	4	1
Rice..............................	4	4	1
Arkansas..........................	5	5	0
Baylor............................	4	5	0
Texas A & M.......................	3	7	0

CONFERENCE	W	L	T
Texas.............................	6	0	0
Texas Tech........................	4	2	0
Rice..............................	2	3	0
SMU..............................	2	3	0
Baylor............................	2	3	0
TCU..............................	2	3	0
Arkansas..........................	2	4	0
Texas A & M.......................	2	4	0

Twelfth Week
November 23, 25

39 YEARS AGO
NOVEMBER 24, 1933
Arkansas 20 - Texas 6
NOVEMBER 25, 1933
Texas Tech 6 - Kansas State 0
TCU 26 - Rice 3
Baylor 13 - SMU 7
NOVEMBER 30, 1933 (THANKSGIVING)
Tulsa 7 - Arkansas 0
Texas A&M 10 - Texas 10

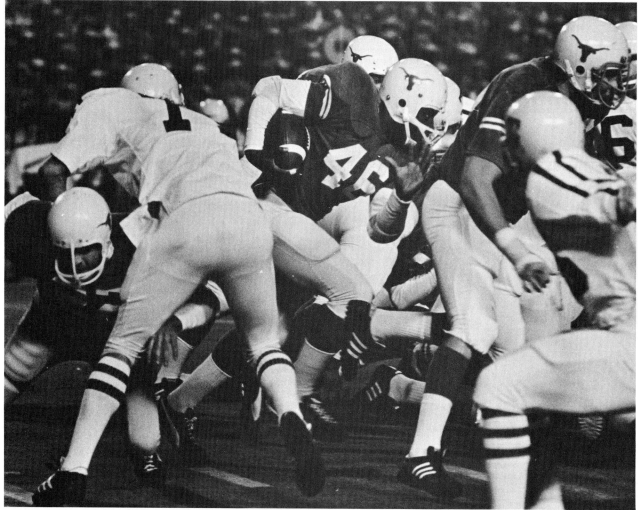

It looks like the 5 o'clock rush hour as Roosevelt Leaks (46) picks his way through A & M traffic. Tommy Landry (22) blocks out Aggie linebacker Ed Simonini (77).

TEXAS 38 - TEXAS A&M 3

Thanksgiving means turkey and Texas - Texas A & M football. These days you cannot always count on having turkey, but you can be sure that on national Alka-Seltzer day the Longhorns and Aggies are going to meet on the football field. They have met on this holiday every year since 1916. This happened to be the first time the game has ever been played at night. For the national television audiences it may have been great, but for the 68,000 "live" audience in Memorial Stadium it was miserable. The temperature was 40 degrees and it rained throughout the game. For the Aggie followers the weather was not the only thing that was miserable.

Lonnie Bennett fumbled the A & M kickoff and Garth TenNapel recovered for the Cadets at the Texas 33. In five plays the Aggies moved to the Longhorn 14 where they faced a third down one. Brad Dusek made the first down, then fumbled and Randy Braband recovered for Texas at his 12. On the Longhorns' first play from scrimmage quarterback Alan Lowry fumbled the snap and Blake Schwarz recovered for A & M at the Texas 11. On the

following play Dusek fumbled and Bruce Cannon recovered for Texas at the 12. Three downs later Lowry punted to Larry Ellis who fumbled the fair catch, and Don Crosslin recovered for Texas at the Aggie 46.

Some may have thought by this time that this was the circus and they had come to the wrong stadium. The Cadets held the Longhorns when Schwarz dropped Lowry for a four yard loss on third down. Lowry's punt was downed at the Aggie one.

A & M moved to the Texas 44 in 15 plays where Robert Murski punted to the Texas 15. After three punt exchanges the Cadets had possession at their 23 early in the second quarter. Skip Walker, on first down, went down the sidelines 38 yards to the Texas 39. A pass interference penalty on Texas moved the ball to the 27. The Longhorns held at that point and Pat McDermott kicked a 45-yard field goal. With 7:55 left in the second quarter A & M led 3-0.

Following the kickoff Texas started at their 31. On first down Lowry dropped back to pass. Schwarz broke

A & M's freshman linebacker Ed Simonini (77) along with Grady Hoermann (31), apply the squeeze play on Texas quarterback Alan Lowry (15) behind the line of scrimmage.

through and grabbed Lowry's leg, but couldn't bring him down. With Schwarz hanging on, Lowry passed to Jimmy Moore for 39 yards to the A & M 30. Three plays later Tommy Landry got outside and ran to the six. On third down, Lowry scored from the three. Billy Schott converted and Texas led 7-3.

The Longhorns came back on their next possession and moved 92 yards in nine plays. The big gainers came on a Lowry to Moore pass of 29 yards, and a 35-yard run by Landry. On third down and eight, at the Aggie 10, Lowry passed to Julius Whittier for the touchdown. Schott kicked good and Texas led 14-3. The first half ended 52 seconds later.

On their first possession in the third quarter, the Longhorns' Billy Schott tried a 36-yard field goal. The ball hit the crossbar and bounced back onto the playing field. On their second possession, they drove 47 yards in nine plays. A 19-yard Lowry to Moore pass was the big play in the drive. Landry got the touchdown on a five-yard run to the left. Schott converted and Texas led 21-3.

Cannon set up the next Longhorn score when he intercepted Cadet quarterback Don Dean at the Aggie 29. On "student body left" Landry ran for 19 to reach the 10.

The Aggies held at their three and Schott kicked a 20-yard field goal. Texas led 24-3.

Early in the fourth quarter another interception set up a Texas touchdown. Tommie Keel stole Dean's pass and returned to the A & M 14. A personal foul on the Aggies put the ball on the seven. Lowry scored from the six on a third down. Schott's kick was good and Texas led 31-3.

When the Aggies couldn't move following the kickoff, Murski punted to Moore who returned 61 yards for a Texas touchdown. Schott kicked good, and the Longhorns led 38-3.

That is the way it ended almost nine minutes later. Roosevelt Leaks carried 230 times during the season, breaking Byron Townsend's team record set in 1950. His 1099 yards rushing broke Chris Gilbert's sophomore record set in 1966.

	A&M	Texas
First downs	13	15
Rushes-yards	57-200	57-228
Passing yards	44	111
Return yards	22	117
Passes	4-13-2	6-10-1
Punts	7-35	5-36
Fumbles lost	3-5	2-3
Penalties yards	5-42	3-40

Texas A&M............0 3 0 0— 3
Texas ....0 14 10 14—38
A&M—FG 45 McDermott
Tex—Lowry 3 run (Schott kick)
Tex—Whittier 10 pass from Lowry (Schott kick)
Tex—Landry 5 run (Schott kick)
Tex—FG 20 Schott
Tex—Lowry 6 run (Schott kick)
Tex—Moore 61 punt return (Schott kick)
A—68,000

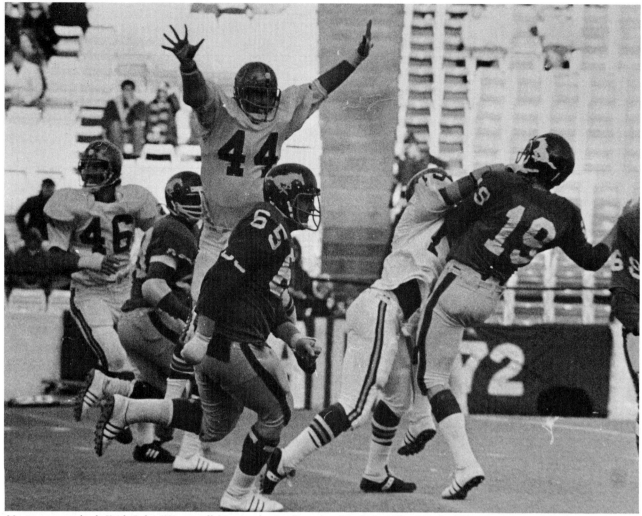

Mustang quarterback Keith Bobo (19) gets off his pass despite the rush of Baylor's Millard Neely (78). The Bears' Ed Taylor (44) leaps to block the ball and Derrel Luce (46) looks downfield to see where it went. Alvin Maxson (28) and Guy Thomas (65) are other Mustangs shown.

SMU 12 - BAYLOR 7

A sparce crowd of 18,035 looked on as the Bears and Mustangs met in the Cotton Bowl. It was a cool 52 degrees and the wind, coming out of the northwest, was gusting up to 38 miles per hour. Baylor was hoping to break a six year drouth against SMU. They only lacked 13 yards in achieving their goal and also SMU's.

Baylor kicked off to start the game and their defense allowed only two yards in three plays. Sam McLarty punted and Tommy Stewart fumbled when hit by Alvin Maxson, and Don Deweber recovered for SMU at the Baylor 37. On first down Maxson hit a hole in the middle and ran 36 yards to the Bear one. On the following play Maxson was stopped for no gain, and on second down Roger Goree shot through and grabbed Maxson at the four. A struggling Maxson flipped a lateral to quarterback Keith Bobo who bobbled the ball, but it bounced back into his hands and he sprinted in for the touchdown. A two-point conversion pass by McLarty failed and with 2:43 gone SMU led 6-0.

Lester Ealey returned the Mustang kickoff to the SMU 48, giving the Bears excellent field position. Gary Lacy picked up a first down at the 38 on two carries, but on the next play a pitchout from quarterback Neal Jeffrey to Ealey was off target, and Kris Silverthorn recovered for SMU.

As the second quarter opened Bobo, from the Baylor 46, passed complete to Randy Goss in the Bear end zone. The play was called back when offensive pass interference was called on Maxson.

Robert Armstrong replaced Jeffrey at quarterback, and took the Bears from their 20 to the Mustang 29, with most of the yardage coming on a 38-yard run by Ealey. On third and eight at the 27 Armstrong was intercepted by Andy Duvall and returned to the SMU 45. A 16-yard run by Maxson reached the Baylor 39, but he fumbled on the next play and Tommy Turnipseede recovered for Baylor.

When SMU gained possession again it was at their 15. Wayne Morris ran for 13, and Maxson followed with a 10 yard carry. Split end Kenny Harrison, on the next play, took the ball on a reverse and threw a pass. Oscar Roan

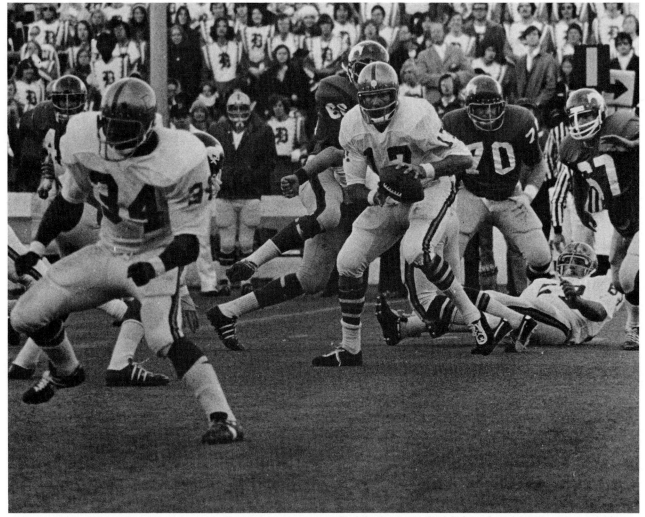

Randy Cavender (17), the third quarterback used by Baylor in the game, rallied the Bears comeback bid. Lester Ealey (34) moves out to block as Mustangs Ed Johnson (66), Steve Morton (70) and Don Randell (67) close in on Cavender.

caught the ball and was downed at the Bear 33. Bobo passed to Harrison for 22 yards, but a clipping penalty brought the ball back to the 23. Morris and Maxson carried the rest of the way with Morris scoring from the four. Bobo's run for two points was stopped by Goree. SMU led 12-0 and that's where it stood at halftime.

In the third quarter Armstrong directed the Bears to the SMU 27. It all came to a halt when Jim Ryan deflected an Armstrong pitchout and Silverthorn recovered for SMU. Midway through the period, with the wind at his back, Baylor's Mike Conradt tried a 62-yard field goal which was short.

As the third quarter came to a close, Randy Cavender became the Bear's third quarterback of the game. Nine plays and 56 yards later Baylor was on the scoreboard. Cavender passed to Lacy for eight yards, then hit Charles Dancer for 13. Gene Wilson ran the middle for 11, and came back later for 12 more and the touchdown. Conradt converted and with 12:37 left in the game SMU led by five points, 12-7.

The Mustangs retaliated by driving to the Bear 30, but Millard Neely and Joe Johnson dropped Bobo for a 12-yard loss. Clint Hackney tried a 57-yard field goal which

was short. Baylor had one chance remaining.

Starting at his 20, Cavender began moving the Bears. He ran for 13, then Lacy took the option pitchout 23 yards. Moments later, Cavender passed to Ealey for 13 yards. This was followed by a run of six yards to the Mustang 13 by Billy Wilson. The Bears were 13 yards from the SMU goal and a victory. Cavender lost a yard on the following play and Baylor used their last time out. Armstrong replaced Cavender (Cavender had been playing with a broken toe, and the pain had become unbearable) and on an option run or pass play was dropped by Randy Savage, Ryan and Steve Morton for a one-yard gain. It was a fourth and four effort, so the Mustangs took over the ball and reached the Baylor 15 before the Bears' hopes and the clock expired.

	Baylor	SMU
First downs	18	19
Rushes-yards	50-223	59-217
Passing yards	53	78
Return yards	—3	41
Passes	5-11-1	5-10-1
Punts	4-43	7-36
Fumbles lost	5-3	4-1
Penalties yards	6-62	5-45

Baylor	0	0	0	7— 7
SMU	6	6	0	0—12

SMU—Bobo 1 run (pass failed)
SMU—Morris 4 run (run failed)
Bay—G. Wilson 12 run (Conradt kick)
A—18,035

Cougar quarterback D. C. Nobles (3) takes off on his second touchdown run, this one for 36 yards. Other Cougars shown are Marty Watts (16), Ken Baugh (63), David Bourquin (68) and Puddin' Jones (30).

HOUSTON 49 - CINCINNATI 0

The Cougars had played the Bearcats 10 times before and lost only one, that coming in 1964. Before 18,795 in the Astrodome Houston closed out its season, and the coaching career of Cincinnati's Ray Callahan, with a victory. This was the defensive unit's first shutout of the season and they also scored the last two touchdowns on pass interceptions. The Cougar offense ran up over 400 total yards as the first unit warmed the bench most of the second half. With the win Houston finished their seventh straight winning season.

On their first possession the Cougars moved from their 13 to the Cincy 14, but the drive ended at that point on two incomplete passes. Forcing the Bearcats to punt after three plays, Houston took over at the Cincinnati 41 and scored in two plays. Quarterback D. C. Nobles kept on option left and ran 39 yards to the two-yard line. He scored, behind David Bourquin's block, on the next play.

Ricky Terrell converted and Houston led 7-0.

Lightning struck again just over two minutes later. The Cougars started scrimmage at the Bearcat 48. Puddin' Jones made two yards up the middle. Nobles passed to Marty Watts for 10 yards to the 36. Next, Nobles ran the option again and blew right by the Cincy secondary for 36 yards and a touchdown. Terrell kicked good and Houston, with 2:18 left in the first quarter, led 14-0.

Early in the second quarter Gerald Hill partially blocked a Cincinnati punt and Houston gained possession at the Bearcat 34. The Cougars drove to the four where Nobles passed to Watts in the end zone, but Watts was charged with offensive pass interference and Cincy took over at their 20. Another long drive from their 27 to the Cincinnati 23 was halted when the Cougars ran out of downs. Finally, with 42 seconds left in the first half, Jones scored from the three to cap a 32-yard drive. The

Houston linebacker Deryl McGallion (1) holds the ball aloft like an Olympic torch after running back an interception 23 yards for a touchdown. David Cruthirds (79), Harold Evans (59) and Robert Giblin (24) are left behind by Deryl's blazing speed.

touchdown was made possible when Robert Ford returned a Bearcat punt 28 yards. Terrell kicked good and Houston led 21-0 at the half.

On their first possession of the second half the Cougars moved 67 yards in six plays. The big gainer came on a Nobles screen pass to Ford, good for 24 yards to the Cincy 29. From the 17 Reggie Cherry went over left tackle and scored untouched. The conversion kick was blocked and Houston led 27-0.

The next time they got the ball the Cougars were again given good field position by a Ford punt return. Terry Peel replaced Nobles at quarterback and guided Houston 32 yards in 10 plays. Milton Ward got the touchdown from the one. Nobles came in to hold for the extra point. He took the snap, raised up, and threw to Jones for a two-point conversion. Houston led 35-0 with 5:13 remaining in the third quarter.

The defense then took over the offense. Bearcat quarterback Mike Shoemaker threw under heavy pressure and linebacker Deryl McGallion intercepted his pass at the Cincinnati 23. He returned untouched into the end zone. Terrell converted and with Houston leading 42-0 the third period had 3:45 left.

Play moved into the final quarter and Shoemaker was still having his problems. A flare pass intended for back Dick James was intercepted in mid-flight by Bill Hamrick, who ran 14 yards for Houston's final touchdown of 1972. Terrell kicked the extra point and Houston had peaked out at 49 points.

The Cougar defense was also playing defense along with their offense. When the clock ran down to all zeros, the Bearcats were still looking for the Houston end zone - maybe there wasn't any Houston end zone.

	Cin	Hou
First downs	9	23
Rushes-yards	42-104	62-389
Passing yardage	44	46
Return yardage	8	144
Passes	7-17-2	4-10-1
Punts	10-37-6	2-47-5
Fumbles lost	2-0	2-1
Penalties-yards	3-15	1-5

Cincinnati . . . . 0 0 0 0— 0
Houston . . . . 14 7 21 7—49

UH—Nobles 2 run (Terrell kick)
UH—Nobles 36 run (Terrell kick)
UH—Jones 3 run (Terrell kick)
UH—Cherry 17 run (kick blocked)
UH—Ward 1 run (Jones pass from Nobles)
UH—McGallion 23 pass interception (Terrell kick)
UH—Hamrick 14 pass interception (Terrell kick)
A—18,795

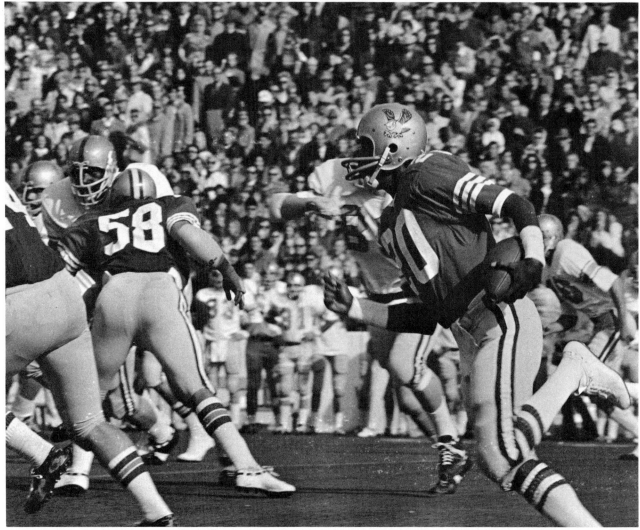

Flanker Ron Arceneaux (20) runs 47 yards on a double reverse play which led to Rice's first touchdown. Owl David Vandiver (58) blocks on the play.

RICE 25 - TCU 21

The Owls and the Horned Frogs put on their fourth barnburner in a row. Last year TCU won by one point, two years ago Rice prevailed by two points and three years back the Frogs had a four-point victory. Only 15,000 were on hand for the Dad's Day game at Rice Stadium. The Owls jumped out ahead, TCU closed the gap and eventually wrested the lead, then like a Hollywood script here came the Owls snatching back their lead and galloping off into the sunset. For the third straight week the Owls proved that they may be one of the best fourth quarter teams in America.

Rice drew first blood on their first possession. They moved from their 28 for the touchdown with the big play coming on a double reverse. Quarterback Bruce Gadd handed off to Edwin Collins who handed off to Ron Arceneaux who ran 47 yards to the TCU 20. Moments later Gadd passed to Collins for 14 yards. Two plays later John Coleman scored from the one. Mark Williams converted and Rice led 7-0.

Early in the second quarter, following a TCU punt, the Owls had good field position at their 49. A pass to Joe Buck carried to the Frog 34 and another to Gary Ferguson reached the 25. The Horned Frogs held, Williams kicked a 42-yard field goal and Rice led 10-0.

Midway through the second quarter the Frogs got on the scoreboard. Quarterback Terry Drennan hit John Ott with a pass down the middle for 50 yards to the Owl 12. Mike Luttrell tried the middle, the ball popped out of his grasp backwards into the hands of teammate Ronnie Webb who gained four yards. The Owls were offsides at the three and Drennan scored on a keeper from the one. Berl Simmons kicked good and Rice led 10-7, which was the score when the first half ended.

TCU moved ahead in the third quarter. First, they drove 73 yards for a touchdown with the second half kickoff. On a fourth down one at the Rice 42, Webb ran for three to keep the drive alive. Drennan got the touchdown as he broke a tackle on a 17-yard run.

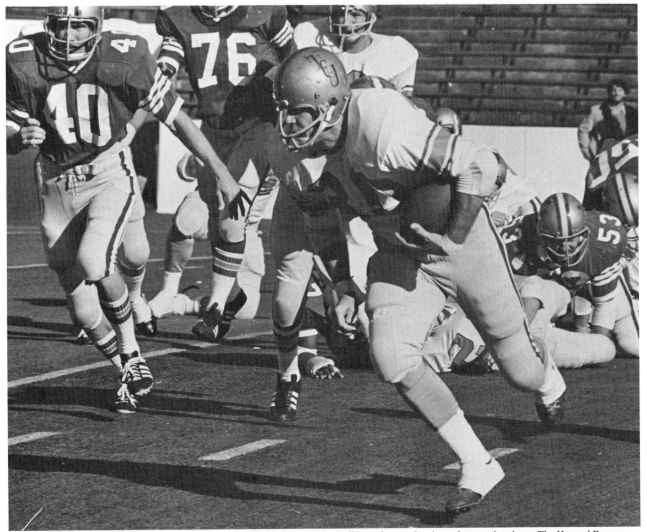

Ronnie Webb (30) saves TCU from disaster as he grabs a fumble by Mike Luttrell in mid-air and picks up four yards to boot. The Horned Frogs went on to score their first touchdown moments later. Owls shown are Preston Anderson (40), Cornelius Walker (76) and Richard Hollas (53).

Simmons converted and TCU led 14-10.

After a punt exchange, Gadd was intercepted by Tookie Berry on a pass tipped by Dede Terveen. Berry returned to the Owl 27. The Frogs scored in five plays. Luttrell got the touchdown from the 11 with Owls hanging onto him as he crossed the goal. Simmons was on target, and with 2:55 remaining in the third quarter TCU led 21-10.

The Owls closed the gap on their next possession. They moved 68 yards mainly on the arm of Gadd and the receiving of Gary Butler, who caught 23 and 19-yard passes, of Collins, who caught a four-yarder, and of Buck, who had a seven-yard reception. Coleman ran the ball over from the three. Ferguson threw a pass to Collins, who made a one-handed reception, for a two-point conversion. TCU led 21-18 with only four seconds gone in the fourth quarter.

Later, the Frogs began moving to what looked like a clinching touchdown. Staying on the ground, with runs by Drennan, Webb, Luttrell and Billy Sadler, TCU moved from their 20 to the Rice 34. An offsides penalty and a stiffening Owl defense were enough to stop the

Frogs. On fourth down and 11, Simmons came in to try a 52-yard field goal. Jody Medford broke through to block the kick, and Rice had the ball on the TCU 40.

Gadd passed to Collins for nine and Coleman ran for a first down at the 28. Butler caught a nine-yard pass and Coleman one of six yards to reach the 13. Three plays later, Gadd found Arceneaux alone in the end zone and hit him with a nine-yard scoring pass. Williams kicked the point after and with 2:36 left Rice led 25-21.

The game ended for TCU when David Snellings stopped Webb on a fourth down play by a foot. Rice took over the football and ran four plays, giving the ball back to the Frogs at the Rice 41 with time left for just one play, which was an incomplete pass.

	TCU	Rice
First downs	21	18
Rushes-yards	69-279	37-145
Passing yards	97	187
Return yardage	56	15
Passes	6-11-1	15-26-2
Punts	6-34	6-53
Fumbles lost	2-0	0-0
Penalties-yards	4-30	6-39

TCU .... 0 7 14 0—21
Rice .... 7 3 0 15—25
Rice—Coleman 1 run (Williams kick)
Rice—FG Williams 42
TCU—Drennan 1 run (Simmons kick)
TCU—Drennan 17 run (Simmons kick)
TCU—Luttrell 11 run (Simmons kick)
Rice—Coleman 3 run (Ferguson pass to Collins)
Rice—Arceneaux 9 pass from Gadd (Williams kick)
A—15,000

177

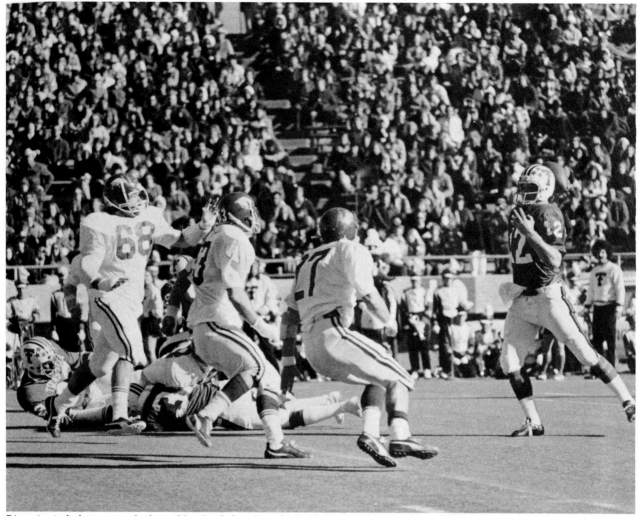

Discretion is the better part of valor and faced with three Razorbacks, Tech quarterback Joe Barnes (12) decides to pass. The confronting Hogs are John Wheat (68), Bill Burns (53) and Kenneth Wallace (27).

ARKANSAS 24 - TEXAS TECH 14

If you live by the pass, you die by the pass and Arkansas had died in three straight games. The Razorbacks put their aerial attack in the hanger and brought out their infantry. Scott Bull, who has played four positions this year, took over at quarterback and led the Hogs to a season ending victory over Sun Bowl bound Tech. They also escaped the SWC cellar after being picked to take the crown in pre-season polls. The Red Raiders lost only three times this year, all three defeats coming at home. A Jones Stadium crowd of 35,275 braved the 41 degree weather with winds gusting up to 35 mph.

Tech kicked off and the Hogs started at their 20. Staying on the ground Bull, Dickey Morton and Marsh White carried the ball to the Raider 19 in 13 plays. On the 14th Bull made five yards before losing the ball to Greg Waters on a fumble. Four plays later the Hogs had the ball back when Cliff Hoskins, who had run for 19 yards on the previous play, fumbled and Doug Yoder recovered for Arkansas at the Tech 42. The Razorbacks scored in nine plays with the biggest being a 10-yard Bull to Jack

Ettinger pass. A Tech face mask penalty moved the ball from the seven to the three and Jon Richardson scored on the next play. Mike Kirkland kicked good and Arkansas led 7-0 with 2:35 left in the first quarter.

The Red Raiders came roaring back, in five plays and 2:20, to tie the game. From their 30 George Smith carried for 33 yards to spark the drive. James Mosley ran for three, then Smith carried three straight times for three, one and 30 yards. The last run was terminated in the Arkansas end zone. Don Grimes converted and the game was tied 7-7.

The second quarter was a study in frustration for both teams. Arkansas received Tech's kickoff and moved from their 23 to their 43 where White's fumble was recovered by Waters. Tech drove to the Hog 34 where quarterback Joe Barnes fumbled and teammate Smith recovered for a seven yard loss. Following the Tech punt, Arkansas started from their 31. On second down Morton made a big gain of 21 yards, but a holding penalty put the ball back on the Hog 14. Drew Toole got off a short punt to

Scott Bull (19), the Razorback's new quarterback, heads upfield behind the blocking of Jon Richardson (32) and Dickey Morton (33). Tech's Gaines Baty (84) gives chase.

the Arkansas 41 and was injured on the play when a Tech player was blocked into him. On Tech's second play they were penalized 15 yards for clipping. On fourth down John Garner punted dead on the Arkansas five. One play later the first half ended.

The third quarter was a punting contest and Kirkland, who took over for Toole, was a pleasant surprise for the Razorbacks. Midway through the quarter he punted from his 28 to the Tech eight. Mosley got the Raiders out of a hole with a 27-yard run, but eventually Tech was forced to punt.

As the third period came to an end the Hogs had moved from their 19 to the Red Raider four, thanks mostly to a pass interference penalty on Tech which cost them 39 yards. On the third play of the fourth quarter White scored from the one. Kirkland converted and Arkansas led 14-7.

Smith fumbled on Tech's second play following the Razorback's kickoff. Louis Campbell recovered for Arkansas on the Raider 26. Morton ran for 12 yards, then one, then 11 to the two. White gained one and Bull scored on the next play. Kirkland kicked the extra point and Arkansas led 21-7.

Smith returned the Hog kickoff to his 39 and Arkansas was penalized to their 46 because of a personal foul on the runback. Tech scored in six plays. Barnes had a run of 10 yards and Mosley one of 20 yards for the big gainers. Barnes was shaken up on his run and was replaced by Jimmy Carmichael, who scored the touchdown from the two. Grimes kicked good and with 8:26 remaining Arkansas led 21-14.

The Razorbacks, following the kickoff, used up 6:20 and all of Tech's timeouts in moving from their 27 to the Red Raider 20. From there Kirkland kicked a 37-yard field goal and Arkansas led 24-14.

Barnes re-entered the game and did a remarkable job of moving Tech from their three to the Arkansas three with no timeouts, before the clock finally ran out. The drive covered 94 yards in 11 plays.

	Ark	Tech
First downs	20	19
Rushes-yards	7-278	41-275
Passing yards	21	100
Return yards	1	5
Passes	2-4-0	12-20-0
Punts	3-44	5-24
Fumbles lost	2-3	2-7
Penalties-yards	5-54	3-58

Texas Tech ....7 0 0 7—14
Arkansas ....7 0 0 17—24
Ark—Richardson 3 run (Kirkland kick)
Tech—Smith 30 run (Grimes kick)
Ark—White 1 run (Kirkland kick)
Ark—Bull 1 run (Kirkland kick)
Tech—Carmichael 2 run (Grimes kick)
Ark—FG Kirkland 37
A—35,275

SYNOPSIS

12

TOP TEN

1. Southern Cal
2. Alabama
3. Oklahoma
4. Ohio State
5. Penn State
6. Texas
7. Michigan
8. Nebraska
9. Auburn
10. Notre Dame

UPSET OF WEEK:

Florida 3 - LSU 3

SWC OFFENSIVE PLAYER OF WEEK

Jim Moore, Split End, Texas

SWC DEFENSIVE PLAYER OF WEEK

Jody Medford, Tackle, Rice

FRESHMAN RESULTS

TCU 17 - SMU 14

SWC TEAM LEADERS FOR SEASON

OFFENSE . . . . **AVG.**
Rushing . . . . Texas 276 yds.
Passing . . . . Rice 217 yds.
Total . . . . Houston 402 yds.

DEFENSE . . . . **AVG.**
Rushing . . . . SMU 130 yds.
Passing . . . . Baylor 84 yds.
Total . . . . Texas 275 yds.

FINAL FRESHMAN RECORDS

	W	L	T
Texas Tech	5	0	0
Texas A&M	4	1	0
Texas	4	1	0
Arkansas	4	1	0
Rice	2	3	0
TCU	2	3	0
Houston	1	4	0
SMU	1	4	0
Baylor	1	4	0

SEASON RECORDS

	W	L	T
Texas	9	1	0
Texas Tech	8	3	0
SMU	6	4	0
Houston	6	4	1
Rice	5	4	1
Arkansas	6	5	0
TCU	5	5	0
Baylor	4	6	0
Texas A&M	3	8	0

CONFERENCE

	W	L	T
Texas	7	0	0
Texas Tech	4	3	0
Rice	3	3	0
SMU	3	3	0
Arkansas	3	4	0
Baylor	2	4	0
TCU	2	4	0
Texas A&M	2	5	0

Thirteenth Week
December 2

39 YEARS AGO
DECEMBER 2, 1933
TCU 26 - SMU 6
Baylor 7 - Rice 6

ONE WEEK LATER
DECEMBER 9, 1933
St Mary's 18 - SMU 6

TCU linebacker Chad Utley (37) grips SMU quarterback John Blackburn's (11) jersey and pulls him to the ground. Rusty Putt (85) looks on as D. Nady (76) watches from the sidelines.

SMU 35 -TCU 22

Mustang coach Hayden Fry won the battle, but lost the war. He won his final game, which gave SMU a tie with Texas Tech for second place in the SWC, and his team finished the season with a winning 7-4 record. On Friday, the day before the TCU game, Coach Fry was notified that his tenure at SMU had come to an end. Needless to say, the Mustangs had all the incentive necessary to demolish the Horned Frogs. A crowd of 18,125 was on hand in Amon Carter Stadium for the season and Hayden Fry's finale.

The Frogs received the opening kickoff and were moving into a 17 mph wind. On their second possession, Greg Anderson's punt went only 19 yards and SMU had the ball on TCU's 45. The Mustangs quickly moved to the Frog 10 with the big plays coming on a 14-yard pass from quarterback Keith Bobo to Rory Best and a run of nine yards by Bobo. John Blackburn replaced Bobo who was injured on the run. The Frogs were offsides twice in a row, which moved the ball to the two. Blackburn sneaked over from there. Clint Hackney converted and SMU led 7-0.

Fumbles kept the Horned Frogs from launching any kind of drive. During the game, they fumbled seven times and things could have been much worse if they had not recovered all seven. Another short punt gave SMU the ball at their 34 and they scored in nine plays. On first down, Wayne Morris gained 21 yards on a Statue of Liberty play. Later, Alvin Maxson had a run of 11 yards and the touchdown came on a 16-yard Bobo pass to Best in the end zone. Hackney converted and SMU led 14-0 with seven seconds gone in the second quarter.

Two and one-half minutes later the Mustangs were again in the TCU end zone. Kris Silverthorn returned a Frog punt 18 yards to the TCU 41. A penalty wiped out one play and moved SMU back to the 46. Bobo then tossed a short pass to tight end Oscar Roan, who broke a tackle and covered 46 yards for the score. Hackney kicked good and SMU led 21-0.

The Mustangs scored once more before halftime. An interception by Silverthorn put the ball on the TCU 29. Bobo passed complete four times. The fourth completion,

After the game Mustang offensive guard, Guy Morriss, hugs Coach Hayden Fry in victory. It was a time for joy and also a few tears. This was Fry's last game as head coach for SMU.

caught by Raymond Mapps, went for 11 yards and the touchdown. Hackney added the conversion and at intermission SMU led 28-0.

The Frogs scored on their first possession of the second half as they drove 79 yards in 10 plays. The big gainers were a 13-yard run by Mike Luttrell and quarterback Terry Drennan's pass to John Ott for 21 yards. At the SMU 16, Drennan passed to Steve Patterson for the touchdown. Berl Simmons converted and SMU led 28-7.

Early in the fourth quarter, TCU failed on a fourth down and three at the SMU 40. On first down Bobo lateraled wide to Kenny Harrison, who passed to Mapps, who ran into the Frog end zone. The play covered 60 yards. Hackney kicked good and SMU led 35-7.

The Horned Frogs, midway through the quarter, moved from their 41 in for a score. A 36-yard pass to Larry Harris reached into Mustang territory. On a fourth down at the 17, Ronnie Littleton ran to the three. On another fourth down, Drennan passed to Lane Bowen for two yards and the touchdown. Simmons kicked good and SMU led 35-14.

Frankie Grimmett recovered TCU's onside kickoff at the Mustang 46. Perry Senn took over at quarterback for

the Frogs. An SMU penalty and a run by Littleton, of 16 yards, helped reach the Mustang five. Littleton then ran the five yards for the touchdown. Senn passed to Billy Sadler for a two-point conversion. That made the final count SMU 35 - TCU 22.

Maxson ended up at 1005 yards rushing for the season which gave him two 1,000 yard seasons in a row. He needs only 124 yards to break Kyle Rote's SMU career rushing record. The Frog's Luttrell ended up with 905 yards rushing for the season. Coach Fry was carried over to shake hands with TCU coach Billy Tohill, then carried off the field by his now ex-players.

	SMU	TCU
First downs	15	14
Rushes-yards	40-123	60-105
Passing yards	230	130
Return yards	17	0
Passes	13-20-1	9-18-1
Punts	7-36	10-37
Fumbles lost	4-2	7-0
Penalties-yards	6-68	4-28

SMU ....7 21 0 7—35
TCU ....0 0 7 15—22
SMU—Blackburn 2 run (Hackney kick)
SMU—Best 16 pass from Bobo (Hackney kick)
SMU—Roan 46 pass from Bobo (Hackney kick)
SMU—Mapps 11 pass from Bobo (Hackney kick)
TCU—Patterson 16 pass from Drennan (Simmons kick)
SMU—Mapps 60 pass from Harrison (Hackney kick)
TCU—Bowen 2 pass from Drennan (Simmons kick)
TCU—Littleton 5 run (Sadler pass from Senn)
A—18,152

Freshman fullback Pat McNeil (31) scores his first touchdown for Baylor as he swings wide to the left on the six-yard run. Rodrigo Barnes (90) chases McNeil. Cullie Culpepper (46) and Billy Wilson (30) are on the ground behind McNeil.

BAYLOR 28 - RICE 14

The season had dwindled down to just one game. For the Bears and Rice it had to be considered a successful season for their new head coaches. With a victory, the Owls could end up in a tie for second place in the SWC. Baylor, in winning, could end up tied for fourth. Both teams were picked at or near the bottom in pre-season polls. A crowd of 26,000 sat in on the season finale at Bear Stadium. The best passing team in the conference, Rice, would be facing the best defense against the pass, Baylor.

Rice won the coin toss and elected to receive. Baylor would have a 19 mph wind at their backs. When the Owls could not move the ball the pressure was on punter Mark Williams. His first three punts into the wind carried 16, 38 and 28 yards. The Bears, with Robert Armstrong at quarterback, couldn't move after the first two punts. After Williams' third punt, which set up Baylor at the Rice 44, Neal Jeffrey came in at quarterback. A 14-yard pass to Charlie Dancer got the Bears to moving. Jeffrey then stayed on the ground, feeding handoffs to Pat McNeil and Gary Lacy, to reach the three. He then faked

to Lacy and went left on a keeper to score standing. Mike Conradt converted but Baylor was penalized for illegal procedure. Conradt kicked good and again the Bears incurred a procedure penalty. On his third attempt, Conradt kicked a 30-yard extra point. Baylor led 7-0 with 27 seconds left in the first quarter.

As play moved into the second period the Owls had the wind and quarterback Bruce Gadd started opening up the Bear defense with passes. Gary Butler caught one for 14 yards and Steve Ogletree grabbed one for seven. Gary Ferguson then found running room as the Owls moved from their 20 to the Baylor eight. A Bear pass interference penalty aided the drive. On third down at the eight, Gadd overthrew Edwin Collins who was wide open in the end zone. Mark Williams came in and kicked a 25-yard field goal. Baylor took a 7-3 lead into the dressing room at the half.

Rice's first possession of the second half came about when McNeil fumbled at the Owl 42. Cornelius Walker recovered for Rice. The Owls drove to the Baylor 15 with

Owls' Preston Anderson (40) and Richard Hollas(53), along with two unidentified teammates, stop Baylor fullback Wayne Presher (45) for short yardage.

most of the yardage coming on a little razzle-dazzle. Gadd lateraled back to Collins who passed downfield to Ron Arceneaux. The play covered 36 yards to the Bear 22. An offensive pass interference penalty killed the drive, and Williams kicked a 47-yard field goal. Baylor led 7-6.

After the kickoff, Baylor drove 76 yards in 13 plays to score their second touchdown. The big gainers came on passes. Jeffrey hit Ken Townsend for 14 yards and Dancer for 11. The Dancer reception produced a first down at the Owl nine. From the nine, Jeffrey passed to Townsend in the end zone for the touchdown. Conradt converted and with 3:15 left in the third quarter the Bears led 14-6.

Moments later, Derrell Luce intercepted Gadd at the Owl 38. Wayne Presher ran for 12 and six yards and Jeffrey picked up a first down at the six on a keeper. He then pitched back to McNeil who went in on the left side. Conradt kicked good and with 1:30 gone in the fourth quarter Baylor led 21-6.

Rice came right back, moving 80 yards to score. Gadd passed to Ferguson for 13, then hit Roland Boyce for eight. Ferguson snagged another pass for 12 yards. After being thrown for a seven-yard loss, Gadd hit Butler for 14 yards to the 14. On fourth and two, Baylor was guilty of

pass interference which advanced the ball to the six. Three plays later Gadd passed three yards to Ferguson for the touchdown. Gadd connected with Ferguson for a two-point conversion. Baylor led 21-14 with 7:41 remaining.

The Bears came back with the clincher as they moved 78 yards to score leaving only 3:43 on the clock. Staying mostly on the ground, a Jeffrey pass to Dancer did pick up a first down at the Rice 21. Billy Wilson ran 11 yards to the 10 and Lacy reached the two on an eight-yard run. Lacy scored from the two and with Conradt's kick Baylor led 28-14.

Rice couldn't move following the kickoff, and when Williams punted to Baylor the Owls' last hope was gone.

With his two field goals, Williams set new conference records for most field goals in one season (15) and career field goals (30). Rice and Baylor wound up in a tie for fourth place in the SWC along with Arkansas.

	Rice	Baylor
First downs	18	20
Rushes-yards	33-113	58-192
Passing yards	157	87
Return yards	16	17
Passes	15-32-2	9-11-0
Punts	6-31	6-38
Fumbles lost	2-0	1-1
Penalties-yards	8-77	6-53

Rice	0	3	3	8	—14
Baylor	7	0	7	14	—28

Bay—Jeffrey 4 run (Conradt kick)
Rice—FG Williams 25
Rice—FG Williams 47
Bay—Townsend 9 pass from Jeffrey (Conradt kick)
Bay—McNeil 6 run (Conradt kick)
Rice—Ferguson 3 pass from Gadd (Ferguson pass from Gadd)
Bay—Lacy 2 run (Conradt kick)
A—26,000 est.

FINAL PRE-BOWL TOP TEN

1. Southern Cal
2. Oklahoma
3. Ohio State
4. Alabama
5. Penn State
6. Auburn
7. Texas
8. Michigan
9. Nebraska
10. LSU

SWC OFFENSIVE PLAYER OF WEEK

Keith Bobo, Quarterback, SMU

SWC DEFENSIVE PLAYER OF WEEK

Paul Savage, Linebacker, Baylor

UPSET OF WEEK:

Auburn 17 - Alabama 16

SWC TEAM LEADERS FOR SEASON

OFFENSE	AVG.
Rushing	Texas 276 yds.
Passing	Rice 211 yds.
Total	Houston 402 yds.

DEFENSE	AVG.
Rushing	SMU 128 yds.
Passing	Baylor 90 yds.
Total	SMU 274.9 yds.

FINAL SEASON RECORDS

	W	L	T
Texas	9	1	0
Texas Tech	8	3	0
SMU	7	4	0
Houston	6	4	1
Arkansas	6	5	0
Rice	5	5	1
Baylor	5	6	0
TCU	5	6	0
Texas A&M	3	8	0

FINAL CONFERENCE

	W	L	T
Texas	7	0	0
Texas Tech	4	3	0
SMU	4	3	0
Baylor	3	4	0
Arkansas	3	4	0
Rice	3	4	0
TCU	2	5	0
Texas A&M	2	5	0

1972
Wrap-Up

1972
SOUTHWEST CONFERENCE
CHAMPIONS

TEXAS LONGHORNS
Head Football Coach: Darrell Royal
Team Captains: Alan Lowry,
Randy Braband, Jerry Sisemore

23	**Miami**	10
25	**Texas Tech**	20
27	**Utah State**	12
0	**Oklahoma**	27
35	**Arkansas**	15
45	**Rice**	9
17	**SMU**	9
17	**Baylor**	3
27	**TCU**	0
38	**Texas A & M**	3
254		**108**

OVERALL STATISTICAL LEADERS

Points Scored . . . . Houston, 325
Points Allowed . . . . Texas, 108
Total Offense . . . . Houston 401.6 avg.
Total Defense . . . . SMU 274.9 avg.
Rushing Offense . . . . Texas 276 avg.
Rushing Defense . . . . SMU 127.6 avg.
Passing Offense . . . . Rice 211 avg.
Passing Defense . . . . Baylor 90.4 avg.
Rushing . . . . Puddin' Jones, Houston, 1216 yds.
Passing . . . . Bruce Gadd, Rice, 2064 yds.
Receiving . . . . Gary Butler, Rice 708 yds.
Total Offense . . . . Bruce Gadd, Rice 2001 yds.
Punt Returns . . . . Carl Roaches, Texas A&M, 15.1 avg.
x Kickoff Returns . . . . Lawrence Williams, Texas Tech, 30.8 avg.
Scoring . . . . Alvin Maxson, SMU, 78 pts.
Punting . . . . Mark Williams, Rice, 38.9 avg.
Touchdowns . . . . Alvin Maxson, SMU, 13
* Field Goals . . . . Mark Williams, Rice, 15
Extra Points . . . . Ricky Terrell, Houston 38
Interceptions . . . . Bruce Henley, Rice, 7
* Career Field Goals . . . . Mark Williams, Rice, 30

* SWC RECORD

x FIRST IN NATION

188

1972 SEASON RECORDS

ARKANSAS

10	Southern Cal	34
24	Oklahoma State	23
21	Tulsa	20
27	TCU	13
31	Baylor	20
15	Texas	35
42	North Texas	16
7	Texas A & M	10
20	Rice	23
7	SMU	22
24	Texas Tech	14
228		230

BAYLOR

14	Georgia	24
27	Missouri	0
10	Miami	3
20	Arkansas	31
7	Oklahoma State	20
15	Texas A & M	13
42	TCU	9
3	Texas	17
7	Texas Tech	13
7	SMU	12
28	Rice	14
180		156

HOUSTON

13	Rice	14
28	Arizona State	33
21	Tulsa	0
27	VPI	27
49	San Diego State	14
13	Miami	33
13	Mississippi State	27
31	Florida State	27
48	Colorado State	13
33	New Mexico	14
49	Cincinnati	0
325		202

RICE

14	Houston	13
29	Clemson	10
36	Georgia Tech	36
6	LSU	12
14	SMU	29
9	Texas	45
6	Texas Tech	10
23	Arkansas	20
20	Texas A & M	14
25	TCU	21
14	Baylor	28
196		238

SMU

56	Wake Forest	10
21	Florida	14
10	VPI	13
55	New Mexico State	6
29	Rice	14
3	Texas Tech	17
9	Texas	17
17	Texas A & M	27
22	Arkansas	7
12	Baylor	7
35	TCU	22
269		154

TEXAS A & M

36	Wichita State	13
7	Nebraska	37
17	LSU	42
14	Army	24
14	Texas Tech	17
10	TCU	13
13	Baylor	15
10	Arkansas	7
27	SMU	17
14	Rice	20
3	Texas	38
165		243

TCU

31	Indiana	28
38	UTA	14
13	Arkansas	27
35	Tulsa	9
13	Texas A & M	10
0	Notre Dame	21
9	Baylor	42
31	Texas Tech	7
0	Texas	27
21	Rice	25
22	SMU	35
213		245

TEXAS TECH

45	Utah	2
41	New Mexico	16
20	Texas	25
35	Tulsa	18
17	Texas A & M	14
35	Arizona	10
17	SMU	3
10	Rice	6
7	TCU	31
13	Baylor	7
14	Arkansas	24
254		156

1972 ALL-AMERICAN TEAMS

AP

OFFENSE
TE Charles Young, Southern Cal
WR Johnny Rodgers, Nebraska
T **Jerry Sisemore, Texas**
T John Hicks, Ohio State
G John Hannah, Alabama
G Ron Rusnak, North Carolina
C Tom Brahaney, Oklahoma
QB John Hufnagel, Penn State
RB Greg Pruitt, Oklahoma
RB Otis Armstrong, Purdue
RB Woody Green, Arizona State

DEFENSE
E **Roger Goree, Baylor**
E Willie Harper, Nebraska
T Greg Marx , Notre Dame
T Derland Moore, Oklahoma
G Rich Glover, Nebraska
LB Randy Gradishar, Ohio State
LB John Skorupan, Penn State
LB Richard Wood, Southern Cal
DB **Robert Popelka, SMU**
DB Calvin Jones, Washington
DB Brad Van Pelt, Michigan State

SECOND TEAM
TE Gary Butler, Rice
RB Roosevelt Leaks, Texas
MG Donald Rives, Texas Tech
LB Glen Gaspard, Texas

THIRD TEAM
DT Charlie Davis, TCU

UPI

OFFENSE
WR Johnny Rodgers, Nebraska
TE Charles Young, Southern Cal
T **Jerry Sisemore, Texas**
T Pete Adams, Southern Cal
G John Hannah, Alabama
G Ron Rusnak, North Carolina
C Tom Brahaney, Oklahoma
QB Bert Jones, LSU
RB Greg Pruitt, Oklahoma
RB Otis Armstrong, Purdue
RB Woody Green, Arizona State

DEFENSE
DE Willie Harper, Nebraska
DE Bruce Bannon, Penn State
DT Greg Marx, Notre Dame
DT Dave Butz, Purdue
MG Rich Glover, Nebraska
LB Randy Gradishar, Ohio State
LB Jamie Rotella, Tennessee
DB Brad Van Pelt, Michigan State
DB Cullen Bryant, Colorado
DB Randy Logan, Michigan
DB Conrad Graham, Tennessee

SECOND TEAM
DE Roger Goree, Baylor
DB Robert Popelka, SMU

HONORABLE MENTION
TE Gary Butler, Rice
RB Roosevelt Leaks, Texas
LB Rodrigo Barnes, Rice
LB Danny Rhodes, Arkansas

GRIDIRON

OFFENSE
TE Charles Young, Southern Cal
WR Steve Sweeney, California
T **Jerry Sisemore, Texas**
T Pete Adams, Southern Cal
G John Hannah, Alabama
G Skip Singletary, Temple
C Tom Brahaney, Oklahoma
QB Gary Huff, Florida State
RB Greg Pruitt, Oklahoma
RB Woody Green, Arizona State
RB **Johnny Rodgers, Nebraska**
P Ray Guy, Southern Mississippi
K Chris Gartner, Indiana

DEFENSE
E Bruce Bannon, Penn State
E John Grant, Southern Cal
T Greg Marx, Notre Dame
T Rich Glover, Nebraska
LB Steve Brown, Oregon State
LB Randy Gradishar, Ohio State
LB Roderick Shoate, Oklahoma
DB Cullen Bryant, Colorado
DB Levi Johnson, Texas A & I
DB Brad Van Pelt, Michigan State
DB **Robert Popelka, SMU**

THIRD TEAM
E Roger Goree, Baylor
LB Randy Braband, Texas
K Don Grimes, Texas Tech

FOOTBALL NEWS

OFFENSE
E Charles Young, Southern Cal
E Steve Holden, Arizona State
T John Dampeer, Notre Dame
T **Jerry Sisemore, Texas**
G Geary Murdock, Iowa State
G John Hannah, Alabama
C Tom Brahaney, Oklahoma
QB Bert Jones, LSU
RB Greg Pruitt, Oklahoma
RB Johnny Rodgers, Nebraska
RB Otis Armstrong, Purdue

DEFENSE
E Willie Harper, Nebraska
E Bruce Bannon, Penn State
T George Hasenohrl, Ohio State
T Greg Marx, Notre Dame
G Rich Glover, Nebraska
LB Jamie Rotella, Tennessee
LB Randy Gradishar, Ohio State
LB Rich Wood, Southern Cal
DB Randy Logan, Michigan
DB Conrad Graham, Tennessee
DB Frank Dowsing, Mississippi State

WALTER CAMP FOOTBALL FOUNDATION

OFFENSE
TE Charles Young, Southern Cal
WR Johnny Rodgers, Nebraska
T **Jerry Sisemore, Texas**
T John Hicks, Ohio State
G John Hannah, Alabama
G Skip Singletary, Temple
C Tom Brahaney, Oklahoma
QB John Hufnagel, Penn State
RB Greg Pruitt, Oklahoma
RB Dick Jauron, Yale
RB Otis Armstrong, Purdue

DEFENSE
E Willie Harper, Nebraska
E Bruce Bannon, Penn State
T Dave Butz, Purdue
T Greg Marx, Notre Dame
G Rich Glover, Nebraska
LB Steve Brown, Oregon State
LB Tom Jackson, Louisville
DB Ray Guy, Southern Mississippi
DB **Robert Popelka, SMU**
DB Brad Van Pelt, Michigan State
DB Randy Logan, Michigan

FOOTBALL WRITERS ASSOCIATION

OFFENSE
TE Charlie Young, Southern Cal
WR Steve Holden, Arizona State
WR Johnny Rodgers, Nebraska
T **Jerry Sisemore, Texas**
T Paul Seymour, Michigan
G John Hannah, Alabama
G Ron Rusnak, North Carolina
C Tom Brahaney, Oklahoma
QB Gary Huff, Florida State
RB Otis Armstrong, Purdue
RB Greg Pruitt, Oklahoma
K Ricky Townsend, Tennessee
P Ray Guy, Southern Mississippi

DEFENSE
E **Roger Goree, Baylor**
E John Grant, Southern Cal
T Bud Magrum, Colorado
T Greg Marx, Notre Dame
G Rich Glover, Nebraska
LB John Skorupan, Penn State
LB Warren Capone, LSU
LB Randy Gradishar, Ohio State
DB Brad Van Pelt, Michigan State
DB Randy Rhino, Georgia Tech
DB **Robert Popelka, SMU**

KODAK AMERICAN FOOTBALL COACHES ASSOCIATION

OFFENSE
F Johnny Rodgers, Nebraska
E Barry Smith, Florida State
E Charles Young, Southern Cal
T Paul Seymour, Michigan
T **Jerry Sisemore, Texas**
G John Hannah, Alabama
G Ron Rusnak, North Carolina
C Jim Krapf, Alabama
QB Bert Jones, LSU
RB Greg Pruitt, Oklahoma
RB Dick Jauron, Yale
FB Sam Cunningham, Southern Cal

DEFENSE
E Bruce Bannon, Penn State
E Greg Marx, Notre Dame
T Dave Butz, Purdue
T John LeHeup, South Carolina
G Rich Glover, Nebraska
LB Jamie Rotella, Tennessee
LB Willie Harper, Nebraska
LB Randy Gradishar, Ohio State
LB John Mitchell, Alabama
DB Cullen Bryant, Colorado
DB Randy Logan, Michigan
DB Brad Van Pelt, Michigan State

1972 ALL-SOUTHWEST CONFERENCE TEAM

OFFENSE

Quarterback: Alan Lowry, Texas

Running Backs: Dickey Morton, Arkansas
Roosevelt Leaks, Texas
Mike Luttrell, TCU
Alvin Maxson, SMU

Center: Russell Ingram, Texas Tech

CONSENSUS

Guards: Travis Roach, Texas
Guy Morriss, TCU
Tom Reed, Arkansas

Tackles: Jerry Sisemore, Texas
Ron Waedemon, Rice

Tight End: Gary Butler, Rice

Split Ends: Edwin Collins, Rice
Kenny Harrison, SMU

DEFENSE

Defensive Backs: Robert Popelka, SMU
Bruce Henley, Rice
Lyle Blackwood, TCU
Robert Murski, Texas A & M
Tommy Stewart, Baylor

Linebackers: Randy Braband, Texas
Grady Hoermann, Texas A & M
Glen Gaspard, Texas

Middle Guard: Donald Rives, Texas Tech

Tackles: Louis Kelcher, SMU
Charles Davis, TCU

Ends: Roger Goree, Baylor
Malcolm Minnick, Texas

Punter-Kicker: Mark Williams, Rice

Coach of the Year:
Grant Teaff, Baylor

Defensive Player of Year:
Roger Goree, Baylor

Offensive Player of Year:
Roosevelt Leaks, Texas

Newcomer of the Year:
Roosevelt Leaks, Texas

Player of the Year:
Roosevelt Leaks, Texas

Freshman of the Year:
Wayne Morris, SMU

SECOND TEAM
CONSENSUS

OFFENSE

SE	Charles Dancer, Baylor
TE	Homer May, Texas A & M
T	Don Deweber, SMU
T	Steve Oxley, Texas
T	Richard Mason, Baylor
G	Harold Lyons, Texas Tech
G	Don Crosslin, Texas
C	Bill Wyman, Texas
QB	Joe Barnes, Texas Tech
RB	Doug McCutchen, Texas Tech
RB	Gary Lacy, Baylor
RB	Wayne Morris, SMU

DEFENSE

E	Gaines Baty, Texas Tech
E	Ed Johnson, SMU
E	Larry Walling, Rice
T	Boice Best, Texas A & M
T	Don Wunderly, Arkansas
T	Doug English, Texas
LB	Dede Terveen, TCU
LB	Leonard Carey, SMU
LB	Quinton Robinson, Texas Tech
LB	Ed Simonini, Texas A & M
DB	Mike Bayer, Texas
DB	Mike Rowan, Texas
DB	Louis Campbell, Arkansas
DB	Ira Dean, Baylor

1973 COTTON BOWL

January 1, 1973

TEXAS 9-1 vs ALABAMA 10-1

Previous Games:

1902	Texas 10 - Alabama 0
1915	Texas 20 - Alabama 0
1948	Texas 27 - Alabama 7 (Sugar Bowl)
1960	Texas 3 - Alabama 3 (Bluebonnet Bowl)
1965	Texas 21 - Alabama 17 (Orange Bowl)

School Nicknames & Colors:

Alabama - Crimson Tide, Crimson & White

Texas - Longhorns, Orange & White

TEXAS			**ALABAMA**		
Head Coach: Darrell Royal			Head Coach: Paul "Bear" Bryant		
23	Miami	10	35	Duke	12
25	Texas Tech	20	35	Kentucky	0
27	Utah State	12	48	Vanderbilt	21
0	Oklahoma	27	25	Georgia	7
35	Arkansas	15	24	Florida	7
45	Rice	9	17	Tennessee	10
17	SMU	9	48	Southern Mississippi	11
17	Baylor	3	58	Mississippi State	14
27	TCU	0	35	LSU	21
38	Texas A & M	3	52	VPI	13
254		108	16	Auburn	17
			393		133

1973 SUN BOWL

December 30, 1972

TEXAS TECH 8-3 vs NORTH CAROLINA 10-1

Previous Games: None
School Nicknames & Colors:
North Carolina - Tar Heels, Blue & White
Texas Tech - Red Raiders, Red & Black

TEXAS TECH			NORTH CAROLINA	
Head Coach: Jim Carlen			**Head Coach: Bill Dooley**	
45	Utah	2	28	Richmond	18
41	New Mexico	16	31	Maryland	26
20	Texas	25	34	North Carolina State	33
35	Tulsa	18	14	Ohio State	29
17	Texas A & M	14	31	Kentucky	20
35	Arizona	10	21	Wake Forest	0
17	SMU	3	26	Clemson	10
10	Rice	6	23	Virginia	3
7	TCU	31	14	Duke	0
13	Baylor	7	42	East Carolina	19
14	Arkansas	24	28	Florida	24
254		156	292		182

HEISMAN TROPHY WINNERS

1935 — Jay Berwanger, Chicago
1936 — Larry Kelley, Yale
1937 — Clint Frank, Yale
1938 — **DAVEY O'BRIEN, TCU**
1939 — Nile Kinnick, Iowa
1940 — Tom Harmon, Michigan
1941 — Bruce Smith, Minnesota
1942 — Frank Sinkwich, Georgia
1943 — Angelo Bertelli, Notre Dame
1944 — Leslie Horvath, Ohio State
1945 — Felix Blanchard, Army
1946 — Glenn Davis, Army
1947 — John Lujack, Notre Dame
1948 — **DOAK WALKER, SMU**
1949 — Leon Hart, Notre Dame
1950 — Vic Janowicz, Ohio State
1951 — Dick Kazmaier, Princeton
1952 — Billy Vessels, Oklahoma
1953 — John Lattner, Notre Dame
1954 — Alan Amache, Wisconsin
1955 — Howard Cassady, Ohio State
1956 — Paul Hornung, Notre Dame
1957 — **JOHN DAVID CROW, TEXAS A & M**
1958 — Pete Dawkins, Army
1959 — Billy Cannon, LSU
1960 — Joe Bellino, Navy
1961 — Ernie Davis, Syracuse
1962 — Terry Baker, Oregon
1963 — Roger Stauback, Navy
1964 — John Huarte, Notre Dame
1965 — Mike Garrett, USC
1966 — Steve Spurrier, Florida
1967 — Gary Beban, UCLA
1968 — O. J. Simpson, USC
1969 — Steve Owens, Oklahoma
1970 — Jim Plunkett, Stanford
1971 — Pat Sullivan, Auburn
1972 — Johnny Rodgers, Nebraska

1973 SCHEDULES

September 15
Houston at Rice
Arkansas at Southern Cal
Oklahoma at Baylor
Santa Clara at SMU
Wichita State at Texas A&M
Utah at Texas Tech

September 21
Texas at Miami

September 22
Oklahoma State at Arkansas
Baylor at Pittsburgh
Montana at Rice
SMU at Oregon State
South Carolina at Houston
Texas A&M at LSU
UTA at TCU
New Mexico at Texas Tech

September 29
Texas Tech at Texas
TCU at Ohio State
Boston College at Texas A&M
Virginia Tech at SMU
Rice at LSU
Baylor at Colorado
Iowa State at Arkansas
Houston at Memphis State

October 6
TCU at Arkansas
Florida State at Baylor
Missouri at SMU
Wake Forest at Texas
Texas A&M at Clemson
Oklahoma State at Texas Tech
Houston at San Diego State
Rice: Open date

October 13
Texas A&M at Texas Tech
Idaho at TCU
Oklahoma vs Texas at Dallas
Notre Dame at Rice
Arkansas at Baylor
Virginia Tech at Houston
SMU: Open date

October 19
Houston at Miami

October 20
Texas at Arkansas
SMU at Rice
Texas A&M at TCU
Texas Tech at Arizona
Baylor: Open date

October 27
SMU at Texas Tech
TCU at Tennessee
Baylor at Texas A&M
Rice at Texas
Tulsa at Arkansas
Houston at Auburn

November 3
Florida State at Houston
Texas A&M at Arkansas
TCU at Baylor
Rice at Texas Tech
Texas at SMU

November 10
Arkansas at Rice
Baylor at Texas
Texas Tech at TCU
SMU at Texas A&M
Houston at Colorado State

November 17
Baylor at Texas Tech
Arkansas at SMU
Texas A&M at Rice
TCU at Texas
Houston:Open date

November 22
Texas at Texas A&M

November 24
Texas Tech at Arkansas
SMU at Baylor
Rice at TCU
Wyoming at Houston

December 1
TCU at SMU
Baylor at Rice
Tulsa at Houston

Past Records

SOUTHWEST CONFERENCE CHAMPIONS

1915 BAYLOR, OKLAHOMA	**1934** RICE	**1953** RICE, TEXAS
1916 TEXAS	**1935** SMU	**1954** ARKANSAS
1917 TEXAS A & M	**1936** ARKANSAS	**1955** TCU
1918 TEXAS	**1937** RICE	**1956** TEXAS A & M
1919 TEXAS A & M	**1938** TCU	**1957** RICE
1920 TEXAS	**1939** TEXAS A & M, SMU	**1958** TCU
1921 TEXAS A & M	**1940** TEXAS A & M	**1959** TEXAS, TCU, ARKANSAS
1922 BAYLOR	**1941** TEXAS A & M	**1960** ARKANSAS
1923 SMU	**1942** TEXAS	**1961** ARKANSAS, TEXAS
1924 BAYLOR	**1943** TEXAS	**1962** TEXAS
1925 TEXAS A & M	**1944** TCU	**1963** TEXAS
1926 SMU	**1945** TEXAS	**1964** ARKANSAS
1927 TEXAS A & M	**1946** RICE, ARKANSAS	**1965** ARKANSAS
1928 TEXAS	**1947** SMU	**1966** SMU
1929 TCU	**1948** SMU	**1967** TEXAS A & M
1930 TEXAS	**1949** RICE	**1968** TEXAS, ARKANSAS
1931 SMU	**1950** TEXAS	**1969** TEXAS
1932 TCU	**1951** TCU	**1970** TEXAS
1933 ARKANSAS	**1952** TEXAS	**1971** TEXAS
		1972 TEXAS

SWC NATIONAL CHAMPIONS

1935 SMU (MADISON BELL)   **1963** TEXAS (DARRELL ROYAL)

1938 TCU (L. R. MEYER)   **1964** ARKANSAS (FRANK BROYLES)

1939 TEXAS A & M (HOMER NORTON) **1969** TEXAS (DARRELL ROYAL)

COTTON BOWL RECORD

The Cotton Bowl Game was first played in 1937 and an agreement to have the Southwest Conference Champion be the host team began with the 1941 game. The 1939 and 1940 games were the only ones in Cotton Bowl history that did not have a Southwest Conference team involved. Texas Tech played in the 1939 game but was not a conference member at that time.

1937—TCU 16, Marquette 6	**1955**—Georgia Tech 14, Arkansas 6
1938—Rice 28, Colorado 14	**1956**—Mississippi 14, TCU 13
1939—St. Mary's 21, Texas Tech 13	**1957**—TCU 28, Syracuse 27
1940—Clemson 6, Boston College 3	**1958**—Navy 20, Rice 7
1941—Texas A&M 13, Fordham 12	**1959**—TCU 0, Air Force 0
1942—Alabama 29, Texas A&M 21	**1960**—Syracuse 23, Texas 14
1943—Texas 14, Georgia Tech 7	**1961**—Duke 7, Arkansas 6
1944—Texas 7, Randolph Field 7	**1962**—Texas 12, Mississippi 7
1945—Oklahoma A&M 34, TCU 0	**1963**—LSU 13, Texas 0
1946—Texas 40, Missouri 27	**1964**—Texas 28, Navy 6
1947—Arkansas 0, LSU 0	**1965**—Arkansas 10, Nebraska 7
1948—SMU 13, Penn State 13	**1966**—LSU 14, Arkansas 7
1949—SMU 21, Oregon 13	**1967**—Georgia 24, SMU 9
1950—Rice 27, North Carolina 13	**1968**—Texas A&M 20, Alabama 16
1951—Tennessee 20, Texas 14	**1969**—Texas 36, Tennessee 13
1952—Kentucky 20, TCU 7	**1970**—Texas 21, Notre Dame 17
1953—Texas 16, Tennessee 0	**1971**—Notre Dame 24, Texas 11
1954—Rice 20, Alabama 6	**1972**—Penn State 30, Texas 6

Since 1941: SWC 14 wins, 14 losses, 4 ties

1. Texas No. 4, TCU No. 7, Arkansas No. 9, 1959
2. Texas A & M (1917 and 1919), Texas (1918 & 1920)
3. Oklahoma, Oklahoma State (A&M), Southwestern and Phillips
4. Arkansas Shoats, Baylor Cubs, Houston Kittens, Rice Owlets, SMU Colts, Texas Shorthorns, Texas A&M Fish, TCU Wogs, Texas Tech Picadores.
5. Baylor
6. Arkansas, Texas, Rice & Baylor - 1960 & 1961
7. Waco, Add Ran
8. SMU in 1935
9. Davey O'Brien, TCU, 1937
10. TCU (1923)
11. TCU (1938) Texas A&M (1939) Texas (1963) Arkansas (1964)
12. Oklahoma (1916, 472 pts. - 1917, 442 pts.), Texas (1969, 414 pts. - 1970, 412 pts.), Arkansas (1970, 402 pts.)
13. Sammy Baugh, TCU, 1935 & 1936; Davey O'Brien, TCU, 1937 & 1938; Kay Eakin, Arkansas, 1939
14. Texas A&M, 1939
15. Clyde Carter and Bobby Wilson of SMU (1934)
16. Arkansas, Texas & TCU - 1959 (5-1-0 records)
17. Bobby Layne, Texas; Dick Harris, Texas; Doak Walker, SMU, 1947
18. Arkansas (1946 - tied Rice for SWC crown)
19. Baylor, 1960-1964
20. Texas (1893 - 1932), 1933 (4-5-2)
21. Arkansas, Texas, Texas A&M
22. Texas A&M, 1917 & 1919
23. Rice 14 - Purdue 0, Texas 7 - Notre Dame 6
24. Texas A&M in 1903 played TCU and Baylor three times each and won five, tying Baylor once.
25. Rice 146 - SMU 3, 1916

Records of SWC teams in other Bowl games:

1921 DIXIE CLASSIC (DALLAS): Texas A&M 21, Centre 14

1934 DIXIE CLASSIC (DALLAS): Arkansas 7, Centenary 7

1936 ROSE BOWL: Stanford 7, SMU 0
SUGAR BOWL: TCU 3, LSU 2

1938 SUN BOWL: West Virginia 7, Texas Tech 6

1939 SUGAR BOWL: TCU 15, Carnegie Tech 7

1940 SUGAR BOWL: Texas A&M 14, Tulane 13

1942 ORANGE BOWL: Georgia 40, TCU 26
SUN BOWL: Tulsa 6, Texas Tech 0

1944 ORANGE BOWL: LSU 19, Texas A&M 14

1947 ORANGE BOWL: Rice 8, Tennessee 0

1948 SUGAR BOWL: Texas 27, Alabama 7
SUN BOWL: Miami (Ohio) 13, Texas Tech 12
DIXIE BOWL: Arkansas 21, William & Mary 19

1949 DELTA BOWL: Mississippi 13, TCU 9
DIXIE BOWL: Baylor 20, Wake Forest 7
RAISIN BOWL: San Jose State 20, Texas Tech 13
ORANGE BOWL: Texas 41, Georgia 28

1950 PRESIDENTIAL CUP: Texas A&M 40, Georgia 20

1951 SALAD BOWL: Houston 26, Dayton 21

1952 ORANGE BOWL: Georgia Tech 17, Baylor 14
SUN BOWL: Texas Tech 25, College of the Pacific 14

1954 GATOR BOWL: Texas Tech 35, Auburn 13

1955 GATOR BOWL: Auburn 33, Baylor 13

1956 SUN BOWL: Wyoming 21, Texas Tech 14

1957 SUGAR BOWL: Baylor 13, Tennessee 7
GATOR BOWL: Tennessee 3, Texas A&M 0

1958 SUGAR BOWL: Mississippi 39, Texas 7

1960 BLUEBONNET BOWL: Texas 3, Alabama 3
GATOR BOWL: Arkansas 14, Georgia Tech 7
BLUEBONNET BOWL: Clemson 23, TCU 7
GATOR BOWL: Florida 13, Baylor 12

1961 GOTHAM BOWL: Baylor 24, Utah State 9
SUGAR BOWL: Mississippi 14, Rice 6
BLUEBONNET BOWL: Kansas 33, Rice 7

1962 SUGAR BOWL: Alabama 10, Arkansas 3
TANGERINE BOWL: Houston 49, Miami, Ohio 21

1963 BLUEBONNET BOWL: Baylor 14, LSU 7
SUN BOWL: Oregon 20, SMU 14
SUGAR BOWL: Mississippi 17, Arkansas 13

1965 SUN BOWL: Texas Western 13, TCU 12
GATOR BOWL: Georgia Tech 31, Texas Tech 21
SUN BOWL: Georgia 7, Texas Tech 0
ORANGE BOWL: Texas 21, Alabama 17

1966 BLUEBONNET BOWL: Texas 19, Mississippi 0

1969 SUGAR BOWL: Arkansas 16, Georgia 2
BLUEBONNET BOWL: SMU 28, Oklahoma 27

1970 SUGAR BOWL: Mississippi 27, Arkansas 22
BLUEBONNET BOWL: Houston 36, Auburn 7

1971 SUN BOWL: Georgia Tech 17, Texas Tech 9

1972 BLUEBONNET BOWL: Colorado 29, Houston 17
LIBERTY BOWL: Tennessee 14, Arkansas 13

SWC: 23 W, 27 L, 2 T

Halftime '72

By William H. Lively, SMU

As the annual whisper of September wends its refreshing path across the scorched and yearning plains of the Southwest, the land begins to transform into its customary unique boundaries. Great communities, streamlined by a spectrum of crimson, orange, maroon, blue, green, and purple emerge and assume traditional combat positions. Stadia, bulging to capacity, from Lubbock to Fayetteville, resound with an almost uncontrollable pandemonium traditionally labeled - College Football - Southwest Conference Style.

A closer analysis, however, of what might initially have been mistaken for the sound track to a Cecil B. DeMille Spectacular, reveals that between the stomping feet and clapping hands is a driving rhythmic pulsation and sound dynamism - indeed, the very soul and spirit of Intercollegiate football - the University Band.

Be it the emotional strains of "The Eyes of Texas", as the Longhorns finally pull it out of reach, or the penetrating sound power of 40 trumpets blistering the Cotton Bowl gridiron with the 50th consecutive chorus of "Peruna", the University Marching Band more than ever before "does its thing."

In an age when collegiate football has assumed an almost exalted position within the realm of American entertainment, the University Marching Band has equally enhanced its station. Realistically, the entertainment product represented in the University Marching Band is the primary distinguishing ingredient that separates collegiate athletics from all other forms. The diversity and originality exemplified by the nine University Bands provides Southwest Conference football fans with the finest gridiron performances in the history of the game.

Golden Wave Band

Baylor University
Gene C. Smith, Director

Marching Band was first introduced to Baylor University in the fall of 1903. Organized and directed by Charles Parker, the early marching band was a 28-piece regulation military band under the auspices of the Baylor R. O. T. C. program where it remained until the end of World War I.

In 1929 Everett McCraken was appointed Band Director and it was under his administration that a new age of development for the Bear Band was initiated. A highly successful ten day tour of several Texas towns by the band, displaying their recently purchased new Golden uniforms, inspired columnists to refer to the organization as making "A Golden Wave through Texas." From that time until the present, the band has been known as the Baylor Golden Wave Band.

Admittance of girls into membership in the band was first allowed in 1933 as the program began to strengthen and stabilize. But it was not until 1948 when Donald I. Moore became Director of Bands at Baylor that the Golden Wave Band really became a quality University musical organization.

Currently, directed by Gene C. Smith, the band is composed of 200 members, the largest in the history of the University, and is fast becoming one of the nation's most popular bands.

96 GUYS AND A DOLL

Southern Methodist University
Irving Dreibrodt, Director

Amidst the melee of sound and color that annually accompanies the collegiate football season, one particular organization remains distinctive. Energized by its jazz-oriented musical repertoire, endowed with a flamboyant wardrobe, including 25 different uniforms, and fortified by an almost fanatical "esprit de corps", Southern Methodist University's Mustang Band continues to supply the American football audience with "Entertainment Extraordinaire."

Its incomparably jazz-flavored heritage dates as far back as the initial game of the 1924 season when, under the direction of Cy Barcus, the band's music so inspired the football team that play was temporarily halted "as the players turned around and cheered." Subsequent overwhelming audience response to Mustang-Jazz ultimately motivated the NBC network to broadcast the "Blowin' Mustangs from Big D" in a nation wide radio series entitled "The Pigskin Review." Shortly thereafter the Band was sponsored on a national performance tour of the Vaudeville capitals across America.

Continuing its musical ascension to the throne of American Entertainment, in 1958 Dr. Irving Dreibrodt became Band Director. Under Dreibrodt's administration the most prolific era in the history of the Collegiate Marching Band was begun. Restricting membership to a rigid audition schedule and limiting Mustang Band participation to 96 men and one girl featured performer, the Band became nationally acclaimed as "96 Guys and a Doll."

FIGHTIN' AGGIE BAND

Texas A&M University
Lt. Colonel Edward V. Adams, Director

Inspired by the brilliant proclamation of twelve silver bugles, the 310 member Fightn' Texas Aggie Band pounds the gridiron in a manner reminiscent of the awesome Roman Legions of another age.

Certainly, in the memories of those who have witnessed them in performance, there is little dispute that the Aggie Band is the unchallenged "Best of its Kind" in the world. The highly intricate maneuvers performed by the nation's largest Military Band have thrilled thousands in audiences from College Station to San Francisco, and literally millions of television viewers across America.

Organized in 1879 with an unspectacular membership of 13 Cadets, the early Aggie Bands were outfitted in Texas militia uniforms and used borrowed instruments. Under the inspirational leadership of such personalities as Colonel R. C. Dunn (director from 1926 through 1945) and present Director, Lt. Colonel E. V. Adams, the "Fightn' Aggie Band" has evolved into an integral part of the University's Corps of Cadets. The last of the great marching military college bands, a veritable giant under perfect discipline, the Texas A & M University Band continues in its quest for military dignity with audience appeal.

GOIN' BAND
FROM
RAIDERLAND

Texas Tech University
Dean Killion, Director

In early October of 1925, the Texas Tech Band under the direction of William R. Waghorne began a new concept in West Texas Football Entertainment. Outfitted in crimson and black Matador uniforms, complete with sombrero, the early Tech Band accompanied the football team to games in Brownwood and Abilene. Later, during the 1926 season, the legendary Will Rogers personally subsidized the Band's trip from Lubbock to Fort Worth for the TCU-Tech game. As he explained in the Fort Worth Star Telegram: "Will Rogers wants Fort Worth to see a West Texas Band' and hear some real West Texas music."

From that early 80 member unit, "The Goin' Band from Raider Land" has developed into one of the nation's largest and finest Marching Bands. Currently under the direction of Dean Killion, the Band's membership is well over 400 students of which 310 normally march in halftime performance. The early Matador costume has been replaced by flashy scarlet and black Military styled uniforms in which the Raider Band annually presents its brand of precision routine.

Showband of the Southwest

University of Texas
Vincent R. DiNino, Director

Two hundred eighty five Marching Collegians, all outfitted in bright orange and white Western trimmed uniforms, topped off with white Stetsons and surrounded by a 40 man Flag Brigade - any native of the Lone Star State would immediately recognize the description that could only belong to the University of Texas Longhorn Band. Now celebrating its 72nd year of existence, the Longhorn Band has become internationally recognized as the "Showband of the Southwest", one of the most respected University Bands in America. Renowned for its large scale precision marching and "Texas-size" sound, the Longhorn Band has successfully achieved a balance of excellence in musicianship as well as showmanship.

One of the nation's oldest college bands, the University of Texas Band was organized in 1900 by Dr. E. P. Schoch to provide music and spirit at the University's football games. Little did these early performances give indication of the ultimate size and scope of the Marching Longhorns.

During the past 17 years the Band has accomplished its highest level of achievement under the very competent direction of Vincent R. DiNino. Ever seeking to maintain the utmost in performance quality, all Longhorn Band members are accepted into membership only through audition and personal interview by the Director. Certainly, these efforts have been justly rewarded as "The Showband of the Southwest" has presented command performances from Washington, D. C. to Lima, Peru.

The Best
in Sight
and Sound

University of Arkansas
Eldon Janzen, Director

With a colorful history dating back to the turn of the century, the Marching Razorback Band made its first uniformed appearance, forty men strong, on a fall football afternoon in 1928. The gray Marine jackets and Pershing caps appropriate for that era, have many years since been replaced by the colorful crimson and white contemporary-styled uniforms of the '72 Marching Razorbacks.

Trademarked as "The Best in Sight and Sound" this nationally acclaimed organization pursues one of the most vigorous performance schedules of any University Band in the country. The extensive preparation and planning required for the pre-game and halftime presentations for the enjoyment of Razorback football fans represents a year-long operation for the 172 bandsmen, staff, and directors.

Under the direction of Eldon Janzen, the Arkansas Band has established a standard of excellence in entertainment, highlighting precision-pageantry with the solid sounds of popular and march music. While its personnel come from every college or campus, and from coast to coast, it serves as a laboratory for a solid core of Music Education Majors.

SHOW WINDOW OF TCU

Texas Christian University
James Jacobsen, Director

Texas Christian University's Horned Frog Band, directed by James A. Jacobsen, boasts a long tradition of achievement. Since its origin in 1905 the band has grown both in quantity and quality of performance, taking its place among the finest bands in the nation.

Currently its three divisions include a jazz ensemble, a symphonic band and a marching unit. The marching band has achieved national recognition in recent years for its unique "moving diamond" precision drills. A technique originated by Jacobsen for TCU's band in 1958, the moving diamond is widely used throughout the United States.

Playing for each of the TCU football games, the band is complimented with a march-twirl-dance unit known as the Band Debs. A colorful feature of the famed half-time productions of the "Show Window of TCU," the Debs were originated last year as TCU's equivalent of nationally famed precision dancers.

During the 67 years since a few boys who had a little time, gathered to blow a horn or beat a drum, the group has seen many transitions.

The first band to play for school functions was originated in 1921, and the first uniforms were worn in 1925. With a host of directors in the next 25 years, the band changed in size and style. Jacobsen claimed the helm in 1955, and with his leadership, the group took on its present "swinging" look.

M.O.B.
marching
owl band

Rice University
Bert Roth, Director

Historically, the first official Marching Band at Rice University was organized by twelve industrious University students who had little else but their own enthusiasm with which to work. Finally, in the fall of 1922, the dedicated efforts of the original twelve resulted in the appointment of Lee Chatham as Owl Band Director. Chatham engineered the growth and development of the

band until 1938 when Kit Reid assumed the responsibilities as Director. Unfortunately, by the time Reid had unveiled his elaborate plans for the expansion of marching activities, the country was engaged in World War II.

The post war years witnessed the inclusion of girls into band membership, and the fall of 1951 marked the beginning of a movement to raise the organization's quality to major University caliber under the new guidance of Holmes McNeely. During the next 16 years McNeely instituted an equipment and personnel building program that surpassed any previous campaign of its kind in the University's history.

Presently, the Owl Band is under the direction of Bert Roth. In an endeavor to dramatically present contemporary-flavored football performances, the band has altered the traditional marching format and introduced timely and sometimes controversial topics into the halftime activities. Tongue-in-cheek parodies on politics and campus life have provided ammunition for what has proved to be a very popular form of football entertainment. In conjunction with its new entertainment concept, the University Band has become infamously known as the M O B, which, aside from its literal meaning, stands for "Marching Owl Band."

Cougar
Marching
Band

University of Houston
William C. Moffit, Director

The newest representative in the Southwest Conference gridiron halftime entertainment comes in the form of the 200 member University of Houston Cougar Marching Band. Strikingly uniformed in crimson, white, and black, the Marching Cougars have introduced a refreshing new concept into the excitement of collegiate halftime pageantry. Performing to the dynamic "Soundpower" musical arrangements of Director Bill Moffit, the Cougar Band annually showcases its kaleidoscopic "Patterns of Motion" marching routine, on the synthetic turf of the world famous Astrodome. Certainly, the unique performance potential represented in such a marvelous facility serves to augment the Houston Band's already diversified brand of marching entertainment.

As with many of the Conference's University Bands, the Cougar Band maintains its membership foundation with students from within the University of Houston's School of Music. These young musicians, together with many non-music majors, jointly compose one of the most impressive marching organizations in the Southwest Conference. No doubt, the University of Houston's continued growth as one of the nation's youngest institutions of higher learning, currently surpassing 27,000 enrollment, will be closely paralleled by even more exciting performances by the Cougar Marching Band.

207

We wish to thank the following Sports Information Directors for their cooperation and assistance on this book:

David Cawood, Arkansas
Don Oliver, Baylor
Ted Nance, Houston
Bill Whitmore, Rice
Bob Condron, SMU
Jones Ramsey, Texas
H. L. Gammon, Texas A & M
Jim Garner, TCU
Ralph Carpenter, Texas Tech

PHOTO CREDITS
ARKANSAS ATHLETIC DEPT.: 20
IKE BARUCH: 52, 53, 82, 83, 94, 95, 108, 109, 170, 171
BAYLOR ATHLETIC DEPT.: 14
RALPH BEARDEN: 9, 10, 11, 16, 38, 39, 60, 61, 86, 87, 100, 101, 110, 111, 128, 129, 134, 135, 152, 153, 164, 165, 174, 175
JOHN BENNETT: 32, 33, 58, 59, 88, 89, 116, 117, 122, 123, 154, 155, 162, 163, 172, 173, 184, 185
CHARLES BICKFORD: 24, 25, 48, 49, 70, 71, 98, 99, 130, 131, 150, 151, 160, 161
STEPHEN BRYANT: 3, 4, 5, 26, 27, 40, 41, 56, 57, 72, 73, 96, 97, 112, 113, 136, 137, 166, 167
RAY CARY: 54, 55
BENNY COLLINS: 6, 7, 8
MIKE FLUITT: 138, 139
WILLIAM KNISLEY: 102, 103
DAVID LOTT: 34, 35, 50, 51, 68, 69, 84, 85, 106, 107, 126, 127, 146, 147
BILL MAHAN: 64, 65
AL PANZERA: 44, 45, 74, 75, 90, 91, 120, 121, 140, 141, 158, 159, 182, 183
SMU ATHLETIC DEPT.: 18
TEXAS ATHLETIC DEPT.: 17
TEXAS A & M ATHLETIC DEPT.: 19
TCU ATHLETIC DEPT.: 15
TEXAS TECH ATHLETIC DEPT.: 21
RAY WESTBRROOK: 36, 37, 66, 67, 78, 79, 114, 115, 148, 149, 178, 179
LOU WITT: 22, 28, 29, 46, 47, 80, 81, 124, 125, 142, 143, 176, 177

Published by Football History, Inc.
E. P. Gemmer, Jr., President
Ray Herndon, Editor & Designer
6300 West Loop South
Bellaire, Texas 77401